Repairing
and Extending
Finishes

VAN NOSTRAND REINHOLD'S
BUILDING RENOVATION AND RESTORATION SERIES

Repairing and Extending Weather Barriers   ISBN 0-442-20611-9

Repairing and Extending Finishes, Part I   ISBN 0-442-20612-7

Repairing and Extending Finishes, Part II   ISBN 0-442-20613-5

Repairing and Extending Non-Structural Metals   ISBN 0-442-20615-1

Repairing and Extending Doors and Windows   ISBN 0-442-20618-6

Repairing, Extending, and Cleaning Brick and Block   ISBN 0-442-20619-4

Repairing, Extending, and Cleaning Stone   ISBN 0-442-20620-8

Repairing and Extending Wood   ISBN 0-442-20621-6

Building Renovation and Restoration Series

Repairing and Extending Finishes

PART I

PLASTER

GYPSUM BOARD

CERAMIC TILE

H. Leslie Simmons, AIA, CSI

 VAN NOSTRAND REINHOLD
New York

Printed in the United States of America

Designed by Caliber Design

Van Nostrand Reinhold
115 Fifth Avenue
New York, New York 10003

Van Nostrand Reinhold International Company Limited
11 New Fetter Lane
London EC4P 4EE, England

Van Nostrand Reinhold
480 La Trobe Street
Melbourne, Victoria 3000, Australia

Nelson Canada
1120 Birchmount Road
Scarborough, Ontario M1K 584, Canada

16 15 14 13 12 11 10 9 8 7 6 5 4 3 2 1

Library of Congress Cataloging in Publication Data

Simmons, H. Leslie.
    Repairing and extending finishes / H. Leslie Simmons.
        p.   cm.—(Building renovation and restoration ; v. 2)
    Bibliography: p.
    Includes index.
    Contents: pt. 1. Plaster, gypsum board, and ceramic tile.
    ISBN 0-442-20612-7 (v. 2)
    1. Buildings—Repair and reconstruction. 2. Finishes and
finishing. I. Title. II. Series.
TH3471.S56   1990   88-36478
698'.028'8—dc19   CIP

Series Foreword

To spite a national trend toward renovation, restoration, and remodeling, construction products producers and their associations are not universally eager to publish recommendations for repairing or extending existing materials. There are two major reasons. First, there are several possible applications of most building materials; and there is an even larger number of different problems that can occur after products are installed in a building. Thus, it is difficult to produce recommendations that cover every eventuality.

Second, it is not always in a building construction product producer's best interest to publish data that will help building owners repair their product. Producers, whose income derives from selling new products, do not necessarily applaud when their associations spend their money telling architects and building owners how to avoid buying their products.

Finally, in the *Building Renovation and Restoration Series* we have a reference that recognizes that problems frequently occur with materials used in building projects. In this book and in the other books in this series,

Simmons goes beyond the promotional hyperbole found in most product literature and explains how to identify common problems. He then offers informed "inside" recommendations on how to deal with each of the problems. Each chapter covers certain materials, or family of materials, in a way that can be understood by building owners and managers, as well as construction and design professionals.

Most people involved in designing, financing, constructing, owning, managing, and maintaining today's "high tech" buildings have limited knowledge on how all of the many materials go together to form the building and how they should look and perform. Everyone relies on specialists, who may have varying degrees of expertise, for building and installing the many individual components that make up completed buildings. Problems frequently arise when components and materials are not installed properly and often occur when substrate or supporting materials are not installed correctly.

When problems occur, even the specialists may not know why they are happening. Or they may not be willing to admit responsibility for problems. Such problems can stem from improper designer selection, defective or substandard installation, lack of understanding on use, or incorrect maintenance procedures. Armed with necessary "inside" information, one can identify causes of problems and make assessments of their extent. Only after the causes are identified can one determine how to correct the problem.

Up until now that "inside" information generally was not available to those faced with these problems. In this book, materials are described according to types and uses and how they are supposed to be installed or applied. Materials and installation or application failures and problems are identified and listed, then described in straightforward, understandable language supplemented by charts, graphs, photographs, and line drawings. Solutions ranging from proper cleaning and other maintenance and remedial repair to complete removal and replacement are recommended with cross-references to given problems.

Of further value are sections on where to get more information from such sources as manufacturers, standards setting bodies, government agencies, periodicals, and books. There are also national and regional trade and professional associations representing almost every building and finish material, most of which make available reliable, unbiased information on proper use and installation of their respective materials and products. Some associations even offer information on recognizing and solving problems for their products and materials. Names, addresses, and telephone numbers are included, along with each association's major publications. In addition, knowledgeable, independent consultants who specialize in resolving problems relating to certain materials are recognized. Where names were not available for publication, most associations can furnish names of qualified persons who can assist in resolving problems related to their products.

It is wished that one would never be faced with any problems with new buildings and even older ones. However, reality being what it is, this book, as do the others in the series, offers a guide so you can identify problems and find solutions. And it provides references for sources of more information when problems go beyond the scope of the book.

Jess McIlvain, AIA, CCS, CSI
Consulting Architect
Bethesda, Maryland

Contents

Preface	xv
Acknowledgments	xxi

CHAPTER 1 Introduction — **1**

What Finishes Are and What They Do	2
Failure Types and Conditions	2
What to Do in an Emergency	4
Professional Help	4
Help for Building Owners	4
Help for Architects and Engineers	9
Help for General Building Contractors	10
Prework On-site Examination	11
The Owner	11
Architects and Engineers	11
Building Contractors	12

CHAPTER 2   Support Systems   14

Structural Framing Systems   15
   Structure Failure   15
   Structure Movement   16
Solid Substrates   17
   Solid Substrate Problems   18
Other Building Element Problems   18
Wood Framing and Furring   19
   General Requirements   20
   Materials   20
   Installation   24
Wood Framing and Furring Failures and What to Do about Them   34
   Wood Framing and Furring Problems   34
   Repairing and Extending Wood Framing and Furring 36
Installing New Wood Framing and Furring over Existing Materials 39
Metal Framing and Furring   41
   Materials   41
   Installation   46
Metal Framing and Furring Failures and What to Do
  about Them   60
   Metal Framing and Furring Problems   60
   Repairing and Extending Metal Framing and Furring 61
Installing New Metal Framing and Furring over Existing Materials 63
Where to Get More Information   64

CHAPTER 3   Lath and Plaster   68

Standard Thickness and Veneer Plaster Materials   69
   Lime and Sand-Lime Plaster   69
   Gypsum Plaster   69
   Cement Plaster   70
   Veneer Plaster   71
Standard Thickness and Veneer Plaster Bases   71
   Solid Substrates   71
   Lath   72
   Veneer Plaster Base Board   73
Accessories and Miscellaneous Materials for Standard Thickness
  and Veneer Plaster   73
   Accessories for Standard Thickness Gypsum Plaster 73
   Accessories for Standard Thickness Portland Cement Plaster (Stucco) 74
   Accessories for Veneer Plaster   75
   Miscellaneous Materials   75

Standard Thickness and Veneer Plaster Installation   75
   Installing and Preparing Bases   75
   Installing Standard Thickness Plaster   77
   Installing Veneer Plaster   84
Standard Thickness and Veneer Plaster Failures and What to Do
  about Them   85
   Why Standard Thickness and Veneer Plaster Fails   85
   Evidence of Failure in Standard Thickness and Veneer Plaster   93
   Repairing and Extending Existing Standard Thickness Plaster   101
   Repairing Existing Veneer Plaster   112
Installing New Standard Thickness and Veneer Plaster over
  Existing Materials   112
   Standard Thickness Plaster   112
   Veneer Plaster   113
Synthetic Stucco Materials   114
   Finish Materials   114
   Base for Synthetic Stucco   115
   Accessories for Synthetic Stucco   115
Synthetic Stucco Installation   116
   Bases for Synthetic Stucco   116
   Installing Synthetic Stucco   116
Synthetic Stucco Failures and What to Do about Them   117
   Why Synthetic Stucco Fails   117
   Evidence of Failure in Synthetic Stucco   119
   Repairing Synthetic Stucco   121
Installing New Synthetic Stucco over Existing Materials   121
Where to Get More Information   122

CHAPTER 4   Gypsum Board   126

Gypsum Board and Accessory Materials   127
   Gypsum Board Products   127
   Accessories   132
   Fasteners   134
   Adhesives   137
   Joint Treatment Materials   138
   Texture Finishes   139
Gypsum Board Installation   140
   Substrate Preparation   140
   Installing Standard Gypsum Board   141
   Installing Veneer Plaster Gypsum Base   163
   Installing Gypsum Sheathing   171
   Installing Gypsum Plaster Lath   173
   Installing Predecorated Gypsum Board   175

Gypsum Board System Failures and What to Do about Them   179
Why Gypsum Board Systems Fail   179
Evidence of Failure in Gypsum Board Systems   191
Repairing and Extending Existing Gypsum Board   207
Installing New Gypsum Board over Existing Materials   220
Installing New Gypsum Board by Lamination   220
Installing New Gypsum Board over New Framing or Furring   221
Glass Mesh Mortar Unit Materials and Installation   224
Materials   224
Installing Glass Mesh Mortar Units   226
Glass Mesh Mortar Unit Failures and What to Do about Them   227
Why Glass Mesh Mortar Units Fail   227
Evidence of Failure in Glass Mesh Mortar Units   228
Installing Glass Mesh Mortar Units over Existing Construction   230
Floors   230
Walls   230
Where to Get More Information   230

CHAPTER 5   Ceramic Tile   233

Ceramic Tile Types and Their Uses   233
Glazed Wall Tile   234
Ceramic Mosaic Tile   234
Quarry Tile   236
Paver Tile   236
Special-Purpose Tile   236
Additional Definitions   236
Mortar and Adhesive Types and Their Uses   237
Portland Cement Mortar   237
Dry-Set Mortar   237
Latex-Portland Cement Mortar   237
Chemical-Resistant Epoxy Mortar   238
Modified Epoxy-Emulsion Mortar   238
Furan Mortar   238
Organic Adhesives   238
Epoxy Adhesives   239
Grout Types and Their Uses   239
Portland Cement Grout   239
Dry-set Grout   239
Latex-Portland Cement Grout   240
Epoxy Grout   240
Furan Grout   240
Silicone Rubber Grout   240

Miscellaneous Tile Installation Materials   **241**
  Membranes   241
  Reinforcement   241
  Board Type Bases   241
  Expansion Joint Sealants   242
  Divider Strips   242
Tile Installation   **242**
  Substrates for Field-Applied Tile   242
  Setting Bed Construction for Field-Applied Tile   243
  Joints for Field-Applied Tile   251
  Prefabricated Exterior Tile Cladding   252
Tile Failures and What to Do about Them   **253**
  Why Tile Fails   253
  Evidence of Failure   266
  Repair, Replacement, and Cleaning of Existing Tile and Joints   271
Installing Tile over Existing Surfaces   **275**
Where to Get More Information   **276**
  Appendix   Data Sources   279
  Bibliography   285
  Index   297

Preface

Architects working on projects where existing construction plays a part spend countless hours eliciting data from materials producers and installers relating to cleaning, repairing, and extending existing building materials and products and data for installing new materials and products over existing materials. The producers and installers know much of the needed data and generally give it up readily when asked, but they often do not include such information in their standard literature packages. As a result, there has been a long-standing need for source documents that included the industry's recommendations for repairing, maintaining, and extending existing materials and for installing new materials over existing materials. This book is one of a series called *Building Renovation and Restoration Series* that was conceived to answer that need.

In the thirty-plus years I have worked as an architect, and especially since 1975, when I began my practice as a specifications consultant, I have often wondered why there is no single source of data available to help architects, engineers, general contractors, and building owners deal with existing building materials. It is often necessary to consult several sources to resolve even apparently simple problems, partly because authoritative sources do not agree on many subjects. The time it takes to do all the necessary research is enormous.

I have done much of that kind of research myself over the years. This book includes the fruits of my earlier research, augmented by many additional hours of recent searching, making the book as broad as possible. In it, I have included as many of the industry's recommendations about working with existing plaster, gypsum board, ceramic tile, and related support systems as I could fit in. The data in this book, as is true for that in the other books in the series, come from published recommendations of producers and their associations; applicable codes and standards; federal agency guides and requirements; contractors who actually do such work in the field; the experiences of other architects and their consultants; and from the author's own experiences. Of course, no single book could possibly contain all known data about these subjects or discuss every potential problem that could occur. Where data are too voluminous to include in the text, references are given to help the reader find additional information from knowledgeable sources. Some sources of data about historic preservation are also listed.

This book, as do the others in the series, explains in practical, understandable narrative, supported by line drawings and photographs, how to extend, clean, repair, refinish, restore, and protect the existing materials that are the subject of the book, and how to install the materials discussed in the book over existing materials.

The audience for the books in the series include building owners; architects; federal and local government agencies; building contractors; university, professional, and public libraries; members of groups and associations interested in preservation; and everyone who is responsible for maintaining, cleaning, or repairing existing building construction materials. The books in this series are not how-to books meant to compete with publications such as *The Old-House Journal* or the books and tapes generated by the producers of the television series, "This Old House."

I hope that if this book doesn't directly solve your current problem, it will lead you to a source that will.

How to Use This Book

This book is divided into five chapters that discuss the subject areas suggested by their titles. Chapter 1 is a general introduction to the subject and offers suggestions as to how a building owner, architect, engineer, or general building contractor might approach solving the problems associated with dealing with existing building materials. It offers advice about seeking expert assistance when necessary and suggests the types of people and organizations that might be able to help.

Each of the other four chapters includes:

- A statement of the nature and purpose of the chapter
- A discussion of materials commonly used to produce the support system (Chapter 2) or type of finish (Chapters 3 through 5) discussed in that chapter and their usual uses
- A discussion of how and why those materials might fail. Chapters 2 through 5 include numbered lists of failure causes, such as "Leaving the base coat too smooth," which are grouped into failure source categories, such as "Structure Failure," "Structure Movement," "Improper System Design," "Bad Workmanship," and so on.

  In Chapters 3 through 5 there is also a list of failure types, such as "Loose Plaster." Thus, a failure that is recognized in the field (loose plaster, for example) can be traced to several possible causes, including in this case "Bad Workmanship: Improper Installation and Curing of Plaster: Cause 24," which is "leaving the base coat too smooth." Where appropriate, there is also an explanation and discussion of the failure causes, so that a reader can see specific examples showing the effects of selecting specific wrong materials.

- A discussion of methods of extending and repairing materials that have failed, as well as information on installing those types of materials over existing surfaces
- An indication of sources of additional information about the subjects in that chapter

The book has an Appendix that contains a list of sources of additional data. Sources include manufacturers, trade and professional associations, standards-setting bodies, government agencies, periodicals, book publishers, and others having knowledge of methods for restoring building materials. The list includes names, addresses, and telephone numbers. Sources from which data related to historic preservation may be obtained are identified with a boldface **HP**. Many of the publications and publishers of entries in the Bibliography are also listed in the Appendix.

The items listed in the Bibliography are annotated to show the book chapters to which they apply. Entries that are related to historic preservation are identified with a boldface **HP**.

Building owners, engineers and architects, and general building contractors will, in most cases, each use this book in a somewhat different way. The following suggestions give some indication of what some of those differences might be.

Owners

It is probably safe to assume that a building owner is consulting this book because the owner's building has experienced or is now experiencing failure of one of the materials discussed here. If the problem is an **EMERGENCY**, the owner should turn immediately to Chapter 1 and read the parts there called "What to Do in an Emergency," and in "Help for Building Owners," the subsection "Emergencies."

When the failure is temporarily under control, a more systematic approach is suggested. An owner may tend to want to turn directly to the chapter containing information about the finish that seems to have failed. An owner who has a good knowledge of such problems, and experience with them, may be able to approach the problem in that manner. Otherwise, it is better to first read and become familiar with the contents of Chapter 1, including those parts that do not at first seem to be applicable to the ʳoblem. The cause of a finish failure is not always readily ᵐping to an incorrect conclusion can be costly.

ᵗᵉʳ 1, the owner should turn to the chapter covering ᵐe point, that chapter may refer to another ˣample, often refer to Chapter 2, and both ᵤₚ ᵣ. When that happens, it is important to also read the cross-referenced material.

A word of caution, however. Unless experienced in dealing with such failures, an owner should not simply reach for the telephone to call for professional help until after reading the chapter covering the failed material. It's always better to know as much as possible about a problem before asking for help.

Architects and Engineers

An architect's or engineer's approach will depend somewhat on the professional's relationship with the owner. For example, an architect who has been consulted regarding a finish failure may approach the problem differently depending on whether the architect was the existing building's architect of record, especially if the failure has occurred within the normal expected life of the failed finish. In such cases, there may be legal as well as technical considerations. This book, though, is limited to a discussion of technical problems.

An architect's or engineer's first impulse may be to rush to the site to determine the exact nature of the problem. For one who has extensive experience with finish failures, that approach may be reasonable. Someone with little such experience, however, should do some homework before submitting to queries by a client or potential client.

That homework might consist of reading the chapters of this book that deal with the apparent problem and consulting the sources of additional information recommended there. Then, if the problem is even slightly beyond the architect's or engineer's expertise, the next step is to read Chapter 1 and decide whether outside professional help is needed. An architect or engineer who has some related experience might delay that decision until after studying the problem in the field. One who knows little about the subject, however, will probably want someone knowledgeable to accompany them on the first site visit. Chapter 1 offers suggestions about how to go about making that decision.

An architect's or engineer's approach will be slightly different when they are commissioned to renovate an existing building. In that case, extensive examination of existing construction documents and field conditions is called for. When finish failures have contributed significantly to the reasons for the renovations, and the architect or engineer is not thoroughly versed in dealing with such conditions, it is reasonable to consider seeking professional assistance throughout the design process. In that event, the architect or engineer should read Chapter 1 first, then refer to other chapters as needed during the design and document production process. Even when there is a consultant on the team, the architect or engineer should have enough knowledge to understand what the consultant is advising and to know what to expect of the consultant.

Building Contractors

How a building contractor uses this book depends on which hat the contractor is wearing at the time and on the contractor's expertise in dealing with existing building materials. For the contractor's own buildings, the suggestions given above for owners apply, except that the contractor will probably have more experience with such problems than many owners do.

When asked by a building owner to repair a failed finish, a contractor's approach might be similar to that described above for architects and engineers.

When repairs to a finish are part of a project for which a contractor is the general contractor of record, the problem is one of supervising the subcontractor who will actually repair the failed finish. Even a knowledgeable contractor will find it sometimes helpful to double-check the methods and materials a subcontractor proposes against the recommendations of an authoritative source, such as those listed in this book. It is also sometimes useful to verify a misgiving the contractor might have about specified materials or methods. In each of those cases, the contractor should read the chapter covering the subject at hand and check the other resources listed, whenever a question arises with which the contractor is not thoroughly familiar. Before selecting a subcontractor for repair work, a contractor might want to review Chapter 1.

Even a contractor who has extensive experience in repairing failed finishes will frequently encounter unusual conditions. Then the contractor should turn to the list of sources of additional information at the end of the appropriate chapter and the Appendix and Bibliography to discover who to ask for advice.

Disclaimer

The information in this book was derived from: data published by trade associations, standards-setting organizations, manufacturers, and government organizations; statements made to the author by their representatives; interviews with consultants and architects; and related books and periodicals. The author and publisher have exercised their best judgment in selecting data to be presented, have reported the recommendations of the sources consulted in good faith, and have made every reasonable effort to make the data presented accurate and authoritative. But neither the author nor the publisher warrant the accuracy or completeness of the data nor assume liability for its fitness for any particular purpose. Users bear the responsibility to apply their professional knowledge and experience to the use of data contained in this book, to consult the original sources of the data, to obtain additional information as needed, and to seek expert advice when appropriate.

Manufacturers and their products are occasionally mentioned in this book. Such mention is intended to indicate the availability of such products and manufacturers. No such mention in this book implies any endorsement by the author or the publisher of the mentioned manufacturer or product, other products of the mentioned manufacturer, or any statement made by the mentioned manufacturer or associated in any way with the product, its accompanying literature, or in advertising copy.

Similarly, handbooks and other literature produced by various manufacturers and associations are mentioned. Such mention does not imply that the mentioned item is the only one of its kind available or, for that matter, even the best available material. The author and publisher expect the reader to seek out other manufacturers and appropriate associations to ascertain if they have similar literature or will make similar data available.

Acknowledgments

A book of this kind requires the help of many people to make it valid and complete. I would like to acknowledge the manufacturers, producers' associations, standards-setting bodies, and other organizations and individuals whose product literature, recommendations, studies, reports, and advice helped make this book more complete and accurate than it otherwise would have been.

At risk of offending the many others who helped, I would like to single out the following people who were particularly helpful:

John Boland, Chicago Plastering Institute, Chicago, Illinois.

Scott Broney, Technical Service Manager, American Olean Tile Company, Inc., Lansdale, Pennsylvania.

Margaret Ficklen, Association of the Wall and Ceiling Industries, International, Washington, D.C.

Larry Horsman, National Concrete Masonry Association, Herndon, Virginia.

John W. Harn, Harn Construction Co., Laurel, Florida.

Bruce McIntosh, Portland Cement Association, Skokie, Illinois.

Walter F. Pruter, Walter F. Pruter Associates, Los Angeles, California.

Helen Richards, Mid-City Financial Corporation, Bethesda, Maryland.

Cathy Sedgewick, Association of the Wall and Ceiling Industries, International, Washington, D.C.

Sally Sims, Librarian, National Trust for Historic Preservation Library and University of Maryland Architectural Library, College Park, Maryland.

Everett G. Spurling, Jr., FAIA, FCSI, Bethesda, Maryland.

George H. Stewart, Sr., Stewart Brothers Photographers, Inc., Rockville, Maryland.

Also, I would like to especially thank Jess McIlvain, AIA, CCS, CSI, Jess McIlvain & Associates, Bethesda, Maryland, for contributing his time, energy, and expertise to help me gather the data about ceramic tile in Chapter 5. Mr. McIlvain is the leading independent consultant on the installation of ceramic tile and causes of installation failures. He is also a registered architect; a member of AIA, CSI, and ASTM; a Certified Construction Specifier; and is listed in the American Bar Association Register of Expert Witnesses in the Construction Industry. He is the author of numerous articles on tile-related subjects, many of which are listed in this book's Bibliography.

CHAPTER 1

Introduction

A building's finishes are affected by many factors, including the construction of the building; the finish materials themselves; the humidity and temperature during and after the application of finishes or installation; the quality of the workmanship used to apply or install the finishes; and how well the finishes are protected after they have been applied or installed. For interior finishes to remain in good condition, the building's shell and those elements, such as doors and windows, used to close openings in the shell must turn away wind and water and protect interior spaces from excessive temperature and humidity levels and fluctuations.

Almost every building will, at some time, experience a finish failure. Most of those failures will manifest themselves as cracks, discolorations, or disintegration of the finish material, or by the finish material separating from its support system. When a finish failure occurs, there is both an immediate problem and a long-range problem.

The immediate problem, of course, is to stop the damage from getting worse. The long-range problem is to repair the damage in such a way that it will not recur.

This chapter includes a brief generic discussion of finishes and their failures and outlines steps that a building owner can take to solve both the short- and long-range problems associated with failure. It also discusses the relationship of architects, engineers, building contractors, and damage (sometimes called forensic) consultants to the owner on projects involving finish failures, and outlines orderly ways in which those professionals can approach the problem-solving process.

This chapter includes an approach to determining the nature and extent of finish failures and suggests the type of assistance that a building owner might seek to help solve the problem.

Chapters 2 through 5 contain detailed remedies and sources of additional data.

What Finishes Are and What They Do

The term "finish" in this book refers to applied materials used as the finished surface on buildings. This book includes plaster, gypsum board, and ceramic tile finishes and their support systems. Other finishes addressed in other books in this series include non-structural metals; wood paneling and flooring; resilient flooring; various materials used as acoustical treatment; and paint and transparent finishes. Materials which act as the final finish, but are often also part of the building shell or structure are also addressed in other books in this series. They include stone, brick, and concrete unit masonry.

The term "failure" in this book refers to every type of failure, from the slight crazing of a surface to total disintegration of the material, and everything in between.

Failure Types and Conditions

A failed finish is often a symptom of an underlying problem, rather than a failure of the finish material itself. Recognizing that a finish failure has occurred often requires no special expertise (Fig. 1-1). Cracked tile, sagging ceilings, and nail pops, for example, are easy to see. Discovering the cause of the failure and determining the proper remedy, however, often requires a detailed knowledge of finishes and their support systems, and often of structural design as well.

When a finish fails, reviewing the appropriate chapter of this book, or another book in this series wherein the failed material is discussed, might help an owner, architect, engineer, or building contractor identify the cause of the failure and solve the problem. If, after reading the material presented

Figure 1-1 This looks unsalvageable, but it's mostly cosmetic. All of the finishes require extensive work, but the structure is essentially sound. (*Photo by Stewart Bros., courtesy of Mid-City Financial Corporation.*)

in this book series and examining the referenced additional data, the reader does not feel competent to proceed, seeking professional help is in order.

What to Do in an Emergency

In an emergency, it is often necessary to act first and analyze later. When action must be taken immediately to stop damage that is already occurring or imminent, whatever is necessary should be done. Emergency action, for example, might consist of shoring a sagging ceiling using wood braces. If the failure is occurring because of a building or plumbing leak, it is, of course, necessary to stop the leak as soon as possible.

A word of caution is in order, however. Unless doing so is absolutely unavoidable, no irreversible remedial action should be taken. Small repairs that cannot be easily removed can become major costs items when permanent repairs are attempted. Hastily tearing holes in a ceiling to gain access to a leaking pipe could damage the ceiling to the extent that it must be completely removed later and a new ceiling installed.

Professional Help

If, after reading the chapters of this book or another book in this series that addresses the identified problem area, the next step is still unclear, or it is not possible to be sure of the nature of the problem, consult with someone else who has experience in dealing with the kind of failure being experienced. Who that is will vary with the knowledge and experience of the person seeking the help.

Help for Building Owners

Building owners can turn to several levels of expert help when finish problems appear.

Emergencies. In emergencies, a building owner should seek help from the most readily available professional person or organization that can stop the damage from continuing. But, even in an emergency it is better to seek help from a known organization than to simply thumb through the telephone book.

The first step is to call someone who can remedy the immediate problem, and worry about protocol later. An exception to this rule should be made, however, if the building is still under a construction warranty. Then the owner should go to the person who is responsible for the warranty, which is usually a general contractor.

In other circumstances, if the owner has a relationship with a building construction professional who is able to solve the immediate problem, then this is the place to start. If the owner has relationships with several building professionals, the place to start is with the most appropriate. For example, if the failed finish was recently installed by a specialty contractor under direct contract with the owner—that is, there was no general contractor involved—the owner should call that specialty contractor.

Unless they are the only building professional that the owner knows, or the owner is unable to find someone to stop damage from occurring, calling an architect or engineer in an emergency is probably not appropriate. The best most of them will be able to do is recommend an organization that might stop the damage from occurring. Going through the building professional could waste valuable time.

In some areas of the country, a call to a local organization representing building industry professionals will net a list of acceptable organizations specializing in repairing the kind of damage that is occurring. Such local organizations might include a local chapter of the Associated General Contractors of America; an association of plastering, gypsum drywall, or tile contractors, as applicable; or the American Institute of Architects.

It might be possible to find a local damage consultant who specializes in the kind of finish that has been damaged, but that person may only be able to recommend someone to repair the damage.

In each case, the methods recommended later in this chapter for contacting the various entities would apply in an emergency. There would not, however, be time to do the double-checking suggested.

Architects and Engineers. Even in nonemergency situations, building owners with easily identifiable finish problems do not always need to consult an architect or engineer. An exception occurs when repairing a finish failure is part of a general remodeling, renovation, or restoration project. Even when the repairs are solely evidenced by finish failure, repairs requiring manipulation of structural systems or which might cause harm to the public may require a building permit. In many jurisdictions, building officials will not accept permit applications unless accompanied by drawings and specifications sealed by an architect or engineer. Sometimes, the scope of the problem warrants hiring an architect or engineer to prepare needed drawings and specifications, even when authorities having jurisdiction do not require such documents.

When the owner hires an architect or engineer, the same standards one would usually follow when hiring such professionals apply. In addition to the usual professional qualifications applicable to any project, however, architects and engineers commissioned to perform professional services related to an existing building should have experience in the type of work needed. It is seldom a good idea to hire an architectural firm with experience solely in office building construction, no matter the scope, to renovate an existing hospital.

General Building Contractors. Simple finish failure problems are often best handled by a building contractor. Depending on the scope, the contractor may be a general contractor or a specialty contractor. If the problem is isolated and involves a single discipline, a single specialty contractor may be all that is needed. If multiple disciplines are involved, a general contractor may be needed to coordinate the activities of several specialty contractors. Owners with experience in administering contracts may be able to coordinate the work without a general contractor.

When selecting a general contractor, it is best to select one that the owner knows. If there is no such contractor, the owner should seek advice in finding a competent firm. Such advice might come from satisfied building owners, architects, or engineers that the owner knows, or from the American Institute of Architects. As a last resort, an owner might ask for a recommendation from a contractor's organization. The owner should bear in mind, however, that asking for a recommendation from an organization that is supported by and that represents the firm being sought will, at best, get a list of firms in the area. This is not a good way to get a recommendation. This is in no way an indictment of contractors or their associations. The same advice applies to doctors, lawyers, and architects. You find the best ones by word of mouth.

If the project is large enough to warrant doing so, an owner might consider seeking competitive bids from a list of contractors. Few finish repair projects are that large or complicated, however. Negotiation is better, if reputable firms can be found with which to negotiate. If all of the parties are unknown, competitive bidding may be the only way to get a reasonable price.

Specialty Contractors. If the finish repair project is small and *simple,* a building owner is usually better off hiring a specialty contractor directly, using the same methods suggested earlier for finding a reputable general contractor. In addition, general contractors the owner knows to be reputable are one source of recommendations for specialty contractors, so long as there is no symbiotic relationship between the general contractor and the specialty contractor. Product manufacturer's representatives are also often a good source of recommendations for installers or applicators of their products.

Competitive bidding is a more acceptable procedure when dealing with specialty contractors for small projects than it is for dealing with a general contractor.

Specialty Consultants. There are three circumstances in which an owner may want to look for a consultant who specializes in the particular type of finish damage that has been encountered.

First, when neither a knowledgeable contractor nor architect is available for consultation. Contractors and architects who have great knowledge about relatively recent materials and their failures may know little about the types of materials and systems used in older buildings. A requirement for historic preservation may be sufficient cause to look for a specialty consultant.

Second, when the owner's contractor and architect cannot agree on the cause of a finish failure or the appropriate means to make repairs.

Third, when the people who are already involved cannot determine with certainty the cause of the damage or the proper method for making repairs.

Consultants who specialize in damage problems are sometimes called forensic consultants. They should be able to determine the nature of a problem and identify its true cause; find a solution to the problem; select the proper products to use in making repairs; write specifications and produce drawings related to the solution; and oversee the repairs.

Unfortunately, all such consultants are not created equal. Many who present themselves as consultants are actually building product manufacturer's representatives trying to increase their sales or specialty contractors trying to enlarge their business. While most of them are reputable and some are competent to give advice, few are sufficiently knowledgeable to identify or advise an owner about solving underlying substrate or structure problems. Following the recommendations of an incompetent consultant can cause problems that will linger for years.

Selecting a consultant can be filled with uncertainty and potential for harm. There are no licensing requirements, and no nationally recognized associations representing consultants who specialize in plaster, gypsum board, or tile problems. While there are some training programs available, in reality, anyone who chooses to do so can hang up a shingle that says "Ceramic Tile Consultant," for example. As a result, a building owner who needs to hire a damage consultant must qualify that consultant with little help. One way to do this is to hire an architect or engineer and let him select and qualify the consultant, subject to the owner's approval, of course.

Some contractor's organizations, such as the Association of Tile, Terrazzo, Marble, Contractors and Affiliates, Inc., can recommend consultants.

Another potential source of recommendations for consultants are standards-setting organizations such as the Tile Council of America and the Materials and Methods Standards Association for ceramic tile consultants.

Asking individual specialty contractors to recommend a consultant may not be a good idea. Although some of them hire damage consultants themselves, many specialty contractors feel that such consultants are, at best, a necessary evil. Their opinion probably stems from the tendency of some manufacturer's representatives to call themselves consultants and then oversell their abilities and knowledge.

Regardless of who makes the recommendation or does the hiring, the consultant should have a demonstrated expertise in dealing with the problems at hand. Obtaining references from the consultant's satisfied clients is an appropriate prequalification tool. A licensed architect or engineer who has extensive experience dealing with existing construction might be acceptable.

A consultant who is qualified to deal with finish failures in relatively new construction may know little about the kinds of materials that might be encountered in very old buildings. This is a particular problem when historic preservation is involved. A consultant for this type of work needs to demonstrate knowledge in dealing with very old materials and systems and the special requirements associated with historic preservation. It may not be possible to find a consultant who is an expert in dealing with old materials and also knowledgeable in general construction principles. In that case, it may be necessary to find two consultants with complimentary knowledge.

A damage consultant should also have extensive knowledge of the material that has failed, general construction principles, and structure physiology. Many finish failures are a result of several problems (Fig. 1-2). The consultant should know enough about buildings as a whole to be able to identify all of the underlying problems, and not just the obvious ones or those directly associated with the finish itself. Many finish problems are caused by structure movement, for example. The consultant should be able to determine whether the responsible movement is normal movement, which has not been accounted for in the finish or its support system, or is a matter of structure failure, which might require repairing the structure itself. The consultant need not, however, be a structural engineer or know how to repair the structure. Usually, the ability to make the diagnoses is sufficient.

Finally, the consultant should have no financial stake in the outcome of the investigation. The owner needs to be sure that the consultant is an independent third party who is selling a professional service and not installation or repair of a product. Neither a product manufacturer's representative nor a contractor who wants to actually make the repairs meets this qualification.

Figure 1-2   Vandals and time are often conspirators in finish failures. The apartment shown in this photograph is repairable, but it won't be cheap. (*Photo by Stewart Bros., courtesy of Mid-City Financial Corporation.*)

Help for Architects and Engineers

Architects and engineers usually get involved in finish repairs only when the repairs are extensive, have occurred on a prestigious building, or are part of a larger renovation, restoration, or remodeling project.

Architects who do not have extensive experience in dealing with finish problems or working with existing finishes should seek outside help from someone who has such experience. The nature of that help and the person selected to consult depends on the type and complexity of the problem.

Other Architects and Engineers.   One source of professional consultation for architects and engineers is another architect or engineer who has experience with the type of finish problem at hand. The qualifications needed are similar to those outlined earlier in this chapter for specialty damage consultants. The other architect or engineer need not be in architectural or engineering practice. Specifications consultants and qualified architects and engineers employed by government, institutional, or private corporate organizations should not be overlooked.

Specialty Consultants.   Architects also can employ specialty damage consultants who are not architects or engineers, when the situation warrants it. The qualifications outlined earlier in this chapter for such consultants apply no matter who is hiring the consultant.

Product Manufacturers and Industry Standards.   Product manufacturers and their associations often produce sufficient information for a knowledgeable architect or engineer to deal with many finish failures. The architect or engineer must, of course, compare product manufacturer's statements with those of other manufacturers and industry standards and exercise good judgment in deciding which claims to believe. The problem is the same as any other where architects and engineers consult producers and their associations for advice. The architect or engineer must study every claim carefully, especially if the claim seems extravagant, and double-check everything.

Help for General Building Contractors

Whether a general building contractor needs to consult an outside expert depends on the complexity of the problem, the contractor's own experience, and whether the owner has engaged an architect or specialty consultant. Duplication of effort is unnecessary, unless the contractor intends to challenge the views expressed by the owner's consultants, or the content of the drawings and specifications.

A general building contractor acting alone on a project where the owner has not engaged an architect, engineer, or consultant must base the need for hiring consultants on such factors as the contractor's experience and expertise with the types of problems to be encountered, the contractor's specialty subcontractor's experience and expertise in dealing with the types of problems involved, and the complexity of the problems.

Hiring a specialty consultant may complicate a general contractor's relationship with subcontractors. Such duplicity is seldom justified and often a bad idea. An experienced and qualified specialty subcontractor is not likely to appreciate a damage consultant hired to tell the subcontractor how to do the job. The general contractor would be better off finding a qualified subcontractor to do the work and rely on that subcontractor's advice. If no such subcontractor is available, and the general contractor is not experienced with the problem at hand, hiring a consultant may be necessary, regardless of the feelings of the subcontractor. Muddling along to salve feelings is wholly incompetent and unprofessional. In these circumstances, the contractor should recommend that the owner employ a qualified architect or engineer to specify the repairs and let the owner and the design professional hire a damage consultant if necessary.

In the event that a contractor should hire a specialty damage consultant, the earlier recommendations in this chapter apply.

Prework On-site Examination

On-site examinations before the work begins are important tools in helping to determine the type and extent of a finish failure and the damage to underlying construction that it might portend. Who should be present during an on-site examination is dictated by the stage at which the examination will take place.

The Owner

The first examination should be by the owner or the owner's personnel to determine the general extent of the problem. This examination should help the owner decide what the next step should be and the type of consultant that the owner needs to contact, if any.

When the owner has selected a consultant, the owner and the consultant should visit the site and define the work to be done. The owner's consultant may be an architect or engineer, general contractor, specialty subcontractor, or specialty damage consultant. This second site examination should be attended by a representative of each expert that the owner has engaged to help with the problem. A specialty damage consultant, if engaged by another of the owner's consultants, also should be present. The general contractor's specialty subcontractors should also be present, if they have been selected.

During the second site visit, the parties should become familiar with conditions at the site and offer suggestions about how to solve the problem.

Architects and Engineers

An architect or engineer hired to repair a failed finish should, before visiting the site if possible, determine the products and systems used in the failed finish and the type of underlying and supporting construction. The architect should then visit the site with the owner to determine the extent of the work and to begin to decide how to solve the problem. Based on discussion with the owner about the nature of the problem, the architect should have decided whether to engage professional help. If a consultant is to be used, that consultant should visit the site with the owner and the architect.

If, as a result of the architect's first site visit, the architect determines that a specialty damage consultant, previously considered unnecessary, is needed, the architect should arrange for another site visit with that consultant.

During the progress of the work, the architect and the architect's consultant should visit the site as often as is necessary to fully determine the nature and extent of the problem and to help arrive at a total solution. These site visits should extend the observation beyond the immediate problem to ascertain whether additional, unseen, damage might be present.

Building Contractors

Non-Bid Projects.   On non-bid projects, a building contractor may wear at least two hats.

The easiest situation to deal with is a negotiated bid based on professionally prepared construction documents. In that case, the contractor should conduct an extensive site examination to verify the conditions shown and the extent and type of work called for in the construction documents. Offering a proposal based on unverified construction documents is a bad business practice that can cost much more than proper investigation would have, if the documents are later found to be erroneous.

When the owner has not hired an architect or consultant to ascertain and document the type and extent of the work, the contractor must act as both designer and contractor. Then, the contractor should visit the site with the owner as soon as possible, and revisit as often as necessary, to determine the nature of the problem and the extent of the work to be done. A carefully drawn proposal is an absolute must to be sure that the owner does not expect more than the contractor proposes to do.

Even when the owner hires an architect or other consultant, the contractor should visit the site with the owner and the owner's consultant as soon as such a visit is permitted. The purpose of the visit is to ascertain the extent and type of work to be done and to recommend repair methods. Invite specialty subcontractors to also visit the site with the owner, the owner's consultants, and the contractor, if possible. The more input the contractor has in the design process, the better the result is likely to be.

Bid Projects.   Even when the contractor is invited to bid on a project for which construction documents have been prepared, a prebid site visit is imperative. No contractor should bid on work related to existing construction without extensive examination of the existing construction. Some construction contracts demand it. Some construction contracts even try to make the failure to discover a problem the contractor's responsibility. Even if the courts throw that clause out, who can afford the time and costs of a lawsuit? A contractor should know the project well and establish exactly what work is to be done before bidding. Insufficient data may be cause for not choosing to bid on a project.

CHAPTER 2

Support Systems

Finishes are supported by the building's structural framing systems; by solid substrates, such as concrete and unit masonry, which may be either structural or nonstructural; or by framing and furring systems erected specifically to support the finishes.

This chapter includes a general discussion of structural systems and solid substrate materials and installation, as well as a more specific discussion of structural systems and solid substrate problems that may lead to finish failures. It also includes descriptions of both wood and framing and furring systems, including the components and materials normally used; potential errors that can lead to failure in the framing, furring, or finish supported; and ways to correct the errors once they have been identified.

Structural system, solid substrate, and framing and furring problems often first appear as a failure in the finish being supported. Chapters 3, 4, and 5 each contain a part ("Evidence of Failure in Standard Thickness and Veneer Plaster" in Chapter 3, for example) where a number of evidences of failure are listed. Each evidence of failure is referenced back to another portion of that chapter ("Why Standard Thickness and Veneer Plaster

Fails'' in Chapter 3, for example) where the possible causes of the failure are listed. Among the causes listed there are "Structure Failure," "Structure Movement," "Solid Substrate Problems," "Wood Framing and Furring Problems," and "Metal Framing and Furring Problems." Those five reasons for failure are addressed in this chapter under their respective headings, and the numbers used for those reasons in Chapters 3, 4, and 5 correspond to the numbers listed for those failure causes in this chapter.

Structural Framing Systems

A building's structural system can have a major impact on whether the building's finishes remain in good condition or fail. The structural system can affect the finishes in two ways: The structure can fail, or the structure can move in ways that are not anticipated for in the finish systems.

Structure Failure

Structures fail because they are improperly designed or because they experience conditions which exceed their design limitations. Design limitations are dictated by legal requirements and economic factors. It is not economically feasible to design every structure to handle every condition that might occur. Even a building designed to withstand an earthquake that measures 8 on the Richter scale may fail if the level reaches 8.5. It might not be possible to design a building that will be completely undamaged in even a small earthquake.

Structure failure may be large in scope, including even complete building collapse. More frequently, however, structure failure is relatively small in magnitude. A single cause may generate failure at any level. An undersized footing, for example, may lead to building collapse or simply more settlement than normal.

Since even minor structural failure will almost certainly damage a building's finishes, especially homogenous finishes such as plaster, it is necessary before repairing failed finishes to determine whether structural failure is responsible for the finish failing. Where structural failure is to blame for finish failure, it is usually necessary to correct the structural failure before repairing the finish. Otherwise, the finish failure will usually recur. In severe cases, structural reconstruction, such as shoring up beams, adding columns, or replacing structural members, may be necessary. When the structure damage is self-limiting and not dangerous to the building or to people, however, it is sometimes possible to modify the existing, or provide a new, finish support system (framing and furring) without making major corrections to the failed structure. An example is a self-limiting minor settlement caused by a small weak spot in the earth beneath a portion of a footing. With a few exceptions, repair of a failed structural system is beyond the scope of this book. The exceptions are wood stud framing of bearing walls and partitions, and light gage metal framing of exterior walls, bearing walls, and partitions. This book has been written with the assumption that, for other structural elements, such as wood and metal trusses and joists, steel framing, wood truss-joists, and heavy timber construction, structural problems have been diagnosed and necessary repairs have been made.

To prevent structural system failure, the following set of conditions must be met:

1. The structure must be properly designed to withstand all loads to be applied with no excess deflection, vibration, settlement (especially differential settlement), expansion, or contraction.

Structure Movement

In addition to finish failures caused by structure failure, damage to finishes can occur because the structure moves, especially if the movement is larger than expected. Unaccounted-for structure movement is probably the major cause of cracking and other plaster failures, for example. It should be suspected when any finish fails, especially if the evidence of the failure is cracks or the finish separating from the substrates. To prevent failure, finishes and their support systems must take structure movement into account.

Undue structure movement is a symptom of structural failure, as discussed in previous paragraphs. Some structure movement, however, is normal and unavoidable. Expected structural movement due to wind, thermal expansion and contraction, and deflection under loads is large in many modern buildings, which are purposely designed to have light, flexible structural frames that are less rigid than the structural systems used in most older buildings. Exterior column movement is a particular problem. Movement may be especially large in high-rise structures where both flexibility and wind loads are large. While these light modern designs are usually structurally safe, they are more likely to contribute to failures in partition systems and interior finishes, unless the designer is aware of the problems they impose and takes steps to head off those problems. Finishes and their support systems must be designed to accommodate the expected movement. Normal structure movement may be caused by one of the following:

1. Variable wind pressure, particularly on high-rise structures.
2. Structure settlement.
3. Thermal expansion and contraction.

4. Deflection of structural members and slabs.
5. Creep in concrete structures. Creep is permanent change in structure shape due to initial deflection in concrete elements.
6. Structure vibration, which is often transferred from operating equipment in the building. Vibration can loosen fasteners.
7. Lumber shrinkage. Even relatively dry lumber will shrink. Shrinking tends to cause lumber to warp or twist.
8. Lumber expansion due to absorption of free water, condensation, or water vapor in high-humidity conditions.

Solid Substrates

The most common solid substrates to which finishes are directly applied are concrete and masonry. Other solid substrates to which other finishes are applied include stone, adobe, and some types of tile, but most of the time those types of solid substrates are furred before finishes are applied. Concrete and masonry are also often furred to receive finishes.

Failures in solid substrates to which finishes are applied either directly or over furring will usually damage the finishes. The possibility of solid substrate failure must be investigated and ruled out before repairs to finishes or furring are attempted. When a damaged solid substrate is responsible for a finish failure, it is often necessary to repair the solid substrate before repairing the finish. When the solid substrate damage is self-limiting and not dangerous to the building or to people, it is sometimes possible to repair an existing, or install a new, furring system to support the finish without repairing the solid substrate.

Repair of solid substrates is beyond the scope of this book. This book has been written with the assumption that damaged solid substrates have been discovered and that the necessary repairs have been made.

Solid substrates include those that are part of the building's structural system and those that are fillers, such as nonbearing walls and partitions. Solid substrates are used in two ways to support finishes. Some finishes, such as paint, are often applied directly to solid substrates.

Finishes consisting of boards or smaller units, such as tile, are also sometimes applied directly to solid substrates using fasteners, adhesives, or both fasteners and adhesives. Those same finishes are also sometimes applied over a support system, such as wood or metal framing and furring.

It is not the purpose of this book to discuss concrete or masonry construction methods. The reader should recognize, however, that the construction and finishing methods used on solid substrates can drastically affect the finishes applied, and contribute to their failure when it occurs.

Solid Substrate Problems

Solid substrate problems that can lead to finish failure include the following:

1. The solid substrates exude materials that affect the finish or cause it to delaminate from the solid substrate. Some substances extruded by solid substrates that can cause harm to applied finishes are not foreign to the substrate material. It is perfectly natural for a concrete wall to evaporate water for an extended period, for example. Applying a finish too early can lead to failure of that finish. Problems of that sort are not, however, actually substrate failures. This book lists those kinds of failures under the heading "Bad Workmanship," and discusses them in the chapters in which each finish appears.

   Some foreign substances that will cause finish failure, however, are the result of bad workmanship in installing the substrate and have nothing to do with the finish installer's workmanship. Efflorescence is an example.

2. The solid substrate material cracks or breaks up, joints crack, or surfaces spall due to bad materials, incorrect material selection for the location and application, or bad workmanship.

3. The solid substrate moves excessively due to improper design or installation. Excess movements that can cause problems include deflection, vibration, settlement (especially differential settlement), expansion, and contraction.

4. Unaccounted-for normal movement. As is true for structural systems, some movement in solid substrates is normal and unavoidable. That movement must be accounted for in the finish systems. Normal movement includes that caused by settlement, thermal expansion and contraction, creep, and vibration.

Other Building Element Problems

Other building elements that are poorly designed, or that fail, can cause finishes to fail. Those other building elements include roofing; flashing; waterproofing; insulation; elements that close openings, such as windows, doors, and louvers; caulking and sealants; and mechanical and electrical systems. The types of failures in those systems that can cause finishes to fail include the following:

1. Other building elements, whether poorly designed or simply failed, that permit water intrusion into the finish, its substrates, or both. Possible sources of water intrusion include roof and plumbing leaks (Fig. 2-1), failed sealants, and leaks through doors, windows, louvers, and other opening closers.

Figure 2-1 A plumbing leak caused this damage. (*Photo by author.*)

2. Designs that permit condensation to form and enter the finish, its
   supports, or both. Condensation can result from selecting the wrong
   materials or installation methods for insulation and vapor retarders,
   or improperly locating those elements. Failing to provide proper ventilation in attic spaces can also lead to condensation affecting
   finishes.
3. Placing unsupported insulation directly on ceiling boards or lath. Under some circumstances, ceilings will support insulation loads. The
   condition should be checked with the finish manufacturer when failure occurs that might be related to applied loads.

Wood Framing and Furring

Wood framing to which finishes are applied includes portions of the structure, such as joints, trusses, and bearing studs, as well as partition framing.
Though there is no attempt here to discuss in detail the many possible
building framing systems, the general requirements related to stability, tolerances, and materials included here apply to the structural portions of the
building when they receive finishes directly.

General Requirements

Wood framing and furring should comply with the building code and the standards and minimum requirements of generally recognized industry standards, such as the following:

- The American Institute of Timber Construction's (AITC) *Timber Construction Standards* and *Timber Construction Manual.*
- The United States Department of Commerce's (DOC) *PS 1—Construction and Industrial Plywood* and *PS 20—American Softwood Lumber Standard.*
- The National Forest Products Association's (NFPA) *National Design Specifications for Wood Construction; Span Tables for Joists and Rafters;* and *Manual for House Framing.*
- The Southern Pine Inspection Bureau's (SPIB) *Standard Grading Rules for Southern Pine Lumber.*
- The Western Wood Products Association's (WWPA) *Grading Rules for Western Lumber; Grade Stamp Manual; A-2, Lumber Specifications Information; Western Woods Use Book;* and *Wood Frame Design.*
- The West Coast Lumber Inspection Bureau's (WCLIB) *Standard Grading Rules for West Coast Lumber.*
- Applicable American Wood-Preservers Association (AWPA) standards.
- Applicable Federal Specifications and ASTM standards.
- Applicable rules of the respective grading and inspecting agencies for species and products indicated.

Materials

Wood and Plywood

Moisture Content of Lumber.   Probably the single largest cause of problems with finishes associated with wood framing or furring are caused by the wood being not properly cured when installed. Wood for framing and furring should be seasoned lumber with 19 percent maximum moisture content at time of dressing. Lumber with a moisture content in excess of 19 percent can be expected to change in size by 1 percent for each 4 percent reduction in moisture content. As the wood changes in size it will usually also warp and twist, especially when held in place at the ends as is the case in framing and furring members.

Lumber Classification and Grades.   Softwood materials should comply with the U.S. Department of Commerce's *PS 20,* and the National Forest

Products Associations *National Design Specifications for Wood Construction.* Each piece of lumber should be grade-stamped by an agency certified by the Board of Review, American Lumber Standards Committee.

Studs, joists, rafters, foundation plates and sills, planking, beams, stringers, posts, structural sheathing, and similar load-bearing members should be of at least the minimum grades required by the building code and the engineering calculations made for the building. Light framing lumber might be, for example, "Stud" or "Standard" grade lumber for studs and "Standard" grade for other light framing, or "Construction," "Standard," or "Utility" grade for all light framing. Heavier structural framing might be "Select Structural Grade" or "Southern Pine No. 1 Dense" grade.

Often, structural lumber is selected by its structural characteristics. It might, for example, have the following minimum allowable stresses and modulus of elasticity:

Fb (extreme fiber stress in bending): 1250 pounds per square inch.

Fv (horizontal Shear): 95 pounds per square inch.

Fc (compression perpendicular to grain) 385 pounds per square inch.

E (modulus of elasticity): 1,500,000 pounds per square inch.

Blocking, nailers, and similar items are usually the same grade as the framing.

Rough carpentry boards might be WWPA "No. 2 Common," or SPIB "Southern Pine No. 2."

Concealed trim and blocking might be Douglas fir "C Select" or equivalent WWPA softwood.

The previous are examples only. The actual lumber used may have different characteristics.

Lumber Species. Lumber for framing and furring may be any of a number of available species, including, but not limited to, Douglas fir, Douglas-fir-larch, hem-fir, southern pine, spruce-pine-fir, and redwood.

Lumber Sizes. In newer buildings, actual wood sizes will probably be in accord with the United States Department of Commerce's *PS 20,* and the lumber will probably be surfaced on all four sides. In older buildings sizes may be actual (a full 2 inch by 4 inch instead of 1-1/2 by 3-1/2 inch) or a different actual dimension for the same nominal size. For many years, the normal actual size for a 2 by piece of lumber was 1-5/8 inches and not today's 1-1/2 inches, for example. Older furring and framing lumber may not be surfaced on any sides, or may be surfaced only where finishes are applied.

Softwood Plywood. While not usually used in furring systems, or as a substrate for finishes, softwood plywood might appear in some framing systems. Much softwood plywood used in framing is Douglas fir manufactured and graded in accordance with the United States Department of Commerce *PS 1.* Each panel should bear the appropriate American Plywood Association (APA) grade trademark, indicating grade, but the grade mark may not be visible after installation.

Miscellaneous Framing Components and Other Materials

Wood Roof Trusses. Trusses should have been designed for the manufacturer by a registered professional engineer to support the loads to be applied and in accordance with building code requirements.

Roof trusses are factory fabricated, often from No. 2 Douglas fir, or equivalent. Connections are usually made with metal plate connectors or plywood gussets. Metal truss plates, whether pressed-in tooth or nail-in types, should comply with the Truss Plate Institute's *Design Specifications for Light Metal Plate Connected Wood Trusses.* Truss plate connectors less than 1/8 inch thick should be zinc coated or noncorrosive metal, and conform to the provisions of ASTM Standard A 525 for Commercial Coating Class.

Wood Truss-Type Floor Joists. Joists should have been designed for the manufacturer by a registered engineer to support the loads to be applied and in accordance with building code requirements. These are proprietary products with unique characteristics. Where it is necessary to work with or alter them, the manufacturer should be ascertained and consulted in advance.

Miscellaneous Materials. The following miscellaneous materials are necessary for wood framing and furring installations:

- Rough hardware, metal fasteners, supports, and anchors.
- Nails, spikes, screws, bolts, clips, anchors, and similar items of sizes and types to rigidly secure framing and furring members in place. These items should be hot-dip galvanized or plated when in contact with concrete, masonry, or pressure treated wood or plywood, and where subject to high moisture conditions or exposed.
- Suitable rough and finish hardware, as necessary.
- Bolts, toggle bolts, sheet metal screws, and other suitable approved anchors and fasteners. These should be located not more than 36 inches on center to firmly secure wood furring, plates, nailers, block-

ing, grounds, and other wood members, and plywood securely in place. Nuts and washers should be included with each bolt. Anchors and fasteners set in concrete or masonry should be hot-dip galvanized, and should be types designed to be embedded in concrete or masonry as applicable and to form a permanent anchorage.

• Special fasteners or framing devices are sometimes used in lieu of conventional types of fasteners (nails, screws, bolts, etc.) to improve installation procedures or to provide higher load values. Such devices should be designed and manufactured to conform with pertinent standards for material selection and performance. Where framing or furring fastened with such devices must be altered or modified, the manufacturer should be consulted for particulars, including bearing and load-carrying capacities and methods to be used in dealing with the devices. Such devices should have the manufacturer's name or identifying mark on them.

• Building paper is often placed between framing and furring and the substrate, especially at exterior walls, to prevent moisture transfer from the substrate to the framing or furring. The material most often used is 15 pound asphalt-saturated unperforated felt complying with ASTM Standard D 226.

Wood and Plywood Treatment

Preservative Treatment.   Treated lumber or plywood should comply with the applicable requirements of the applicable standards of the American Wood Preservers Association (AWPA) and the American Wood Preservers Bureau (AWPB). Each treated item should be marked with an AWPB "Quality Mark," but the markings may not be visible after installation.

Most recently treated framing and furring will have been treated in compliance with AWPA standards C2 for lumber and C9 for plywood, using water-borne preservatives complying with AWPB standard LP-2. Some installations might be treated using other AWPA or AWPB recognized chemicals. Older applications may have been treated in accordance with other standards and using other chemicals, sometimes even creosote.

After treatment, treated wood should be kiln-dried to a maximum moisture content of 19 percent.

Most framing and furring will not be pressure preservative treated. Treated portions of framing and furring usually include wood and plywood near or in contact with roofing or associated flashing; and wood sills, sleepers, blocking, furring, stripping, foundation plates, and other concealed members in contact with masonry or concrete.

Treated items should be fabricated before treatment where possible.

Where treated material is later cut, the cut surfaces should be coated with a heavy brush coat of the same chemical used for the initial treatment.

Fire-Retardant Treatment. Fire-retardant treated lumber and plywood should comply with AWPA standards for pressure impregnation with fire-retardant chemicals, and should have a flame spread rating of not more than 25 when tested in accordance with Underwriter's Laboratories Incorporated's (UL) Test 723 or ASTM Standard E 84. It should show no increase in flame spread and no significant progressive combustion when the test is continued for 20 minutes longer than those standards require. The materials used should not have a deleterious effect on connectors or fasteners.

Treated items that are exposed to the exterior or to high humidities should be treated with materials that show no change in fire-hazard classification when subjected to the standard rain test stipulated in UL Test 790.

Fire-retardant treatment chemicals should not bleed through or adversely affect the type of finish used.

Each piece of fire-retardant treated lumber and plywood should have a UL label, but the labels may not be visible after application.

After treatment, treated wood should be kiln-dried to a maximum moisture content of 19 percent.

Framing and furring in walls and floors where fire rated construction is required by the building code will probably be treated.

Installation

General Requirements. Lumber and plywood with defects that might impair the quality of the finished surfaces, or that are too small to use in fabricating the framing or furring with the minimum number of joints possible or with the optimum joint arrangement, should not be used.

The framing or furring should be laid out carefully and set accurately to the correct levels and lines. Members should be plumb, true, and accurately cut and fitted. Openings should be framed and blocking provided for the related work of other trades.

Framing materials should be sorted so that defects will have the least detrimental effect on the stability and appearance of the installation. Large or unsound knots should be avoided at connections. Materials at corners should be straight.

Framing and furring should be securely attached to the substrates in the proper locations, and should be level, plumb, square, and in line. Anchoring and fastening should be done in accordance with applicable recognized standards. Nailing, for example, should be done in accordance with the "Recommended Nailing Schedule" in the National Forest Products Association's *Manual for House Framing*. Flat surfaces should not be warped, bowed, or out of plumb, level, or alignment with adjacent pieces by more than 1/8 inch in every 8 feet.

Nailing should be done using common wire nails. Fasteners should be of lengths that will not penetrate members where the opposite side will be exposed to view or will receive finish materials. Connections between members should be made tight. Fasteners should be installed without splitting of wood, using predrilling if necessary. Work should be braced to hold it in proper position, nails and spikes driven home, and bolt nuts pulled up tight with heads and washers in contact with the work. Shims and wedges should be avoided.

Framing and furring should be spiked and nailed using the largest practicable sizes of spikes and nails. The recommendations of the applicable recognized standards should be followed.

Plywood should be installed in conformance with the recommendations of the American Plywood Association.

Framing and furring that abuts vertical or overhead building structural elements should be isolated from structural movement sufficiently to prevent transfer of loads into the framing or furring. Open spaces and resilient fillers are often used to fill spaces while preventing load transfer. Care must be taken to ensure that lateral support is maintained.

Both sides of control and expansion joints should be framed independently. The joints should not be bridged by framing or furring members.

Anchors and Fastening Systems.   Bolts, lag screws, and other anchors should be used to anchor framing and furring in place. Generally, fasteners are placed near the top and bottom or ends of items and not more than 36 inches on center between. Shorter members, however, should be anchored at 30 inches on center.

Bolts should have nuts and washers.

Anchor bolts should not be less than 1/2 inch in diameter with the wall end bent 2 inches. They should extend not less than 8 inches into concrete and 15 inches into grouted masonry units. They should be placed at 48 inches on center with not less than 2 bolts in each member.

Expansion bolts should be not less than 1/2 inch in diameter and should be placed into expansion shields. The expansion shields should be accurately recessed at least 2-1/2 inches into concrete.

Exterior wall sills should be anchored with anchor bolts as indicated above.

Interior bearing wall sills should be anchored using expansion bolts into concrete at 48 inches on center with not less than two bolts in each member; or with shot pins with cadmium washers into concrete 6 inches from corners and splices and not less than 36 inches on center with not less than 2 pins in each member.

Interior nonbearing partition sills should be installed as described in the previous paragraph for bearing walls, except that shot pin spacing may be increased to 48 inches on center.

Bolts in wood framing should be standard machine bolts with standard malleable iron washers or steel plate washers. Steel plate washer sizes should be about 2-1/2 inches square by 5/16 inch thick for 1/2- and 5/8-inch diameter bolts, and 2-5/8 inches square by 5/16 inch thick for 3/4-inch diameter bolts. Bolt holes in wood shall be drilled 1/16 inch larger than the bolt diameter.

Lag bolts should be square headed and of structural grade steel. Washers should be placed under the head of lag bolts bearing on wood.

Framing and Furring Spacings.   Spacings requirements are generally the same for framing or furring, but may vary in practice with the substrate and the supported material. Structural considerations may dictate framing spacings. Wood studs are often placed at 16 inches on center, for example, even though the finish used might well be capable of safely spanning 24 inches. Conversely, wood trusses may be spaced at 24 inches on center to satisfy economic requirements, thus forcing use of cross furring members to support a ceiling that requires a closer spacing. The following spacings are usual industry-recommended requirements. They may not reflect the actual condition found at a project. Variance from them does not automatically mean that failure will occur. When failure has occurred, however, deviation from normal industry recommendations should be examined as a potential cause.

Spacings for Standard Gypsum Board.   The spacing varies depending on the location, the thickness of the board, and whether the installation is single-ply or double-layer.

On ceilings, framing and furring should be spaced not more than 16 inches on center for single-ply 3/8-inch thick board.

On ceilings, framing and furring should be spaced not more than 16 inches on center for 1/2- or 5/8-inch thick board placed with the long dimension of the board parallel (see Fig. 2-2) with the framing or furring.

On ceilings, framing and furring should be spaced not more than 16 inches on center for 1/2-inch-thick board with a textured finish applied and the board placed with its long dimension perpendicular (Fig. 2-3) to the framing or furring.

On ceilings, framing and furring for all other single-ply applications should be placed not more than 24 inches on center.

Figure 2-2 Boards applied with long dimension parallel with supports.

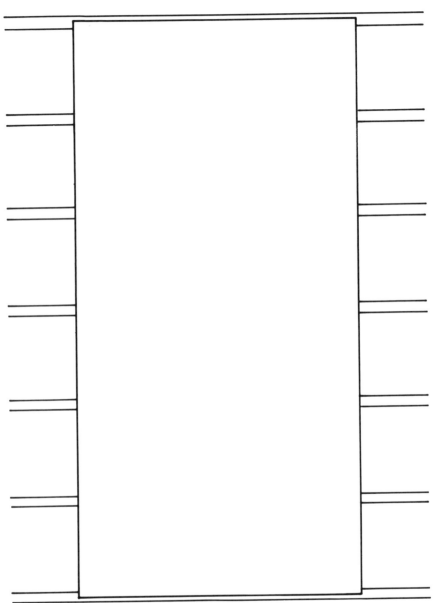

Figure 2-3   Boards applied with long dimension perpendicular to supports.

On walls, framing and furring should be placed not more than 16 inches on center for single-ply 3/8-inch thick board and not more than 24 inches on center for all other single-ply applications.

On ceilings, framing and furring should be placed not more than 16 inches on center for double-layer applications where adhesives are not used between plies and where the installation consists of two plies of 3/8-inch thick board.

On ceilings, framing and furring should be placed not more than 16 inches on center for double-layer applications where adhesives are not used between boards and where the installation consists of a base ply of 1/2-inch thick board placed with the long dimension parallel (see Fig. 2-2) with the framing or furring and a face ply of either 3/8- or 1/2-inch thick board with the long dimension placed perpendicular (see Fig. 2-3) to the framing or furring.

On ceilings, framing and furring should be placed not more than 16 inches on center for double-layer applications where adhesives are not used between boards and where the installation consists of a base ply of 1/2-inch thick board placed with the long dimension perpendicular (see Fig. 2-3) to the framing or furring and a face ply of 1/2-inch thick board with the long dimension placed perpendicular (see Fig. 2-3) to the framing or furring and with a textured finish applied.

On ceilings, framing and furring should be placed not more than 24 inches on center for all other double-layer applications where adhesives are not used between plies.

On walls, framing and furring should be placed not more than 16 inches on center for double-layer applications, whether or not adhesives are used between plies when the face layer is 3/8-inch thick board, and 24 inches on center for all other applications.

On ceilings, framing and furring should be placed not more than 16 inches on center for double-layer applications where adhesives are used between plies and where the installation consists of two plies of 3/8-inch thick board or a base layer of 1/2-inch thick board and face layers of either 3/8- or 1/2-inch thick board.

On ceilings, framing and furring should be placed not more than 24 inches on center for all other double-layer applications where adhesives are used between plies.

Spacings for Veneer Plaster Gypsum Base. On ceilings, framing or furring may be placed 16 inches on center for single-ply or double-layer installations of any thickness veneer plaster base.

On ceilings, framing or furring may be placed at 24 inches on center for either single-layer or double-layer installations with either 1/2- or 5/8-inch thick base.

On walls, framing or furring spacings may be either 16 or 24 inches for either single-ply or double-layer installations and for either 3/8-, 1/2-, or 5/8-inch thick base.

Spacings for Gypsum Sheathing. Gypsum sheathing is seldom applied over furring. The spacing of framing supporting gypsum sheathing is often dictated by structural considerations, but will usually be either 16 or 24 inches on center.

Spacings for Gypsum Plaster Lath. On ceilings, framing or furring to receive gypsum lath should be spaced at 16 inches on center.

On walls, framing or furring to receive gypsum lath should be spaced at 16 inches on center for 3/8-inch thick lath and 24 inches on center for 1/2-inch thick lath.

Spacings for Metal Lath. On ceilings, supporting framing should not exceed 36 inches on center.

On ceilings, where suspended wood furring is used, the usual spacing is either 16, 19, or 24 inches on center. Hangers should be spaced not to exceed 36 inches on center along, and about 6 inches from each end of, each furring member.

On walls, the normal wood furring spacing is 12, 16, 19, or 24 inches on center. Studs could be placed at those same spacings, but they normally would be placed 16 inches on center and the lath weight adjusted to accommodate the stud spacing.

On both ceilings and walls, the actual framing or furring spacing used depends on the weight and type of the lath to be supported and the location. Heavier lath is capable of supporting plaster over a longer span than a lighter weight lath. Ribbed lath will span farther than standard diamond lath. For example, the required framing spacing for 2.5 pound lath on walls may be 12 inches; the spacing for 3.4 pound expanded metal lath might be 24 inches on walls, but 16 inches on ceilings; the spacing for 3.4 pound flat rib diamond mesh lath on ceilings might be 16 inches.

Refer to the sources identifed in Chapter 3 for detailed information about the recommended support spacings for each type and weight of metal lath that should be used in each circumstance. In addition, the Ramsey/Sleeper *Architectural Graphic Standards* includes a basic primer on such requirements.

Spacings for Ceramic Tile. Framing or furring for application of tile over gypsum should be as indicated earlier for gypsum board. Framing or furring spacing for tile applied using a mortar setting bed on metal lath should be spaced not to exceed 16 inches on center.

Wood Furring. Wood furring should be installed as appropriate to support finishes. It should be placed on lines and levels necessary to cause finishes to fall into the proper location. It should correct unevenness in a supporting wood structure or solid substrate. The surface of wood furring to which a finish material will be fastened should be not less than 1-1/2 inches wide. Generally, 2 by 2 lumber is used for furring that is attached to a supporting structure, and 1 by 2 or 1 by 3 lumber is used where furring is laid directly over solid substrates. Nominal 1-inch thick lumber should not be used over framing, because its flexing during nailing will loosen already driven nails. Other sizes may be found in existing construction, however, especially in older construction.

Sometimes ceilings are furred using 2 by 4's hung from structural floor or roof framing by hangers spaced not more than 48 inches on center (Fig. 2-4). Frequently in older buildings, the hangers used were wood members instead of wire as shown in Figure 2-4.

Furring should form a complete system adequate to properly support the finish to be applied. Closers should be installed at edges and openings. Wall furring should be firestopped at the ceiling line.

Wood Framing.   Framing includes wood stud walls and partitions; floor and roof framing; columns, posts, beams, and girders; and trusses. In general, framing design and member sizes, spacings, and locations should comply with recognized standards such as the National Forest Products Association's *Manual for House Framing.*

Framing should be anchored, tied, and braced in such a way that it

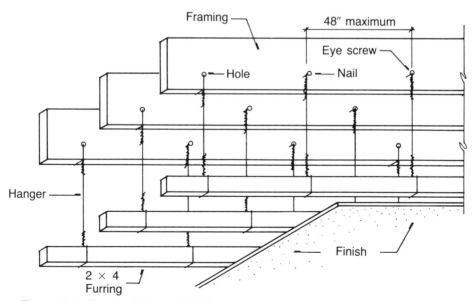

Figure 2-4 Suspended wood furring.

will develop the strength and rigidity necessary for its purpose. Members should not be spliced between supports.

The information that follows is not intended to give the reader enough information to build wood framing. The intent here is to highlight those aspects of wood framing that, if not properly done, might cause applied finishes to fail. Refer to the sources mentioned in "Where to Get More Information" at the end of this chapter for detailed data about constructing wood framing.

Stud Walls and Partitions.   Sills should be securely fastened in place. Where subflooring occurs, the sills should be placed over the subflooring.

Usually, interior stud partitions are framed with 2 by 4 lumber, but sometimes 2 by 3 lumber is used. Exterior walls and some interior bearing walls are often framed with 2 by 6 lumber. Partitions containing pipes are also sometimes framed with 2 by 6 lumber.

Interior wall and partition studs are ordinarily placed 16 inches on center. Exterior wall studs are usually placed either at 16 inches on center or 24 inches on center, depending on the wall's construction and the stud sizes.

Studs should be securely nailed to a sill plate and a top plate. In bearing walls, after the wall framing has been secured in place, a second top plate should be added and securely nailed to the first top plate. Double top plates are also sometimes used in nonbearing walls and partitions (Fig. 2-5).

Walls and partitions should be set level, plumb, true to line, in the proper location, and should be properly braced to prevent later movement. All members in walls and partitions should also be in alignment with each other and free from twist or warp. There faces should be flush with each other.

Every opening should be framed with at least two studs at the jambs and a wood lintel consisting of as many members as necessary to ensure that the lintel finishes flush with the studs on each side of the wall. Three or more studs may be needed at the jambs of wide openings, especially in load-bearing walls.

The bottom of each window opening should have a rough sill consisting of two stud-size horizontal members.

Where plumbing, heating, or other pipes occur in walls and partitions, the studs should be placed to accommodate the pipes while still giving the proper support for the finishes.

Bridging should be provided in stud walls and partitions where recommended to produce a stable wall or partition.

Corners and intersections should be framed with at least three studs (Fig. 2-6) to produce a stable corner or intersection and to provide appropriate fastening surfaces for the finish material.

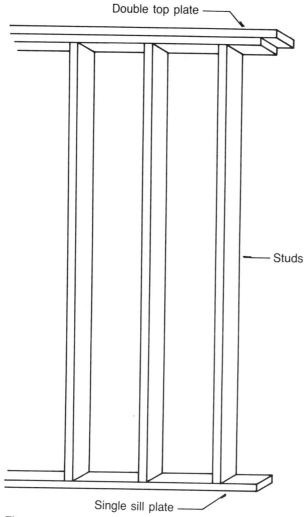

Double top plate

Studs

Single sill plate

Figure 2-5 Typical wood stud wall and partition framing.

Loads imposed by deflecting structural elements should be prevented from being passed down into stud walls. One way to prevent stress from being applied to the partition framing or finish is to provide a space at the top of the framing, which is then filled with a compressible material. Lateral stability of the partition must, of course, be maintained.

Other Structural Framing Elements. Finishes are often fastened directly to wood floor and ceiling joists, roof trusses, columns, beams, and girders.

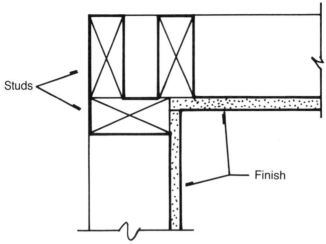

Figure 2-6 Typical wood stud wall or partition corner construction.

To provide an appropriate base for fastening finishes, such framing should be level or in plane, stable, plumb, true, securely fastened in place, and at proper spacings.

Where pipes or other items interrupt the spacing of framing components, additional framing or furring must be provided to stabilize the framing and to properly support the applied finishes.

Framing must be doubled or otherwise increased beneath unusual loads to provide a properly stable and level surface for the finish to be applied.

Bridging should be provided in floor and roof framing to ensure stability and to help prevent warp or twist in framing members.

Wood Framing and Furring Failures and What to do about Them

Wood Framing and Furring Problems

Wood framing and furring systems may fail because of structure failure, structure movement, or solid substrate problems as discussed earlier in this chapter, or because of problems inherent in the framing and furring itself.

Wood framing and furring problems that can cause finish failures include the following:

1. Misaligned, twisted, or protruding wood framing or furring (Fig. 2-7). Where these occur, fasteners may not seat properly and may break

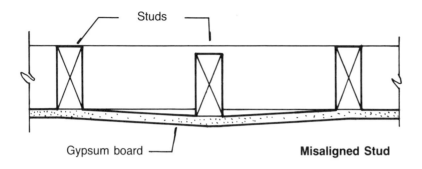

Studs

Gypsum board

Misaligned Stud

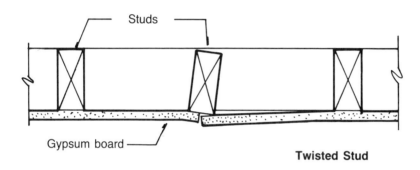

Studs

Gypsum board

Twisted Stud

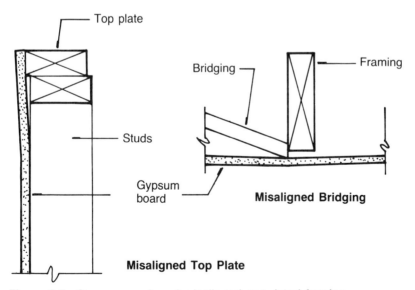

Top plate

Studs

Gypsum board

Misaligned Top Plate

Bridging

Framing

Misaligned Bridging

Figure 2-7 Some examples of misaligned or twisted framing.

the paper surface of board products such as standard gypsum board, veneer plaster gypsum base, gypsum plaster lath, or gypsum sheathing.
2. Lumber shrinkage. Even relatively dry wood will shrink.
3. Flexible or extremely hard wood framing or furring.
4. Wet lumber in the support system.
5. Wood framing that is too dry when the finish is installed. When the wood expands, fastener heads are pulled deeper into gypsum board, for example, depressing the compound over the head and sometimes breaking the paper facing.
6. Supports that are placed too far apart. This can cause nail pops or loose board products and cracking plaster.
7. Failed support system. When the support system loses stability or separates from the substrates, finish failure is inevitable.
8. Wood framed or furred walls, partitions, or ceilings installed in such a way that loads from a deflecting or otherwise moving structure will be passed into the wall, partition, or ceiling framing, furring, or finish. Examples include wedging the ends of furring against masonry or concrete; building the ends of furring members into masonry; and building a stud partition tightly against the bottom of a concrete slab.

Repairing and Extending Wood Framing and Furring

Most failed wood framing or furring members are removed and new material installed, because even when doing so is possible, it is not often reasonable to repair damaged wood framing or furring members. Straightening a warped or twisted stud, for example, will probably prove to be impracticable. So, most of the references in the following paragraphs to repairing framing or furring mean removing the damaged pieces and installing new pieces in their place.

The following paragraphs assume that damaged structure or solid substrate has been repaired and presents a satisfactory support system for the framing or furring being repaired.

Where existing framing or furring in a system having a fire- or sound-rating is to be altered, patched, or extended, and in other locations where assemblies with fire-resistance ratings are required to comply with governing regulations, materials and installation should be identical with applicable assemblies which have been tested and listed by recognized authorities and are in compliance with the requirements of the building code. Materials for use in existing fire-rated assemblies should, unless doing so violates the previous sentence, exactly match the materials in the existing fire-rated assembly.

Materials. Materials used to repair existing wood framing or furring should match those in place as nearly as possible, but should not be lesser in quality, size, or type than those recommended by recognized authorities or required by the building code. Where the existing materials are fire-retardant treated, the new materials must be similarly treated. Where the existing material is pressure-preservative treated, the new should be also.

It is usually best to match lumber sizes exactly when installing a new member in an existing framing or furring system. In older installations, however, the existing lumber may be of sizes that are no longer standard. Members that are nominally 2 by 4 may be actually 2 by 4 inches if the building is old; 1-5/8 by 3-5/8 inches, as was once the standard; or 1-1/2 by 3-1/2 inches, as is the current standard. When lumber of the exact size to match that existing is not available, there are three ways to solve the problem. A larger member can be cut down to the size of the existing members. This may be an expensive solution, however. It will usually be less expensive to shim the new member so that the face surfaces are in alignment with the faces of the existing members. The third alternative is to build up a new member from two standard-sized members.

Repairs. In general, repairs should be made in accordance with the rec-ommendations of recognized standards, such as those mentioned earlier in this chapter or in "Where to Get More Information" at the end of this chapter, or both, and the standards referenced in the Bibliography as applicable to this chapter.

The following paragraphs contain some generally accepted suggestions for repairing wood framing and furring systems. Because the suggestions are meant to apply to many situations, they might not apply to any specific case. In addition, there are many possible cases that are not specifically covered here. When a condition arises in the field that is not addressed in this book, the additional data sources mentioned in this book should be consulted for advice. Often, consultation with the manufacturer of the finish being supported will help. Sometimes, it is necessary to obtain professional help (see Chapter 1). Under no circumstances should the specific recom-mendations in this chapter be followed without careful investigation and application of professional expertise and judgment.

Preparation. Where existing framing or furring members are damaged, the covering plaster and lath, gypsum board, tile, or other finish must be removed to the extent necessary to permit the repairs to be made. Then the damaged existing framing or furring can be removed, along with related suspension systems. Damaged elements that should be removed include wood members that are twisted, warped, broken, rotted, wet, out of align-ment, or otherwise unsuitable for use. Existing hangers that are sound, adequate, and suitable for reuse may be left in place, or removed, cleaned, and reused.

Hangers and hanger attachments that have been left in place where suspended ceiling furring has been removed should be examined to verify their adequacy and suitability to support the new furring. Those found to be unsuitable should be removed.

Existing hangers and hanger attachments in good condition may be used to support new ceiling furring. New hangers and hanger attachments should be provided, of course, where existing hangers and attachments have been removed, where existing hangers or attachments are improperly placed or otherwise inappropriate, and where there are no existing hangers. New hangers should be attached to the structure, never to pipes, conduits, ducts, or mechanical or electrical devices. Existing hangers so attached should not be used.

Misaligned, Warped, or Twisted Framing (see Fig. 2-7) or Furring. Wood framing or furring that is so misaligned, twisted, or warped as to cause damage to the applied finish is often left in place and the finish reattached in such manner that the poor condition of the framing or furring is overcome. When repair to the finish alone will not prevent failure from recurring, it will be necessary to remove the damaged framing or furring and provide new materials.

Shrinkage. Where finish failure is caused by shrinkage in the lumber used in framing or furring, it is often possible to repair and reattach the finish without removing the lumber. Where finish repairs cannot be accomplished satisfactorily, it may be possible to remove a portion of the finish and shim the framing or furring to produce a flush surface for finish application. Where shimming does not solve the problem, it may be necessary to remove the damaged lumber and provide new framing or furring.

Incorrectly Constructed Framing or Furring. Where the framing or furring was originally built in such a way that the finish becomes damaged, the necessary corrective measures depend on the type of error. The possibilities are many, and the solutions even more numerous. They range from simply planing down a projecting brace to reconstructing a stud wall.

Each case must be examined to determine the true cause before steps are taken to correct supposed errors. The extent of the damage must be also taken into account. If it might be possible to prevent the failure from recurring by simply refastening the finish, for example, that should be done before expensive reconstruction of the framing or furring is undertaken.

Failed Ceiling Furring. In Chapter 3, a condition is mentioned whereby plaster that was installed on a ceiling over suspended nailers and wood lath becomes loose or bowed. Often, as discussed in Chapter 3, the problem is caused by the plaster separating from the lath or the lath separating from the furring. In other cases, however, such sagging plaster occurs because the furring system has failed.

Wood ceiling furring supporting gypsum board, wood, or other types of ceilings may also fail, which will result in sagging or bowed ceilings.

Ceiling support systems fail for several reasons, including loads placed on the ceiling furring from above, such as storage; people crawling around; structure deflection; differential movement in the structure; improper attachment of the support system; and other trauma. Failure includes broken wire hangers; broken wood hangers; and wood hangers that have dried out, shrunk, and split away from the nails fastening the ceiling furring nailers to the hangers.

When a ceiling finish failure is due to ceiling furring system failure, repairs may be made by lifting the ceiling back into place and repairing the failed support system. The first step is to stabilize the ceiling. To do so, access to the space above the ceiling must be obtained. When access is not otherwise possible, it will be necessary to remove portions of the ceiling finish. When access to the space above the ceiling is assured, the next step is to wedge the ceiling up from below into proper alignment. Wedging is often accomplished using T-shaped wood braces.

When the ceiling is once again in its proper position, lag bolts are driven into the supporting structure above and the horizontal ceiling furring members are wire-tied to the lag bolts.

Installing New Wood Framing and Furring over Existing Materials

Where a new finish is to be applied over an existing material, a new framing or furring system is often needed. Installing new, and repairing and extending existing, structural framing systems are beyond the scope of this book. The principles for installing, in existing construction, new framing and furring systems that are not part of the main structural system are similar to those for installing framing and furring systems in new construction.

Except for a few different requirements related to fastening them to the existing construction, the same requirements apply to stud partitions in new and existing buildings.

Even in new buildings, furring is always applied over something else. The problems vary only slightly when the something else is old. More shimming may be necessary when new furring is applied on existing substrates, of course, and sometimes an existing surface will be in such poor shape that it cannot be satisfactorily furred. When that happens, it may be necessary to fur the surface with an independent partition, or to remove the existing construction completely and build it new.

It is not always necessary to remove existing trim when installing a new furring system. Items that will be concealed in the finished installation can be left in place.

New wood furring can be applied directly onto ceilings that are themselves directly applied to wood framing, such as joists or trusses, when the framing is sufficiently strong to hold both new and existing ceilings. When the new finish is a gypsum board product, new furring strips should be laid perpendicular to the existing framing at a spacing appropriate for the new finish and nailed through the existing finish to the existing framing. Where the new ceiling is plaster, a layer of polyethylene should be installed over the existing ceiling. Then, furring can be installed as just described to receive the gypsum lath or veneer plaster base, or 3.4 pound metal lath can be installed directly over the polyethylene and nailed through the existing ceiling to the underlying framing. In each case, the nails should extend into the existing framing by at least 1-1/4 inches.

New wood ceiling furring can also be suspended from existing wood framing. The new furring should be 2 by 4's placed at 16 or 24 inches on center, depending on the finish to be supported. Where the existing framing is exposed, the new furring can be hung by 9-gage wires from fasteners driven into the framing. The wire may be tied to nails driven downward into the existing framing, but eye screws are preferable.

Where the existing framing or furring is both sound and strong enough, it is sometimes preferable to leave an existing ceiling in place and hang the new ceiling through it from the existing framing or furring. This may be done in two ways. Large eye screws can be driven through the existing ceiling into the left-in-place wood framing or furring, and the new suspended ceiling furring members hung from them. Such eye screws should penetrate at least a full inch into the existing framing or furring. The second method is to punch sufficient holes of large enough size in the existing ceiling to permit suspending the new system from the existing structural framing.

In every case, care must be taken to ensure that new hangers are attached to sound framing elements that are of sufficient strength. Hangers should not be attached to pipes, conduit, ducts, or mechanical or electrical devices, or to framing or furring that is damaged or too weak to carry the loads to be supported.

Metal Framing and Furring

The metal framing discussed here includes nonbearing wall and partition framing, which consists of C-shaped and truss studs and special studs used in shaft wall systems. It also includes metal stud-type framing designed to bear loads, which is constructed of heavier gage components and often requires different attachment devices than nonbearing framing. The latter is commonly called "cold-formed metal framing."

The metal furring discussed here includes wall, ceiling, soffit, beam, bulkhead, and column enclosure furring.

Metal structural framing, such as steel beams and girders, and bar joists, are not included in the following discussion.

Materials

Metals and Finishes

Metal Framing and Furring Finishes. In exterior installations and in interior installations where high humidity will be present, such as in swimming pool areas or commercial kitchens, metals should be either zinc alloy or hot-dip galvanized steel. The galvanized finish should be equal to that stipulated in ASTM Standard A 525 as G90 for 18-gage and lighter formed metal products, and ASTM Standard A 123 galvanized after fabrication for 16-gage and heavier products.

In locations other than those mentioned in the preceding paragraph, the manufacturer's standard steel products with manufacturer's standard galvanized finish may be used where light gage metals are required. Where 16-gage or heavier sheet metal is required in locations other than those mentioned in the above paragraph, products should be rolled steel and formed sheet steel with a rust-inhibitive paint finish; where 7-gage, 3/16-inch thick, or heavier rods and bars are required, the finish may also be rust-inhibitive paint.

Furring Members. Furring members used in wall and ceiling furring include studs, channels, and various other metal shapes (Fig. 2-8). They should be as listed in the following paragraphs.

Studs. When used for furring, studs should be the same type studs used in nonbearing partitions.

Channel Furring. Most metal furring is composed of sheet metal channels (see Fig. 2-8).

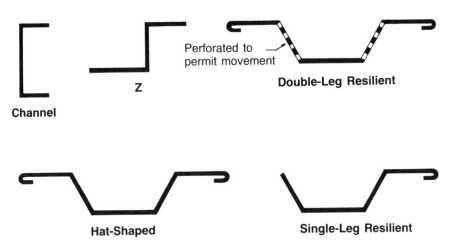

Perforated to
permit movement

Z

Channel

Double-Leg Resilient

Hat-Shaped

Single-Leg Resilient

Figure 2-8 Metal furring members.

Main runner channels, which are sometimes called "carrying" channels, should be at least 16-gage hot-rolled or cold-rolled steel channels.
When painted, 1-1/2-inch deep channels should not weigh less than 475
pounds per 1000 linear feet; 2-inch deep channels should weigh at least 590
pounds per 1000 linear feet. Galvanized channels will be slightly heavier.

Cross furring channels should not be less than 3/4 inch deep. They
should be at least 16-gage, hot- or cold-rolled steel channels, weighing not
less than 300 pounds per 1000 linear feet when painted; slightly heavier
when galvanized.

Other Furring Members.   There are several other types of furring members used in special circumstances.

Furring to receive screw fasteners should be nominally 20- or 25-gage,
hat-shaped channels complying with ASTM Standard C 645 (see Fig. 2-8).
Most hat-shaped furring members have 1-3/8-inch wide by 7/8-inch deep
crowns and flanges for fastening in place, but 1-1/2-inch deep hat-shaped
furring members are also available.

The furring members used on the interior face of exterior walls where
insulation occurs are often Z-shaped members formed from 25-gage sheet
steel (see Fig. 2-8). Their wall legs should be not less than 3/4 inch wide.
The facing legs should be at least 1-1/4 inches wide. Z-shaped furring
member depths vary, depending on the insulation thickness.

Corner furring members are used at corners where other types of furring
members will not provide sufficient support for the finish to be applied.
They are formed from 25-gage commercial quality cold-rolled sheet steel.
They usually have 1-1/4-inch wide knurled nailing faces, two 1/2-inch wide
nailing flanges, and a 7/8-inch furring depth.

Resilient furring members intended to reduce sound transmission are usually a proprietary product made by the manufacturer of the other furring members used. They are formed from sheet steel to various shapes, including an asymmetrical single-leg configuration and a double-leg configuration that has a design similar to that of hat-shaped furring members (see Fig. 2-8). Resilient furring members are designed to receive screw fasteners.

Wall furring brackets should be a nominal 20-gage serrated-arm type, which is adjustable to provide between 1/4-inch and 2-1/4 inch clearance between the wall and the attached channel furring.

Pencil rod furring should be galvanized hot-rolled steel rods.

Grid Suspension Systems.   In addition to the metal ceiling furring systems discussed in the rest of this chapter, which are built up of the components mentioned, there are proprietary ceiling suspension systems designed to support gypsum board products. These systems consist of interlocking main beams and cross-furring framing members similar to those used to support acoustical ceiling systems.

Nonbearing Wall and Partition Framing.   There are three types of steel studs that might be encountered in an existing building (Fig. 2-9). Each type has its own distinctive floor and ceiling runners.

Open-Web Stud Framing Systems.   There are several different open-web stud designs, including the currently popular wire truss-type. Figure 2-9 shows three designs, but others may be found in an existing project. Most open-web studs are non-load bearing.

Wire truss-type studs include those with double wire flanges and those with steel angle flanges. Wires are usually 7 gage. Angle flanges are usually 16 gage.

Open-web studs also include those with hollow sheet metal tube flanges designed to accept fasteners. These latter are sometimes called "nailable."

The webs of open-web trusses are either wire woven across the gap between the flanges to form a truss or flat sheet metal strips welded to or clamped in place by the flanges.

Open-web studs have floor and ceiling runners specifically designed to receive them. The runners are often notched or otherwise configured to control stud spacing. Some open-web studs are anchored to runners by specially designed shoes. Others are held in place by wire ties, clips, screws, or locking tabs. Open-web studs are used primarily beneath standard thickness plaster.

Channel Stud Framing Systems.   Channel studs are open C-shaped sheet metal studs designed for screw attachment of board materials, and are used

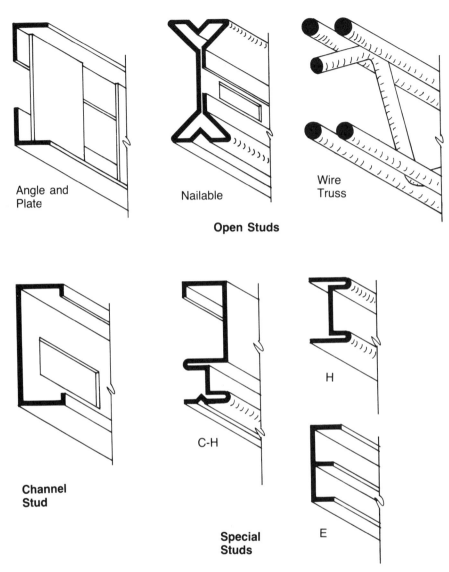

Angle and Plate

Nailable

Wire Truss

Open Studs

Channel Stud

C-H

H

E

Special Studs

Figure 2-9   Steel stud types.

primarily for that purpose (see Fig. 2-9). They are also used for clip attachment of gypsum lath, and wire and screw attachment of metal lath for plaster.

Non-load bearing channel studs should comply with ASTM Standard C 645. Load bearing studs are addressed later in this chapter under "Cold-Formed Metal Framing." Most non-load bearing studs are formed from either 20, 21, 25, or 26 nominal gage steel sheets into C-shaped units. The better studs have each flange returned to form a stiffening lip parallel to the web. Channel studs have knockouts or preformed holes in their webs to permit pipes and conduits to pass through.

Floor and ceiling runner channels for channel studs are C-shaped units with flanges about 1-1/4 inches high. They are designed to receive the studs.

Special Stud Framing Systems.   Special studs include special-shaped (H, C-H, etc.) studs designed for use in shaft wall systems (see Fig. 2-9). Types vary with each manufacturer. Shaft wall systems also include special-shaped runners, such as J-shaped units. The special runners vary in size and weight with each shaft wall system manufacturer.

Sheet metal angles are also sometimes used as floor and ceiling runners for special applications such as solid gypsum board walls. Angle runners are usually formed from 24-gage metal into 1-3/8 by 7/8 inch or larger angles.

Cold-Formed Metal Framing Members.   Components falling into the cold-formed framing category are used for stud walls, joists, metal wall panel back-up, and many other support conditions.

Studs for use in cold-formed metal framing are load bearing in both transverse and axial directions. Studs and runners should comply with ASTM Standard C 955. Cold-formed metal framing studs are usually formed from nominal 18- or heavier gage sheet steel. Incidental parts, however, such as some bracing members, may be formed from nominal 20-gage sheet steel.

Cold-formed metal framing studs may be either C-shaped or punched-channel studs. Runners are C-shaped.

Cold-formed joists and other framing components are formed from sheet metal. The component parts making up such elements are often, but not always, C-shaped.

The size, thickness, and shape of cold-formed metal framing components is dictated by the type of component and the loads supported. Framing components are usually prefabricated, often in the shop. Like members should be fastened together by welding. Dissimilar parts may be fastened together by welding, screwing, or bolting. Components should not be fastened together with wire.

Framing and Furring Accessories and Other Materials.   Accessories include fasteners, bolts, screws, anchor clips, wire, and other items necessary for the complete installation of framing and furring.

Hangers and Fasteners. The types of hangers and fasteners needed include those listed in the following paragraphs.

Hanger wire should be not less than 8-gage wire complying with ASTM Standard A 641. For general use, wire should be Class 1 galvanized soft temper steel. In air plenums, exterior soffits, and under roofs, hanger wire should be of corrosion-resisting (stainless) steel.

Tie wire should be Class 1 galvanized soft temper steel wire which complies with ASTM Standard A 641. Ties for use with studs should be not less than 18-gage wire; for use with furring, not less than 16 gage.

Hanger rods and flat bars should be zinc- or cadmium-coated mild steel. Alternatively, bars may be finished with rust-inhibitive paint.

Angle-shaped hangers should be formed from nominal 15- or 16-gage galvanized sheet steel. Legs should not be less than 7/8 inch wide.

Hanger anchorage devices should be rust-inhibitive screws, clips, bolts, concrete inserts, expansion anchors, or other devices. They should be sized to support five times the calculated hanger loading.

Clips should be the framing or furring manufacturer's standard galvanized wire-type clips.

Fasteners should comply with ASTM Standard C 754. Screws should be rust-inhibitive, oval pan-head, self-drilling, and self-tapping types designed for use with special power-driven tools. They should comply with ASTM Standard C 646. Bolts should be suitable for the purpose.

Other Materials. Several other materials are used in framing and furring systems, including those in the following paragraphs.

Asphalt-saturated felt should be 15 pound nonperforated roofing felt which complies with ASTM Standard D 226.

Acoustical sealant should be a water-based, nondrying, nonbleeding, nonstaining type which is permanently elastic.

Most sound attenuation blankets are semirigid mineral fiber blankets with no membrane facing. They should have a Class 25 flame-spread. They should be 1-1/2 inches thick or more.

Installation

General Requirements. Framing and furring systems for use where fire-resistance ratings are required should comply with governing regulations, and their materials and installations should be identical with assemblies that have been tested and listed by recognized authorities, such as Underwriter's Laboratories.

Framing and furring systems for support of gypsum board products should at least comply with the applicable requirements of ASTM Standard C 754 and ASTM Standard C 840. In addition, load-bearing framing to receive gypsum board products should be installed in compliance with ASTM Standard C 1007. Gypsum board manufacturers may, however, have more stringent requirements.

Non-load bearing steel studs for standard thickness plaster (see Chapter 3 for definition) should be installed in accordance with ASTM Standard C 754.

Load-bearing steel studs for standard thickness plaster should be installed in accordance with ASTM Standard C 1007.

Furring for interior standard thickness gypsum plaster should be installed in accordance with ASTM Standard C 841.

Furring for Portland cement plaster should be installed in accordance with ASTM Standard C 1063.

In addition, light steel framing and furring for plaster to be installed using metal lath should be installed in compliance with the Metal Lath/Steel Framing Association's *Specifications for Metal Lathing and Furring.*

Framing and furring that abuts vertical or overhead building structural elements should be isolated from structural movement sufficiently to prevent transfer of loads into the framing or furring (Fig. 2-10). Open spaces and resilient fillers are often used to fill spaces while preventing load transfer. Care must be taken to ensure that lateral support is maintained.

Both sides of control and expansion joints should be framed independently. The joints should not be bridged by framing or furring members. Adequate space should be left for sealants where they are required.

Flat surfaces of framing and furring should not be warped, bowed, or out of plumb or level by more than 1/8 inch in 12 feet in both directions, or by more than 1/16 inch across any joint or 1/8 inch total along any single member.

On exterior walls, a sheet of 15 pound asphalt felt should be placed between each metal framing or furring member and the interior face of the exterior wall.

Framing and Furring Spacings. Spacing requirements are generally the same for both framing or furring, but may vary in practice with the substrate and the material being supported. Structural considerations may dictate framing spacings. Load-bearing stud spacings, for example, will be determined based on the loads to be applied and the stud spans. Sometimes, even non-load bearing spacings will be determined by stud lengths. The following spacings are usual industry-recommended requirements. They may not reflect the actual condition found at a project. Variance from the following recommendations does not automatically mean that failure will occur. When failure has occurred, however, deviation from industry recommendations should be examined as a potential cause.

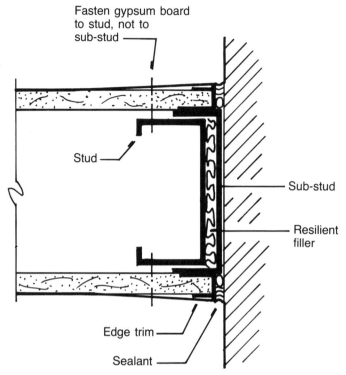

Figure 2-10   One method of isolating framing from the structure.

Spacings for Standard Gypsum Board.   The spacing varies depending on the location, the thickness of the board, and whether the installation is single-ply or double-layer.

Main runner (carrying) channels in ceiling support systems should be placed at not more than 48 inches on center and supported by hangers at not more than 48 inches on center along, and about 6 inches from each end of, each main runner.

On ceilings, furring channels should be spaced not more than 16 inches on center for single-ply 3/8-inch thick board.

On ceilings, furring channels should be spaced not more than 16 inches on center for 1/2- or 5/8-inch thick board placed with the long dimension of the board parallel (see Fig. 2-2) with the furring.

On ceilings, furring channels should be spaced not more than 16 inches on center for 1/2-inch thick board with a textured finish applied and the board placed with its long dimension perpendicular (see Fig. 2-3) to the furring.

On ceilings, furring for all other single-ply applications should be placed not more than 24 inches on center.

On walls, framing and furring should be placed not more than 16 inches on center for single-ply 3/8-inch thick board and not more than 24 inches on center for all other single-ply applications.

On ceilings, furring should be placed not more than 16 inches on center for double-layer applications where adhesives are not used between plies and where the installation consists of two plies of 3/8-inch thick board.

On ceilings, furring should be placed not more than 16 inches on center for double-layer applications where adhesives are not used between boards and where the installation consists of a base ply of 1/2-inch thick board placed with the long dimension parallel (see Fig. 2-2) with the furring and a face ply of either 3/8- or 1/2-inch thick board with the long dimension placed perpendicular (see Fig. 2-3) to the furring.

On ceilings, furring should be placed not more than 16 inches on center for double-layer applications where adhesives are not used between boards and where the installation consists of a base ply of 1/2-inch thick board placed with the long dimension perpendicular (see Fig. 2-3) to the furring and a face ply of 1/2-inch thick board with the long dimension placed perpendicular (see Fig. 2-3) to the furring and with a textured finish applied.

On ceilings, furring should be placed not more than 24 inches on center for all other double-layer applications where adhesives are not used between plies.

On walls, framing and furring should be placed not more than 16 inches on center for double-layer applications, whether or not adhesives are used between plies when the face layer is 3/8-inch thick board, and 24 inches on center for all other applications.

On ceilings, furring should be placed not more than 16 inches on center for double-layer applications where adhesives are used between plies and where the installation consists of two plies of 3/8-inch thick board or a base layer of 1/2-inch thick board and face layers of either 3/8- or 1/2-inch thick board.

On ceilings, furring should be placed not more than 24 inches on center for all other double-layer applications where adhesives are used between plies.

Spacings for Veneer Plaster Gypsum Base.   Support spacing varies depending on the location, the thickness of the board, and whether the installation is single-ply or double-layer.

Main runner (carrying) channels in ceiling support systems should be placed at not more than 48 inches on center and supported by hangers at not more than 48 inches on center along, and about 6 inches from each end of, each main runner.

On ceilings, furring may be placed 16 inches on center for single-ply or double-layer installations of any thickness veneer plaster base.

On ceilings, furring may be placed at 24 inches on center for either single-layer or double-layer installations with either a 1/2- or 5/8-inch thick base.

On walls, framing or furring spacings may be either 16 or 24 inches for either single-ply or double-layer installations and for either a 3/8-, 1/2-, or 5/8-inch thick base.

Spacings for Gypsum Sheathing.   Gypsum sheathing is seldom applied over furring. The spacing of framing supporting gypsum sheathing is often dictated by structural considerations, but will usually be either 16 or 24 inches on center.

Spacings for Gypsum Plaster Lath.   The spacing varies depending on the location and the thickness of the board.

Main runner (carrying) channels in ceiling support systems should be placed at not more than 48 inches on center and supported by hangers at not more than 48 inches on center along, and about 6 inches from each end of, each main runner.

On ceilings, furring to receive gypsum lath should be spaced at 16 inches on center.

On walls, framing or furring to receive gypsum lath should be spaced at 16 inches on center for 3/8-inch thick lath and 24 inches on center for 1/2-inch thick lath.

Spacings for Metal Lath.   On ceilings, normal main runner (carrying) channel spacing is 36 inches on center. Hangers are usually spaced 48 inches on center along, and about 6 inches from each end of, each hanger.

On ceilings, usual metal furring channel spacings for metal lath support are 16, 19, or 24 inches on center; for walls, 12, 16, 19, or 24 inches on center. Studs could be placed at those same spacings, but they normally would be placed 16 inches on center and the lath weight adjusted to accommodate the stud spacing.

The actual spacing used depends on the weight and type of the lath to be supported, and the location. Heavier lath has the capability of supporting plaster over a longer span than lighter lath. Ribbed lath will span farther than standard diamond mesh lath. For example, the required framing spacing for 2.5 pound lath on walls may be 12 inches; the spacing for 3.4 pound expanded metal lath might be 24 inches on walls, but 16 inches on ceilings;

the spacing for 3.4 pound flat rib diamond mesh lath on ceilings might be 16 inches.

Refer to the sources identified in Chapter 3 for detailed information about the recommended support spacings for each type and weight of metal lath that should be used in each circumstance. In addition, the Ramsey/Sleeper *Architectural Graphic Standards* includes a basic primer on such requirements.

Spacings for Ceramic Tile. Framing or furring for the application of tile over gypsum base should be as suggested earlier for gypsum board. Framing or furring spacing for tile applied using a mortar setting bed on metal lath should be spaced not to exceed 16 inches on center.

Metal Furring. Metal furring should be installed as appropriate to support finishes. It should be placed on lines and levels necessary to cause finishes to fall into the proper location. It should correct unevenness in a supporting structure or solid substrate.

Ceiling and Soffit Suspension Systems. Suspension systems are used for gypsum board products, plaster, and ceramic tile on ceilings and soffits.

Suspension system hangers should be secured to wood, concrete, or steel structural supports by connecting directly to the structure where possible. Where direct connection is not possible, the hangers should be connected to inserts, clips, anchorage devices, or fasteners. Except for hanger attachments installed specifically for the purpose by the steel deck installer, hangers should not be attached to steel decks. Since failures have occurred even when deck tabs acceptable to the deck manufacturer have been used, some sources recommend that ceilings not be supported from steel deck under any circumstances. Hangers should never be attached to pipes, conduit, ducts, or mechanical or electrical devices.

Main runner and furring channels should be placed in proper positions, leveled, and saddle-tied to each other using wire hangers or clipped together (Fig. 2-11). They should not be built into, or permitted to come into contact with, masonry or concrete walls, but should instead be permitted to float freely. The first and last rows of runner channels should be located within 6 inches of parallel walls to properly support the ends of the furring members.

Hat-shaped metal furring channels should be securely clipped to main runners and other supports using channel clips, or they should be saddle-tied in place using two strands of 16-gage wire (Fig. 2-12).

End splices in furring members should be made by overlapping (nesting) the two pieces no less than 8 inches and securely wire-tying the two together.

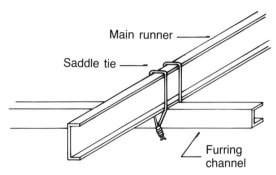

Figure 2-11   Ceiling furring for plaster.

Where furring clips are used, they should be placed on alternating sides of main runner channels. Where clips cannot be alternated, the furring channels should be wire-tied to the main runners.

At light troffers, access panels, and openings that interrupt the carrying or furring channels, additional cross-reinforcing should be installed to restore the lateral stability of the furring system.

On exterior ceilings and soffits, cross-bracing and rigid (compression) supports should be provided to resist wind uplift loading.

Metal Wall Furring.   Where the existing solid substrates are not appropriate for direct application of the finish, metal wall furring should be used. Furring members should be spaced as recommended for the finish being supported.

Where thicker furring depth is not required to accommodate insulation or mechanical, electrical, or other devices, hat-shaped furring channels are usually used to support board products. They are normally attached ver-

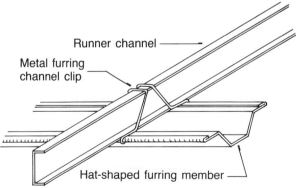

Figure 2-12   Ceiling furring for gypsum board.

tically at 16 inches on center, using hammer-set or power-activated stud fasteners, or concrete stub nails on concrete, solid masonry, stone, ceramic tile, and plaster directly applied over solid bases. Toggle bolts are usually used when the supports are metal or hollow masonry. Fasteners should be staggered on alternate wing flanges of the furring and placed not more than 24 inches on center. End splices should be made by overlapping (nesting) channels no less than 8 inches and fastening them together with two fasteners per wing.

Where insulation occurs on the inner surface of an exterior wall, Z-shaped furring members are often used. They are usually placed vertically and attached at 16 inches on center to concrete or masonry using hammer-set or power activated stud fasteners, or concrete stub nails, spaced at not more than 24 inches on center. End splices should be made by overlapping (nesting) the Z's no less than 8 inches and fastening the sections together using two fasteners.

Where more furring depth is required, studs of the same or similar type to those used in partition framing are used.

Corner furring members are used with hat-shaped furring channels. Wood furring is used at jambs and ends where Z-shaped furring members are used and it is not practicable to use Z-furring members.

Wall furring should extend from the floor to the underside of the structure above.

Duct, Beam, Pipe, Conduit, and Other Furring.   Where they are not otherwise enclosed with masonry or other materials, furring is often used to conceal horizontal and vertical ducts, pipes, conduit, backs of electrical panels, and other utility and service devices which extend below finished ceilings, or occur at walls, partitions, columns, or other locations within finished spaces. Furring may also occur in other locations.

Horizontal furring is usually constructed using main runner channels or cross-furring channels, or both. Where gypsum board occurs, hat-shaped furring channels are used as the top layer of furring members. Furring should be anchored securely to wall and overhead surfaces. Longitudinal runners should be braced diagonally where practicable. Intersections of metal channels should be secured using sheet metal screws. Hat-shaped channels should be secured with screws or clips.

Furring at vertical locations is usually constructed using main runner channels, cross-furring channels, or both. Where board products are to be supported, hat-shaped furring channels are usually the top layer of furring. The furring should be anchored securely at the top and bottom and braced intermediately.

Formed metal channels equal to those used for channel stud partition framing are sometimes used for duct, beam, column, and other furring.

Nonbearing Stud Wall and Partition Framing. Besides the normal use for nonbearing walls and partitions, nonbearing metal stud framing is also used for building chases and shafts; for wall furring; and for furring at columns, pipes, bulkheads, and soffits.

Typical Nonbearing Metal Stud Walls and Partitions. Except where the ceiling is specifically designed to support the framing, metal partition framing should extend to the underside of the structural slab or structural members above. Framing should be aligned and plumbed accurately. Metal floor and ceiling runners should be securely fastened to cast-in-place concrete slabs using stub nails or power-driven fasteners, and to other substrates using suitable fasteners. They should be located near ends of runner members and between, at spacings not to exceed 24 inches on center.

Metal channel studs should be attached to masonry and concrete walls using power-actuated fasteners or stub nails.

Metal studs should be positioned vertically in floor and ceiling runners with all flanges in any single wall or partition pointing in the same direction at the spacing recommended by the referenced standards (Fig. 2-13). Studs located adjacent to partition intersections and corners should be anchored to floor and ceiling runner flanges with locking metal fasteners or by positive screw engagement through each stud flange and runner flange. Stud splices should be avoided, but when necessary should be made by overlapping (nesting) two studs with a minimum lap of 8 inches and attaching the flanges together with two screws in each flange.

Where metal studs are installed in ceiling runners mounted on the bottom of concrete slabs or other structural elements, a 3/8-inch to 1/2-inch wide space should be left between the top of the stud and the web of the runner so that loads resulting from deflection of the concrete slab will not be transferred into the studs (Fig. 2-14).

Studs should be located no more than 2 inches from abutting partitions, partition corners, and other construction.

Door and other openings should be framed in accordance with the recommendations of the referenced standards. Double studs and runners should be provided where recommended. All elements should be screw fastened together and to the adjacent floor and ceiling runners. The opening above opening headers should be framed with short studs. Door frames should be spot grouted at jamb anchor clips using joint compound, plaster, or mortar, depending on the finish.

Suspended stud framing should be installed using methods recommended by the gypsum board manufacturer.

Chase Walls. Stud partitions that form chases are usually similar to typical partitions. The maximum width of a chase is controlled by the size

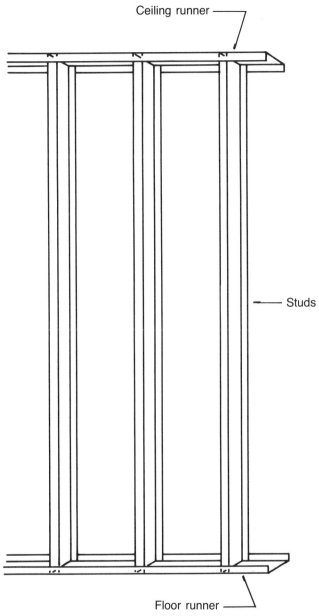

Ceiling runner

Studs

Floor runner

Figure 2-13 Typical metal stud wall or partition.

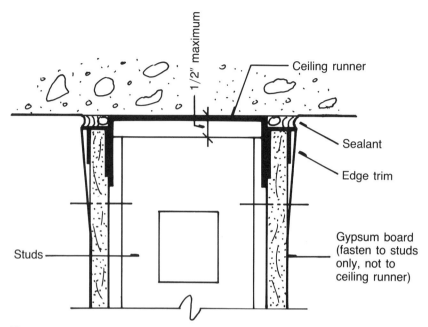

Figure 2-14 Top of metal studs beneath a concrete slab or other structural element.

and height of the studs used. It should be in accordance with the referenced standards and the published requirements of the stud and finish manufacturers.

The studs on opposite sides of a chase should be in alignment across the chase and their flanges should all be pointed in the same direction (Fig. 2-15). The studs should be anchored to the floor and ceiling runner flanges with screws or lock fasteners. Overhead structure deflection should be allowed for in the same way as in a typical partition.

Chases should be internally braced. The type of bracing depends somewhat on the configuration of the chase. Where both sides of a chase are unfaced on the chase side, the braces may be either sections of gypsum board or small (often 2-1/2 inch) metal studs placed at about 48 inches on center vertically (see Fig. 2-15). The braces should span horizontally between the studs on opposite sides of the chase and should be screw fastened to each stud. Studs used as braces should be fastened with two screws in each end.

When chase wall studs are not opposite each other, 2-1/2 inch or larger continuous runner channels should be applied in the chase across the studs on each side of the chase at about 4 foot intervals vertically and securely anchored with screws to each stud. The two continuous runners should be

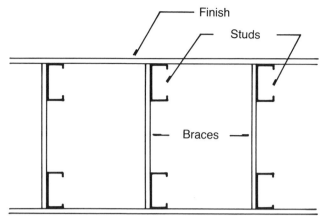

Figure 2-15   Chase construction with metal studs.

at the same level. Cross-braces made of 2-1/2 inch or larger runner sections should then be screw attached to each continuous runner at the same intervals as the stud spacing.

When one side of a chase is solid or has had a layer of gypsum board applied on the chase side of its studs, one runner should be applied within the chase to the face of the exposed studs and a second runner should be applied within the chase to the face of the solid board or other substrate. The two runners should be at the same level. Runners applied at exposed studs should be attached to those studs with screws. Runners applied at studs covered with gypsum board should be fastened through the gypsum board to the underlying studs using screws. Runners applied at solid sub-strates should be attached with appropriate fasteners. Cross-braces made of 2-1/2 inch or larger runner sections should then be screw attached to each continuous runner at the same intervals as the stud spacing.

Partition Reinforcing.   Additional studs, metal blocking, plates, and headers should be installed within partitions to frame openings and to provide for secure and rigid attachment of both recessed and surface mounted fixtures, handrails, accessories, and equipment. The kind of items requiring additional supports includes, but is not limited to, bath and toilet accessories, wall mounted cabinets, shelving, chalkboards and tackboards, fire-extinguisher cabinets, handrails, and other specialties and equipment. The layout of the channel studs should be coordinated with the requirements for such items. Single or multiple studs should be installed as required for their support. At least two studs should be provided at locations where wall-mounted plumbing fixture supports are attached.

Cold-Formed Metal Framing. Cold-formed metal framing is used where studs or other light framing must bear loads either in the transverse or axial directions. It should be installed in accordance with ASTM Standard C 1007.

Stud Assemblies. Before erection, cold-formed metal studs and runners are often preassembled in jigs into panels, which are then braced to prevent racking. The completely assembled panels are then lifted into place and fastened to the substrates. Panel size is dictated by the structure, but should be adjusted to suit the finish material. Where plaster on metal lath occurs, for example, the prefabricated panels should be smaller than normal, and they should be installed so as to permit movement between panels. Too rigid a support system will probably result in movement and subsequent cracking of the plaster.

Floor and ceiling runner tracks for cold-formed metal stud assemblies should be fastened in place using appropriate fasteners. The fasteners should be placed in accordance with the structural design and the system manufacturer's recommendations, but nails and power-driven fasteners should not be placed more than 24 inches on center, and other fasteners should not be placed more than 16 inches on center.

Panels should be erected with studs set plumb (or in the correct plane) and in proper alignment and spacing and with the panels plumb (or in the correct plane) and in proper location and alignment. The stud spacing will often be dictated by structural considerations. When the spacing is not so dictated, it should be in accordance with the finish manufacturer's recommendations.

Many of the requirements indicated earlier in this chapter for nonbearing studs also apply to cold-formed metal framing. Bracing for fixtures, equipment, services, cabinets, handrails, and similar items must be provided, for example. Differences occur in the thickness of the metal used in the framing members and in the method of fastening used within the systems.

Screws are used for most connections within nonbearing stud systems. In cold-formed metal framing, connections between like members (two sheet metal components, for example) are usually welded. Studs are usually welded to the floor and ceiling runners. Connections between unlike members (sheet metal and structural steel, for example) are usually bolted, but even they are sometimes welded. Wire ties should not be used.

Framing members around openings are often heavier and more complex in cold-formed metal framing applications than in nonbearing stud assemblies, because the cold-formed assemblies frequently carry loads in addition to their own weight.

Horizontal or diagonal bracing, which is needed only in tall nonbearing partitions, is usually required in all cold-formed assemblies.

Other Cold-Formed Framing.   Cold-formed metal joists should be installed plumb and level within acceptable tolerances for the finish to be supported. Ends should bear not less than 1-1/2 inches on solid supports. Joist ends should be reinforced. Common methods include imposing clips, hangers, wood blocking, and sheet steel channels or angles. Joists that support concentrated loads or crossing loads such as transverse partitions may require additional bracing at the point of the applied load. Such bracing might consist of a section of sheet metal channel or angle placed vertically within the joists. Joists must also be braced and secured to prevent lateral movement.

Sound Insulation and Caulking

Sound Insulation.   Where they are used, sound insulation blankets should be installed over the full height and width of the framing or furring.

Where gypsum board is the finish, sound insulation in partitions is usually installed between the studs and fastened to the concealed face of the gypsum board on one side of the partition, using staples or adhesive. In some cases, sound insulation can be friction fit. In others, it may be fastened in place with pins, clips, adhesives, or wire.

Insulation should be tightly butted with joints in solid contact and without voids. It should be fitted neatly to studs and opening framing and packed tightly around penetrations and between back to back penetrations through walls and partitions.

Adhesive Sealant.   Where sound ratings are required, a 1/4- to 1/2-inch space should be left between the partition framing and the adjacent construction, where possible. The space should be filled with resilient material and sealed with acoustical sealant. At floor and ceiling runners and end studs which must be held tightly to the adjacent construction, a 1/4- to 3/8-inch diameter bead of acoustical sealant should be installed at both sides of the runner or stud before the finish is applied.

Shaft Wall Construction.   Shaft walls are used as lightweight fire-resistive enclosure walls for stair, elevator, and dumbwaiter shafts; chutes; and service shafts for air, pipes, conduit, and ducts. They are also used as column fireproofing, fire separation between tenant spaces, and as corridor walls.

The term "shaft wall" generally implies a proprietary system of components, including gypsum board and metal framing members furnished by the gypsum board manufacturer. Some are solid construction. Others are cavity walls. Framing and board application should be in accord with the manufacturer's recommendations to provide the fire-rating required by code and the desired sound transmission class. Most installations are fire-rated for two hours or more.

Shaft wall assemblies and each component should be rated by Underwriter's Laboratories or another recognized agency at the required fire-resistance and sound transmission levels. Structural performance must be adequate for the purpose used.

Shaft walls may be finished with painted or otherwise decorated gypsum board, veneer plaster, or ceramic tile over water-resistant gypsum board.

Many of the requirements for other gypsum board systems also apply to shaft wall systems. For example, isolation from the structure and supplementary blocking and framing to support applied items such as cabinets and toilet fixtures are required.

Metal Framing and Furring Failures and What to Do about Them

Metal Framing and Furring Problems

Metal framing and furring systems may fail due to the types of structure failure, structure movement, or solid substrate problems discussed earlier in this chapter. In addition, framing and furring may fail because of problems inherent in the framing and furring systems themselves.

Metal framing and furring problems that can cause finish failures include the following:

1. Metal framing or furring that is out of alignment.
2. Supports that are placed too far apart. This can cause loose boards or nail pops.
3. Failed support system. When the support system loses stability or separates from the substrates, finish failure is inevitable.
4. Metal framed or furred walls, partitions, or ceilings installed in such a way that loads from a deflecting or otherwise moving structure will be passed into the wall, partition, or ceiling framing, furring, or finish. One way to prevent stress from being applied to wall or partition framing or finish is to provide a space at the top of the framing, which is then filled with a compressible material. Lateral stability of the wall or partition must, of course, be maintained. Partition, wall, and ceiling furring should be held away from adjacent solid substrates and structural elements.
5. Welded stud systems installed too rigidly with prefabricated panels too large and insufficient provisions for movement.

Repairing and Extending Metal Framing and Furring

It may not be feasible to repair failed metal framing or furring members. Even when such is possible, for example, it is seldom practicable to clean and repaint severely rusted furring channels. So, most of the time when this text refers to repairing framing or furring it means removing the damaged pieces and installing new pieces in their place.

The following paragraphs assume that structure and solid substrate damage has been repaired and that there is satisfactory support for the framing or furring being repaired.

Where existing framing or furring in a system having a fire or sound rating is to be altered, patched, or extended, and in other locations where assemblies with fire-resistance ratings are required to comply with governing regulations, materials and installation should be identical with applicable assemblies which have been tested and listed by recognized authorities and are in compliance with the requirements of the building code. Materials for use in existing fire-rated assemblies should, unless doing so violates the previous sentence, exactly match the materials in the existing fire-rated assembly.

Materials.   Materials used to repair existing metal framing or furring should match those in place as nearly as possible, but should not be lesser in quality, size, or type than those recommended by recognized authorities or required by the building code. Errors in the original application should not be duplicated purely for the sake of matching the original.

Damaged existing materials should not be used in making repairs or in extending the existing surfaces.

Repairs.   In general, repairs should be made in accordance with the recommendations of recognized standards, such as those mentioned earlier in this chapter or in "Where to Get More Information" at the end of this chapter, or both, and the standards referenced in the Bibliography as being applicable to this chapter.

The following paragraphs contain some generally accepted suggestions for repairing metal framing and furring systems. Because the suggestions apply to many situations, they might not apply to a specific case. In addition, there are many possible cases that are not specifically covered here. When a condition arises in the field that is not addressed here, advice should be sought from the additional data sources mentioned in this book. Often, consultation with the manufacturer of the finish being supported will help. Sometimes, it is necessary to seek professional help (see Chapter 1). Under no circumstances should the specific recommendations in this chapter be followed without careful investigation and application of professional expertise and judgment.

Preparation.   Where existing framing or furring members are damaged, the covering plaster and lath, gypsum board, tile, or other finish must be removed to the extent necessary to permit the repairs to be made. Then the damaged existing framing or furring can be removed, along with their hangers and hanger attachments. Removed damaged elements should be discarded. Damaged elements that should be removed include, but are not limited to, furring members that are broken, bent, or otherwise physically damaged, rusted beyond repair, or otherwise unsuitable for reuse; and hangers and hanger attachments that are rusted, broken, or otherwise damaged. Existing hangers that are sound, adequate, and suitable for reuse may be left in place, or removed, cleaned, and reused.

Hangers and hanger attachments that have been left in place where suspended ceiling furring has been removed should be examined to verify their adequacy and suitability to support the new furring. Those found to be unsuitable should be removed.

Existing hangers and hanger attachments in good condition may be used to support new ceiling furring. New hangers and attachments should be provided, of course, where existing hangers and attachments have been removed or are improperly placed or otherwise inappropriate, and where there are no existing hangers. New hangers should be attached to the structure, never to pipes, conduits, ducts, mechanical or electrical devices, or steel decks. Existing hangers so attached should not be used.

Misaligned, Bent, or Twisted Framing or Furring.   Even metal framing or furring that is misaligned, bent, or twisted enough to cause damage to the applied finish can sometimes be left in place and the finish reattached in such a manner that the poor condition of the framing or furring is overcome. When repair to the finish alone will not prevent the failure from recurring, it will be necessary to remove the damaged framing or furring and provide new materials. Sometimes, removed metal framing or furring that was only misaligned can be properly reinstalled.

Incorrectly Constructed Framing or Furring.   When existing framing or furring was built in such a way that the finish becomes damaged, the necessary corrective measures depend on the type of error. The possibilities are many, and the solutions even more numerous.

Each case must be examined to determine the true cause before steps are taken to correct supposed errors. The extent of the damage must also be taken into account. If it is possible to prevent the failure from recurring by simply refastening the finish, for example, that should be done before expensive reconstruction of the framing or furring is done.

Failed Ceiling Furring.   Metal ceiling furring systems may fail for several reasons, including loads placed on the ceiling furring from above, such as those from items stored there; structure deflection; differential movement in the structure; improper attachment of the support system; and other trauma.

When a ceiling finish failure is due to ceiling furring system failure, repairs may be made by lifting the ceiling back into place and repairing the failed support system. The first step is to stabilize the ceiling. To do so, access to the space above the ceiling must be obtained. When access is not otherwise possible, it will be necessary to remove portions of the ceiling finish. When access to the space above the ceiling is assured, the next step is to wedge the ceiling up from below into proper alignment. Wedging is often accomplished using T-shaped wood braces.

When the ceiling is once again in its proper position, the furring can be secured in place using tie wire or clips.

Installing New Metal Framing and Furring over Existing Materials

Where a new finish is to be applied over an existing material, a new framing or furring system is often needed. Installing new structural framing systems and repairing and extending the existing structural framing system are beyond the scope of this book. The principles for installing the types of metal framing and furring systems that are discussed in this book in existing construction are similar to those for installing new framing and furring systems.

Except for a few different requirements related to fastening them to the existing construction, the same requirements apply to stud partitions in new and existing buildings.

Even in new buildings, furring is always applied over something else. The problems vary only slightly when the something else is old. More shimming may be necessary when new furring is applied on existing substrates, of course, and sometimes an existing surface is in such poor shape that it cannot be satisfactorily furred. When that happens, it may be necessary to fur the surface with an independent partition, or to remove the existing construction completely and build it anew.

It is not always necessary to remove existing trim at openings when installing a new furring system over an existing surface. Items that will be concealed in the finished installation can be left in place.

New ceiling furring can be installed by suspending it from the existing framing. The new furring should be a system of main runner (carrying) channels and furring members suspended from the structure above or a proprietary direct grid suspension system. The requirements for spacing of the furring members and their hangers is the same as for new furring, as discussed earlier in this chapter. When the existing framing is exposed, the new furring should be installed exactly as it would be in all-new construction.

It is sometimes preferable to leave the existing ceiling in place. That can be done by penetrating the existing ceiling only as necessary to install hangers. The number of hangers, and thus penetrations through the existing ceiling, can sometimes be reduced by using channel studs as the furring members, and thus increasing the spacing of the main runners.

In every case, care must be taken to ensure that new hangers are attached to structural framing elements. Hangers should not be attached to steel decks, pipes, conduit, ducts, or mechanical or electrical devices.

Where to Get More Information

The National Forest Products Association's *Manual for House Framing* contains a comprehensive nailing schedule and other significant data about wood framing. It is a useful tool for anyone who must deal with wood construction.

Ramsey/Sleeper's *Architectural Graphic Standards* contains data about nailing arrangements and nail sizes for many framing situations.

The Commerce Publishing Corporation's *The Woodbook* is a wood products reference book published annually. It contains specifications, application recommendations, span tables, and other data about a number of wood products. It contains mostly fliers and product data published by wood product producers and their associations. Unfortunately, there is a fee for this book, which, while annoying, follows the trend so successfully pursued by McGraw-Hill (with their *Sweet's Catalog File*) and others, of selling manufacturer's product literature to architects and others who need the material to select and specify the product. Whether this is a case of biting the hand that feeds you is subject to the reader's judgment. McGraw-Hill has been getting away with it for years with little protest from architects. While the author has "subscribed" to *Sweet's Catalog File* because it is difficult to practice without doing so, he has so far refused to pay for the product data contained in *The Woodbook*.

The Forest Products Laboratory's *Handbook No. 72—Wood Handbook* contains a detailed discussion of wood shrinkage.

Some of AIA Service Corporation's *Masterspec* basic sections contain excellent descriptions of the materials and installations that are addressed in this chapter. Unfortunately, those sections contain little that will help with trouble-shooting failed framing or furring systems. Sections that have applicable data are:

- Section 09200, Lath and Plaster.
- Section 09215, Veneer Plaster.
- Section 09250, Gypsum Drywall.
- Section 09270, Gypsum Board Shaft Wall Systems.

Every designer should have the full complement of applicable ASTM Standards available for reference, of course, but anyone who needs to understand framing and furring for finishes should definitely own a copy of the following ASTM Standards:

- Standard C 11, "Definition of Terms Relating to Gypsum and Related Building Materials."
- Standard C 645, "Specifications for Non-Load (Axial) Bearing Steel Studs, Runners (Track), and Rigid Furring Channels for Screw Application of Gypsum Board."
- Standard C 754, "Specifications for Installation of Steel Framing Members to Receive Screw-Attached Gypsum Wallboard, Backing Board, or Water-Resistant Backing Board."
- Standard C 840, "Specifications for Application and Finishing of Gypsum Board."
- Standard C 841, "Specifications for Installation of Interior Lathing and Furring."
- Standard C 955, "Specifications for Load-Bearing (Transverse and Axial) Steel Studs, Runners (Track), and Bracing or Bridging, for Screw Application of Gypsum Board and Metal Plaster Bases."
- Standard C 1007, "Installation of Load-Bearing (Transverse and Axial) Steel Studs and Accessories."
- Standard C 1063, "Specifications for Installation of Lathing and Furring for Portland Cement-Based Plaster."

ASTM Standards for framing and furring materials and their finishes, and for fasteners and other devices used in framing and furring systems, and other ASTM Standards that are of interest to anyone involved with framing and furring for plaster, gypsum board, and tile, are listed in the

Bibliography and marked with a [2]. They may also be mentioned in this and other chapters.

The following Gypsum Association documents are applicable to the subjects discussed in this chapter:

- The 1984 *Fire Resistance Design Manual: Eleventh Edition (GA-600-84)* is a guide to the fire- and sound-resistance of wall, ceiling, and furring assemblies containing plaster or gypsum board. Anyone designing or maintaining a building containing fire-rated plaster or gypsum board should own a copy.

- The 1985 *Gypsum Board Products Glossary of Terminology (GA-505-85)* is an excellent reference.

- The 1986 *Recommendations for Covering Existing Interior Walls and Ceilings with Gypsum Board (GA-650-86)* goes directly to one of the subjects in this book. It is a "must have" for anyone responsible for installing new gypsum board over existing surfaces. It includes some basic data about supporting construction, including framing and furring.

- The 1988 *Recommended Specifications: Recommendations for Installation of Steel Fire Door Frames in Steel Stud-Gypsum Board Fire-Rated Partitions (GA-219-86)* contains data about steel framing around fire doors.

All Gypsum Association publications mentioned above may be obtained from the Gypsum Association at the address listed in the Appendix.

The Metal Lath/Steel Framing Association's publications *Lightweight Steel Framing Systems Manual* and *Specifications For Metal Lathing and Furring* should be available to everyone responsible for metal framing or furring systems.

The United States Gypsum Company's publications *Gypsum Construction Handbook* and *Red Book: Lathing and Plastering Handbook* are excellent data sources. Everyone concerned with designing, specifying, installing, or maintaining framing or furring for gypsum board or plaster should have them available.

The Western Lath, Plaster, and Drywall Contractors' Association (formerly California Lathing and Plastering Contractors' Association), is responsible for an excellent 1981 publication called *Plaster/Metal Framing System/Lath Manual*. A new edition was published in late 1988 by McGraw-Hill, but was not available at the time of this writing. While the 1981 edition of *Plaster/Metal Framing System/Lath Manual* does not cover repairing existing materials, it is a good source of information about metal framing.

At the time of this writing, Mr. J. R. Gorman, the director of the Lath, Plaster, and Drywall Information Bureau (at the address listed in the Appendix for the International Institute for Lath and Plaster) was available to answer questions about existing materials problems. Also contact the Lath, Plaster, and Drywall Information Bureau for information about the *Plaster/Metal Framing System/Lath Manual* mentioned in the previous paragraph.

Mr. Walter F. Pruter of W. F. Pruter Associates (see International Institute for Lath and Plaster in the Appendix) would also, at the time of this writing, answer questions about lath and plaster problems on behalf of the International Institute for Lath and Plaster.

Patricia Poore's 1983 article, "What's Behind Sagging Plaster," contains recommendations for reattaching wood support systems.

The Exterior Insulation Manufacturers Association, at the address listed in the Appendix, has produced guides for exterior insulation and finish systems.

Also refer to "Where to Get More Information" in Chapters 3, 4, and 5 for additional sources of data about framing and furring for the finishes discussed in those chapters, and to items marked [2] in the Bibliography.

3

Lath and Plaster

This chapter includes wood and metal lath for plaster; standard thickness, veneer, and skim-coat plasters; and synthetic stucco. Insulation for use in exterior insulation and finish systems (EIFS) which are finished with synthetic stucco is also discussed in this chapter. Other construction associated with the subjects discussed in this chapter, such as the building's structural system; solid substrates, such as masonry and concrete; other building elements; and both wood and metal framing and furring are addressed in Chapter 2. Veneer plaster gypsum base; gypsum plaster lath; and gypsum sheathing for use in EIFS are discussed in Chapter 4.

The term "standard thickness plaster" in this book refers to plaster systems that are field installed with a total thickness exceeding 1/4 inch. Excluded are skim coat and veneer plasters, and synthetic stucco.

The term "synthetic stucco" refers to the finish portion of exterior insulation and finish systems (EIFS), and to thin cementitious coatings installed over masonry or concrete.

Standard Thickness and Veneer Plaster Materials

Lime and Sand-Lime Plaster

Sand-lime plaster (sometimes called lime plaster), which consists of lime, sand, and usually hair, is not generally used today because it is extremely slow drying and not particularly strong. An existing building, however, may well have sand-lime plaster that needs repair. While older sand-lime plaster will be found on wood lath, plaster installed in the last part of the nineteenth and early twentieth centuries may well have wire or expanded metal lath bases.

Some sand-lime plaster used in the past for general plastering of walls and ceilings had a small amount of gypsum or Keene's cement plaster added to speed the setting process. Some old ornamental plaster may not be a lot different from gypsum plasters available today.

Gypsum Plaster

The term "gypsum plaster" is used to describe both a final product and one of the components used to produce that product. When this book refers to the final product, it uses the term without a modifier. References to the material are specifically so noted.

Gypsum plaster is a mixture of a material called "gypsum plaster," an aggregate, hydrated lime, and water. Some of the formulations commonly used are discussed in this chapter under "Standard Thickness and Veneer Plaster Installation."

The material name "gypsum plaster" is actually a generic name given to a variety of products. The name is derived from the mineral gypsum, which is the basic material used to make all the products called "gypsum plaster."

The basic material used to manufacture all gypsum plaster products is *plaster of Paris*, which is made by crushing and heating the mineral gypsum in a process called "calcining," until it loses about 75 percent of its water. The *plaster of Paris* is then crushed to a powder and mixed with various additives which control setting time, strength, and other properties.

A material called gypsum Keene's cement, which produces a plaster that is harder and more resistant to water absorption than other types of gypsum plaster, is also a gypsum product. It is made by heating crushed gypsum until it loses almost all its water.

Other materials are added to some gypsum plaster materials at the factory to impart specific characteristics in addition to those already mentioned. Wood fiber is added to give the material greater strength and impact resistance. Lightweight aggregates are added to increase the material's fire resistance and decrease its weight. When this book refers to lightweight aggregates and plaster made using them, the only material it mentions by name is perlite, because at this writing perlite was the only lightweight aggregate being added at the factory to commercially available gypsum plaster materials. Vermiculite is also used as a lightweight aggregate, but today must be added in the field.

Acoustical plaster, a specially formulated and placed gypsum plaster seldom used today, is a lightweight sound absorbent material with a rough textured surface. Most current installations called acoustical plaster are actually standard gypsum plaster with a finish that resembles true acoustical plaster.

While earlier products may vary, gypsum plaster materials generally used today are divided into the following two categories:

- Base coat materials, which include:
  Read-mixed gypsum plaster, with perlite aggregate
  Neat gypsum plaster
  High-strength neat gypsum plaster
  Wood-fibered gypsum plaster
- Finish coat materials, which include:
  Gypsum gauging plaster
  Ready-mixed gauged gypsum plaster
  High-strength gypsum plaster
  Gypsum Keene's cement plaster
  Casting and molding plaster

High-strength plasters are usually limited in use to areas where they are subjected to high impact. Such locations might include corridors, lobbies, and similar areas. Keene's cement plaster is primarily used in areas that must be cleaned frequently and which are subject to medium humidity conditions, such as toilet rooms and kitchens. Perlite aggregate plaster is frequently used where fire resistance is needed.

Gypsum plaster mixes also contain either Type S or Type N hydrated lime in accordance with ASTM Standard C 206, and either sand or perlite aggregate in accordance with ASTM Standard C 35.

Cement Plaster

Cement plaster is a mixture of Portland cement or masonry cement, sand, and hydrated lime. Sometimes fiber is used for strength. Glass fiber is usually used today, but old plaster may have jute or hair fiber instead.

Portland cement may be either Type I or III according to ASTM Standard C 150.

Masonry cement used in cement plaster is usually Type N in accordance with ASTM Standard C 91.

The lime used in cement plaster should be Type S, but may comply either with ASTM Standard C 206 or ASTM Standard C 207.

The sand aggregate in cement plaster should comply with ASTM Standard C 897. In finish coats, the sand may be either natural, white, or colored manufactured sand.

Veneer Plaster

Veneer plaster includes a group of proprietary gypsum plaster products formulated for application in thin layers over specially prepared base board, concrete, or unit masonry. Veneer plaster is available as single or two-coat systems, and in high-strength as well as standard formulations. Specially prepared veneer plaster is also available for use with electric radiant heat coils. Some veneer plaster materials contain silica sand to produce a sand finish plaster. Sand is also sometimes added in the field to produce a sand finish.

Veneer plaster applied over concrete or unit masonry is sometimes called "skim-coat plaster." This should not be confused with slurry bond coats used to bond plaster to solid substrates. Some older skim-coat plaster may be standard gypsum plaster rather than the veneer plaster materials used today.

Standard Thickness and Veneer Plaster Bases

Standard thickness plaster may be installed over a solid base, such as masonry or concrete, or lath. Skim-coat plaster is installed over a solid base. Veneer plaster is installed over unique base board designed for the purpose.

Existing standard thickness gypsum base coat plaster may have been installed directly over solid substrates or over wood, metal, or gypsum lath.

Existing standard thickness Portland cement plaster may have been installed over a solid base or metal lath.

Solid Substrates

Monolithic concrete or unit masonry may be used as solid substrates for either standard thickness gypsum or Portland cement plaster, and for veneer (skim-coat) plaster. Gypsum plaster, including veneer plaster, should not, however, be applied directly to concrete or unit masonry that is part of an exterior wall or roof deck.

Very smooth concrete surfaces are not good plaster bases. They should be roughened by bushhammering, sand blasting, or acid etching before plaster is applied. A bonding agent might also be required. When the material cannot be properly roughened, metal lath should be used. Care must be exercised, however, to not leave bases so rough, especially when veneer plaster will be installed, that the plaster finish is affected.

Lath

Lath may be either wood, metal, or gypsum.

Wood Lath.   Wood lath is seldom used today, but old plaster may have been installed using it.

Early wood lath was just sticks and tree branches. By the late nineteenth century, however, wood lath had become hand- or saw-split slats 1-3/8 or 1-1/2 inches wide, 5/16 or 3/8 inch thick, and 48 inches long. It was cut from a variety of softwoods.

Metal Lath.   At least three kinds of metal lath are regularly used for plaster:

1. Expanded Metal Lath: This lath is produced by cutting and pulling apart (expanding) steel sheets. It may be either painted after fabrication or galvanized. Expanded metal lath includes diamond mesh lath and rib lath.

   Diamond mesh lath may be either flat- or self-furring, and may weigh either 2.5 or 3.4 pounds per square yard. Some Diamond mesh lath is backed at the factory with an asphalt impregnated paper.

   Rib lath is a herringbone mesh lath that is reinforced with evenly spaced solid steel strips. It may have flat ribs less than 1/8 inch high or have ribs that are 3/8 or 3/4 inch deep. The flat variety weighs either 2.75 or 3.4 pounds per square yard. The 3/8-inch high rib type weighs either 3.4 or 4 pounds per square yard. The 3/4-inch high rib lath weighs .6 to .75 pound per square foot.

2. Sheet Lath: Sheet lath is made by stamping, or by punching and forming, metal sheets to form keys for plaster and make the material self-furring. It is an early lath form that has regained popularity as a base for sprayed plaster systems.

3. Wire Mesh Lath: This is made in two types, woven wire and welded wire mesh. Both are made from galvanized wire.

Woven wire mesh is twisted into hexagonal shapes that give it a classic "chicken wire" shape. It is often applied over asphalt-impregnated building paper or sheathing as a base for stucco. It is also used as corner and opening reinforcement over gypsum lath.

Welded wire mesh is interwoven into squares and fastened to a paper, aluminum foil, *Sisalkraft,* or plastic sheet backing. Welded wire mesh is often used as a stucco lath over open studs.

Metal lath is used over unsound solid bases and over wood and metal studs. Most metal lath complies with ASTM Standard C 847.

Gypsum Lath. Gypsum lath is a sheet consisting of a core of gypsum plaster enclosed between layers of paper. Gypsum plaster forms a chemical bond with gypsum lath as the plaster sets. Gypsum lath is discussed in Chapter 4.

Veneer Plaster Base Board

Veneer plaster base board is gypsum board with a specially treated paper finish which is designed to permit thin plaster to bond readily. It is often called "blue board" because of the distinctive bluish-gray color of the paper. It is discussed in Chapter 4.

Accessories and Miscellaneous Materials for Standard Thickness and Veneer Plaster

Accessories for Standard Thickness Gypsum Plaster

Accessories include corner beads, corner and strip reinforcement, casing beads, control joints, and screeds.

Corner Beads. Corner beads may be metal or plastic. Metal beads are usually galvanized steel. They may be small-nosed with either expanded or perforated flanges, or bull-nosed with expanded flanges. Metal corner beads at masonry corners and at columns may have expanded flanges reinforced by ribs.

Plastic corner beads are usually fabricated from polyvinyl chloride into small nosed beads with perforated flanges.

Reinforcement. Reinforcement for plaster is either pre-bent or flat strips of expanded metal lath. It may be either painted or galvanized. Corner reinforcement is used in internal corners between walls. Strip reinforcement is used over the junction of dissimilar bases, over chases, and at the corners of openings.

Casing Beads. Casing beads may be either metal or plastic. Edges are usually square, but bullnosed edges are sometimes used. Flanges may be either solid or expanded.

Metal beads may be either galvanized steel or plastic-coated aluminum. Plastic beads are usually polyvinyl chloride.

Control Joints. Control joints may be of the prefabricated type or made in the field from two casing beads spaced about 1/4 inch apart. Prefabricated control joints are often M-shaped and have expanded or perforated flanges. They may be either metal or plastic.

Metal control joints may be either galvanized steel or plastic-coated aluminum.

Plastic control joints are usually polyvinyl chloride.

Screeds. Screeds are metal strips used to end plaster. Base screeds are used between plaster and terrazzo or cement bases. Screeds are available with expanded flanges and with perforated flanges.

Accessories for Standard Thickness Portland Cement Plaster (Stucco)

Accessories include metal strip and corner reinforcement, metal corner beads, metal and plastic casing beads, and metal screeds.

Corner Beads. Corner beads are usually fabricated from zinc alloy. They have small noses and diamond mesh expanded metal flanges.

Reinforcement. Reinforcement for opening corners or external wall corners is either large-mesh expanded diamond mesh metal lath or welded wire mesh. It is fabricted from either zinc alloy or galvanized steel.

Casing Beads. Casing beads should be either zinc alloy, galvanized steel, or plastic-coated aluminum. Edges are usually square.

Control Joints. Control joints may be prefabricated or made in the field from two casing beads spaced about 1/4 inch apart. Prefabricated control joints are often M-shaped and have expanded or perforated flanges. They may be either zinc alloy, galvanized steel, or plastic-coated aluminum.

Screeds. Screeds are metal strips used to end plaster. Base screeds are used between plaster and terrazzo or cement bases. Sill screeds are used at the bottom of exterior plaster. Screeds are available with expanded flanges.

Accessories for Veneer Plaster

Corner beads, edge trim, and control joints formed to work with veneer plaster are available. They are made from galvanized steel, galvanized steel combined with paper, aluminized steel, or plastic. Flanges for veneer plaster accessories must be perforated.

Miscellaneous Materials

Bonding Agents. Bonding agents for gypsum plaster should comply with ASTM Standard C 631.

Bonding agents for Portland cement plaster should comply with ASTM Standard C 932.

Standard Thickness and Veneer Plaster Installation

The following installations are generally used today. Existing plaster may have been installed using a different mix or system.

Installation methods for new plaster are only generally addressed in this text, since this book is not about new work. Refer to the referenced sources for specific instructions about installing new work.

The descriptions in the following paragraphs are included to help the reader identify existing conditions and to be a ready reference for some materials and systems that may be present.

Installing and Preparing Bases

Solid Substrates. Solid substrates to receive plaster must be clean, free from dirt, oil, grease, curing compounds, form-release agents, other foreign matter, protrusions higher than 1/8 inch, and depressions greater than 1/4 inch. Protrusions should be knocked off. Holes should be filled.

Smooth and clean solid substrate surfaces should receive a bonding agent or slurry bond coat of plaster to produce a secure bond between the plaster and the substrate. Often, a proper bond is possible only when metal lath is applied over the solid substrates. Veneer plaster, which will not permit the use of metal lath, should be bonded to concrete substrates using a bonding agent.

Wood Lath.   Wood lath was generally laid with a 3/8 inch space between the slats and nailed in place to wood supports (Fig. 3-1).

Metal Lath.   Metal lath may be applied over open supports, depending on the substrate, using screws, nails, or clips. It is often applied over open framed wood studs, using No. 18 gage or heavier wire (line wire), which is stretched horizontally across the studs at 6 inches on center and nailed or stapled in place (Fig. 3-2). The lath is then wire-tied to the line wire. On ceilings, metal lath should be installed so that the plastered ceiling will float freely in panels, which lessens the possibility of cracking.

Metal lath should be anchored directly to solid substrates using power-actuated fasteners or hardened concrete nails.

Recommendations for installing metal lath for gypsum plaster are included in ASTM Standard C 841; for cement plaster, in ASTM Standard C 1063.

In every case, metal lath should provide a complete network over the entire surface. It should not, however, extend across expansion or control joints in the substrate.

Gypsum Lath and Veneer Plaster Base.   Refer to Chapter 4 for the installation of gypsum lath and veneer plaster base.

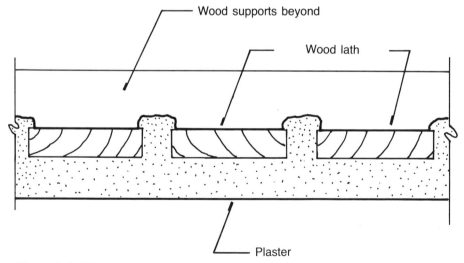

Figure 3-1   Wood lath.

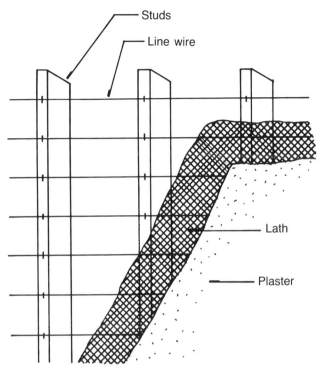

Figure 3-2   Metal lath installed using line wire.

Installing Standard Thickness Plaster

Gypsum Plaster.   Gypsum plaster may be either machine or hand applied.

Gypsum Plaster over Solid Substrates.   Installation may be two- or three-coat work. Three-coat work is seldom used, however, over a concrete substrate. Two-coat work (Fig. 3-3) will usually have a base coat consisting of one of the following:

- Wood-fibered plaster with sand added in the field.
- Neat plaster with sand added in the field. This is the option usually selected where the substrate is concrete.
- Ready-mixed plaster with perlite aggregate added at the factory.

   Three-coat work (Fig. 3-4) will usually have one of the following scratch and brown coat combinations:

- Scratch coat consisting of wood-fibered plaster either neat or with sand

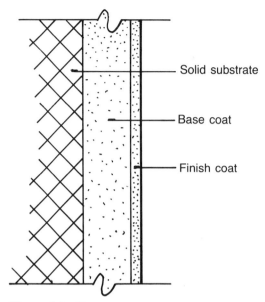

Solid substrate

Base coat

Finish coat

Figure 3-3   Two-coat plaster over solid substrate.

added in the field, and brown coat consisting of wood-fibered plaster with sand added in the field.

- Scratch and brown coats consisting of gypsum neat plaster with sand added in the field.

Gypsum Plaster over Metal Lath.   Gypsum plaster over metal lath should always be applied in three coats. Three-coat work (Fig. 3-5) will usually have one of the following scratch and brown coat combinations:

- Scratch and brown coats consisting of high-strength gauging plaster with sand added in the field.

- Scratch and brown coats consisting of wood-fibered plaster with sand added in the field.

- Scratch and brown coats consisting of gypsum neat plaster with sand added in the field.

- Scratch coat consisting of wood-fibered plaster, either neat or with sand added in the field, and brown coat consisting of neat plaster with sand added in the field.

- Scratch coat consisting of wood-fibered plaster, either neat or with sand added in the field, and brown coat consisting of ready-mixed plaster with perlite aggregate added at the factory. This combination should only occur where the finish is a sand float type.

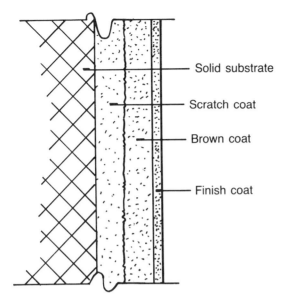

Figure 3-4   Three-coat plaster over solid substrate.

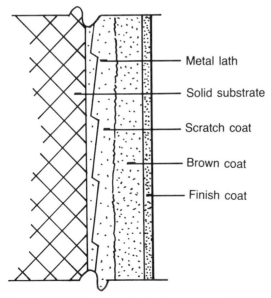

Figure 3-5   Three-coat plaster over metal lath.

- Scratch coat consisting of wood-fibered plaster, either neat or with sand added in the field, and brown coat consisting of neat plaster with lightweight aggregate added in the field. This combination should only occur where the finish is a sand float type.

Gypsum Plaster over Gypsum Lath.   Installation may be two- or three-coat work, but will usually be two-coat work. Two-coat work (Fig. 3-6) will usually have a base coat consisting of one of the following:

- Neat plaster with sand added in the field.
- Ready-mixed plaster with perlite aggregate added at the factory.
- Neat plaster with lightweight aggregate added in the field.

Three coat work (Fig. 3-7) will usually have one of the following scratch and brown coat combinations:

- Scratch and brown coats consisting of ready-mixed plaster with perlite aggregate added at the factory.
- Scratch and brown coats consisting of gypsum neat plaster with sand added in the field.
- Scratch and brown coats consisting of neat plaster with lightweight aggregate added in the field.

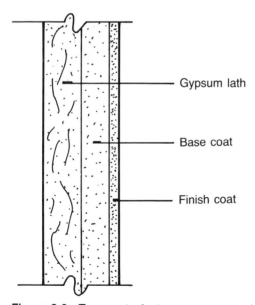

Figure 3-6 Two-coat plaster over gypsum lath.

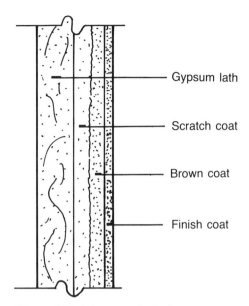

Gypsum lath

Scratch coat

Brown coat

Finish coat

Figure 3-7   Three-coat plaster over gypsum lath.

Gypsum Plaster Finishes.   Gypsum plaster finish coats may be either troweled or floated. Troweled finishes are smooth. Floated finishes bring the aggregate to the surface to impart a texture to the plaster. Additional textures can be, and often are, added by increasing the finish coat thickness and producing texture by means of trowel, stippling with sponge, brush, or wadded paper, brushing with a bricklayers trowel, brushing with a paint brush, hand daubing (pressing human hands into the plaster), and many other techniques. Plaster may be grooved to simulate stone or brick jointing, and even grained to simulate stone.

In addition to the actual plaster textures possible, texture may be added by applying one of the many textured paints on the market in a variety of patterns.

In some cases, the finish texture will dictate the installation methods used.

Existing finish coat mix proportions may be one of the following:

- Troweled gauging plaster mixed with 2 parts (1:2) lime.
- Troweled gauging plaster with 2 parts (1:2) lime and 1/2 cubic foot of lightweight aggregate or 50 pounds of No. 1 white silica sand per 100 cubic feet of plaster. This mix is used when the base coat contains lightweight aggregate.
- Troweled neat ready mixed finish plaster.
- Troweled high-strength gauging plaster. Mix may be 1 part (1:1) lime

or 2 parts (1:2) lime. Twice as much lime makes the plaster one-half as hard.

- Troweled Keene's cement mixed with 1/4 part (4:1) lime or 1/2 part lime (2:1). More lime makes weaker plaster.
- Floated sand-finish gauging plaster. Mix may be 2 parts lime and 8 parts sand (1:2:8) or 1/2 part lime and 4 parts sand (2:1:8).

Fiber.   Modern gypsum plasters do not generally contain such fibers, but existing gypsum plaster may contain hair or sisal fiber reinforcement.

Thicknesses.   Standard thickness gypsum plaster is usually installed in the following total thicknesses. Thickness is measured from the back of metal lath or the face of solid substrates or lath to the face of the plaster.

- Over solid substrates: 5/8 inch.
- Over metal lath: 5/8 inch.
- Over gypsum lath: 1/2 inch.

Fire-retardant plaster may vary from the above to comply with the building code or assembly rating. Plaster in solid partitions will also vary from the above thicknesses.

Face coats should be at least 1/8 inch thick.

Portland Cement Plaster.   Portland cement plaster may be either machine or hand applied.

Portland Cement Plaster over Solid Substrates.   Portland cement plaster may be applied directly to solid substrates in either two or three coats.

In two-coat work (see Fig. 3-3), the base coat may or may not contain lime. The mix proportions are usually 1 part Portland cement and between 3 and 4 parts sand. When lime is added, the quantity is usually between 3/4 and 1-1/2 parts. Masonry cement may be used in lieu of Portland cement, but then the lime is omitted.

In three-coat work (see Fig. 3-4), the scratch and brown coats may or may not contain lime. The mix proportions of the scratch coat are usually 1 part Portland cement to between 2-1/2 and 4 parts sand. The mix proportions for the brown coat are usually 1 part Portland cement to between 3 and 5 parts sand. The proportion of sand in the brown coat should be the same or more than was used in the scratch coat. Where lime is used, the quantity is usually between 3/4 and 1-1/2 parts. Where lime is used, it should be used in both scratch and brown coats.

Existing Portland cement plaster over a solid substrate may also contain fiber, in an amount usually less than 2 pounds per cubic foot of plaster.

Portland Cement Plaster over Metal Lath. Portland cement plaster should always be applied in three coats when over metal lath (see Fig. 3-5). A variety of mixes are used in the scratch and brown coats. In the mixes used, for each part Portland cement there should be between 2-1/2 and 5 parts sand. The proportion of sand in the brown coat should be the same or more than was used in the scratch coat. The mixes also contain between 3/4 and 1-1/2 parts lime. More lime usually means more sand. Masonry cement may be used in lieu of Portland cement. Masonry cement may also be used in addition to the Portland cement, using either the same amount of each or twice as much masonry cement as Portland cement. Where masonry cement is used, lime is omitted.

Existing Portland cement plaster over metal lath may also contain fiber, in an amount usually less than 2 pounds per cubic foot of plaster.

Portland Cement Plaster Finishes. Portland cement plaster may be either trowel applied or sprayed in place. It is generally float finished, but that is just the beginning stage. Often, the finish texture will dictate the installation methods used. Dash finishes are usually machine applied, for example. Final Portland cement finishes are extremely varied, including: float finishes leaving a grainy plaster; finishes made by manipulating the trowel strokes to create textures such as those known by such names as "lace," "glacier," and "Monterey," or random "Spanish" textures consisting of overlapping strokes of the trowel; heavy or light dash textures achieved by varying the air amount at the gun nozzle in sprayed work; combed finishes made by combing the surface vertically or horizontally with a templet; scraped textures made by scraping the finish coat with a steel trowel or joint rod, leaving a torn surface; and burlap rubbed fnishes, sometimes called "California" finishes. Portland cement plaster is also finished to simulate brick and stone, and exposed aggregate finishes are used as well.

Portland cement finish coats may be field mixed or factory mixed. Factory mixed finish coats are mixed at the job site with water only. Field mixed Portland cement plaster finish coats may be made with either Portland cement or masonry cement. In Portland cement mixes, sand is usually added in an amount equal to three times the amount of Portland cement. Lime is also used. The amount of lime varies from 3/4 to 2 parts for each 1 part Portland cement. Mixes may also contain equal amounts of Portland cement and masonry cement and 3 parts sand. Masonry cement may be used with 1-1/2 parts and to each part of cement. Where masonry cement is used, lime is omitted.

Thicknesses. Existing Portland cement plaster may be found in any one of the following total thicknesses. Thickness is measured from the back of metal lath or the face of solid substrates to the face of the plaster.

- Over solid substrates: Usually 5/8 inch; occasionally 7/8 inch; sometimes 3/8 inch over monolithic cast-in-place concrete.
- Over solid substrates with metal lath: 7/8 inch.
- Over metal lath: Some projects may have 5/8 inch thick plaster here, but most will be 7/8 inch thick.

Face coats should be at least 1/8 inch thick.

Installing Veneer Plaster

Veneer plaster is installed by trowel over veneer plaster gypsum base, concrete, or masonry. One or two coat systems are used over veneer plaster gypsum base (Fig. 3-8). Two coat systems are used over concrete and masonry. The thickness may vary from 1/16 to 3/32 inch.

Veneer plaster is usually given a smooth troweled finish, but some sand finish applications also exist.

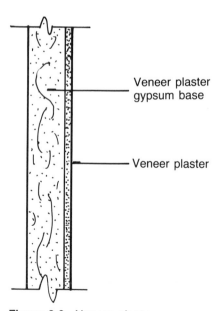

Veneer plaster gypsum base

Veneer plaster

Figure 3-8   Veneer plaster over veneer plaster gypsum base.

Standard Thickness and Veneer Plaster Failures and What to Do about Them

Why Standard Thickness and Veneer Plaster Fails

Most standard thickness and veneer plaster failures are caused either by structure failure; structure movement; solid substrate problems; other building element problems; framing or furring problems; veneer plaster gypsum base failure; gypsum plaster lath failure; bad materials; improper system design; or bad workmanship.

Many plaster failures result from problems with the plaster itself or its installation, which are discussed in this chapter. Other plaster failures result from problems with the construction underlying the plaster. Those problems include structure failure and movement, and problems associated with solid substrates, other building elements, and wood and metal framing or furring, all of which are discussed in Chapter 2.

Some of the problems discussed in Chapter 2, especially structure movement (Fig. 3-9) and solid substrate problems, are as likely to cause plaster failure as problems with the plaster or its installation. Consequently, the

Figure 3-9 This damage was caused by differential movement. (*Photo by author.*)

possibility that the types of problems discussed in Chapter 2 are responsible for a plaster failure should be investigated and ruled out or, if found to be at fault, rectified before plaster repairs are attempted. It will do no good to repair plaster when a failed, uncorrected, or unaccounted-for problem of the types discussed in Chapter 2 is present. The repair will also fail.

Another source of plaster failures that must be considered is the base to which the plaster is applied. Wood and metal lath are discussed in this chapter. Veneer plaster gypsum base and gypsum plaster lath, and possible problems associated with them, are discussed in Chapter 4.

The problems with veneer plaster gypsum base and gypsum plaster lath discussed in Chapter 4 are likely causes for plaster failure. They should be investigated and ruled out as failure causes or, if found to be at fault, rectified as a part of the necessary plaster repairs. Plastering over failed veneer plaster gypsum base or gypsum plaster lath will result in recurrence of the original plaster failure.

After the types of problems discussed in Chapter 2 and Chapter 4 have been investigated and found to be not present, or repaired if found, the next step is to discover causes for the plaster failure that are related to metal or wood lath or the plaster itself, and repair them. Possible failure causes include those in the following paragraphs, which contain numbered lists of errors and situations that can cause plaster failure. Refer to "Evidence of Failure in Standard Thickness and Veneer Plaster" later in this chapter for a listing of the types of failure to which the numbered failure causes in this part apply.

Bad Materials.   Improperly manufactured or prepared materials can result in plaster failures. Bad materials may result from one of the following:

1. Bad plaster is certainly not unheard of. There might have been too much retarder added, for example, which will result in plaster that will not set. But bad plaster is not nearly as common as the other failure causes we will discuss in this chapter.
2. A more common materials failure is improperly graded aggregate. The most common improper gradation problem is sand that has too many fine particles.
3. Water may contain enough dirt, iron, or other impurities to produce plaster failure or discoloration.
4. Lime may contain improperly burned particles.
5. Materials may become contaminated in the field. Insects may fly or crawl into the sand, or seed, leaves, dirt, or other debris may blow into the sand. Plaster materials may be contaminated by oil, tar, creosote, soot, or other foreign materials commonly found on construction sites.

Improper System Design.   In addition to improper design of the parts of a plaster finish system, discussed in Chapters 2 and 4, improper design might also include selection of the wrong accessories, fasteners, or plaster material; failing to require proper preparation; and selecting an improper installation.

Wrong Accessories or Fasteners.   Accessories and fasteners must be appropriate. Errors include:

1. Selecting accessories or fasteners that will rust.
2. Using accessories with nonperforated flanges with veneer plaster.
3. Using accessories of improper depth.
4. Using the wrong accessories for the job at hand. Using a parting screed as an expansion joint is an example.
5. Failing to require weep screeds at grade in exterior plaster.

Wrong Plaster Material.   Selecting the wrong plaster material or mix for a particular location or condition can lead to plaster failure. Errors that will lead to failure include:

1. Mistaking gypsum Keene's cement for a Portland cement product. Errors include using Keene's cement in exterior applications or in interior applications where the material is subject to wetting or high humidity. While Keene's cement is hard and somewhat more resistant to water penetration than other types of gypsum plaster, it is, nevertheless, a gypsum product subject to the same types of water damage as other gypsum plasters.
2. Selecting gypsum plaster for use in wet or exterior locations.
3. Selecting different mix strengths for coats in the same system. This is a particular problem in Portland cement plaster. While setting, different mixes will contract at different rates and crack the plaster.
    Requiring that some lightweight fines or silica sand be included in finish coats over base coats containing lightweight aggregate will help reduce map cracking.
4. Selecting or permitting the use of a veneer plaster material made by a different manufacturer than the producer of the veneer plaster gypsum base.
5. Requiring that cement plaster be used over gypsum lath.

Failing to Require Proper Preparing Methods.   Proper preparation is essential to prevent plaster failure. Problems will result if the designer:

1. Does not require proper preparation of surfaces.

Selecting an Improper Application.   This category includes the following types of problems:

1. Failing to take normal structure movement into account. Preparation should be made in the design to take care of settlement, shrinkage, expansion, warping, and deflection.
2. Applying Portland cement plaster directly to both sides of an exterior wall.
3. Applying gypsum plaster directly to an exterior wall.
4. Specifying a base coat that is too weak for the finish coat.
5. Failing to require expansion joints, or spacing expansion joints too far apart. Expansion joints in Portland cement plaster should usually be not more than 10 feet apart with no panel exceeding 100 square feet. In addition, panels should not have one dimension more than twice the length of the other dimension. Where wood or gypsum sheathing is used, and where the finish texture is heavy, the distance between expansion joints can sometimes be increased without damage. Some finishes, however, require spacings closer than 10 feet.
6. Failing to specify corner reinforcement.
7. Failure to specify opening reinforcement.
8. Failing to provide flashing and drips to prevent water from getting behind exterior plaster.
9. Specifying a plaster coat or total thickness that is too thin or too weak for the situation as recommended by ASTM and other applicable standards.
10. Failing to specify using bonding agents in accordance with ASTM and other applicable standards and the plaster manufacturer's recommendations.

Bad Workmanship.   Proper workmanship is essential to prevent plaster failures. A major problem is not following the design and recommendations of recognized authorities, such as ASTM, Portland Cement Association, and Gypsum Association. A similar problem is not following the manufacturer's recommendations. Specific reasons for failure due to bad workmanship include improper substrate preparation, improper lathing, improper accessory and fastener application, improper proportioning and mixing of plaster ingredients, and improper plaster installation and curing procedures.

Improper Substrate Preparation.   Examples of improper substrate preparation include:

1. Failing to remove dirt, oil, tar, grease, efflorescence, loose particles, and foreign substances.

2. Failing to achieve the correct surface tolerance.
3. Failing to eliminate gloss from an existing surface.
4. Failing to cut back and clean out cracks and holes.
5. Failing to fill depressions deeper than 1/4 inch.
6. Failing to remove protrusions.
7. Failing to provide proper suction on a solid substrate. This problem may be caused by not wetting the substrate, thus providing too much suction, applying too much water, thus providing too little suction, or providing an unequal amount of suction on different parts of the same surface.

Improper Wood or Metal Lath Installation.   Examples include:

1. Improperly installing lath so that it is insufficiently supported, or later sags.
2. Providing insufficient fastening to properly support lath.
3. Failing to drive fasteners in far enough.
4. Applying lath to wet wood supports.
5. Using fasteners that are too large.
6. Using fasteners that are too short.
7. Using fasteners that will rust.
8. Placing wood lath strips too close together, preventing proper keying of plaster to the lath.
9. Extending lath across an expansion joint. Paper backing on metal lath, however, should continue across expansion joints.

Improper Accessory Application.   Examples include:

1. Using fasteners that will rust.
2. Using accessories of the wrong type. Using corner beads with no perforations with veneer plaster is an example. Using beads designed for gypsum plaster with Portland cement plaster is another.
3. Using accessories of the wrong size.
4. Failing to install proper expansion joints in correct locations.

Improper Proportioning and Mixing of Plaster.   Examples of improper proportioning or mixing include:

1. Adding too much sand to the mix. Over-sanding is a common problem, which produces weak plaster that will often craze, and sometimes causes the finish coat to separate from the base coat. Over-sanded gypsum plaster can be scratched deeply with a nail, and the scratched mortar will crumble.

Over-sanding, within reason, may not weaken Portland cement plaster but may make it more difficult to apply and cause weak spots because of thinner application in some locations than in others.

A common problem caused by over-sanding is a base coat that is too weak for the finish coat.

2. Using too much retarder. Plaster with too much retarder may dry out but not properly cure, which results in soft and powdery plaster. Over-retarded plaster, if discovered in time, may be accelerated to a proper cure by spraying with water to which alum had been added. Over-retarded veneer plaster will develop blisters and produce an unsatisfactory surface.

3. Using the incorrect amount of pigment. Too much pigment can result in weak plaster. Differing amounts of pigment in different batches will result in plaster that varies in color.

4. Failing to properly mix the plaster. Leaving particles of unsoaked lime or undissolved retarder are common problems, as is failing to distribute components equally throughout the mix.

5. Adding water to a colored mortar mix after mixing. Additional water will produce a washed out color in that batch, creating a mismatch with other plaster.

6. Allowing either gypsum or Portland cement plaster materials to freeze during mixing. Frozen plaster mix will be weak and must be discarded. Permitting the mix to thaw out will not help.

7. Using different strength mixes for coats in the same system, especially in Portland cement plaster. This fault is included under ''Improper System Design,'' but bears mentioning here also, because it is so common a fault. Different mixes will contract at different rates while setting and crack the plaster. The cement-to-aggregate ratio should be the same for all coats. Water content should be consistent.

8. Not including enough gauging plaster in the finish coat.

9. Retempering Portland Cement finish coats, Portland cement patching plaster, gauged lime putty, or gypsum plaster base coats after mixing.

10. Using a finish coat mix that is too plastic.

Improper Installation and Curing of Plaster.   Examples of improper plaster installation and curing include:

1. Allowing plaster materials to freeze during application or curing. Both gypsum and cement plasters are subject to damage by freezing.

Frozen plaster will be weak and must be discarded. Permitting the plaster to thaw out will not help. Installed plaster which freezes before it has set must be removed. Frozen gypsum plaster may burst, scale, or peel. When Portland cement plaster is allowed to freeze, the coats may separate, or the plaster may crumble.

Sometimes the damage from permitting plaster to freeze will not be apparent for some time. Freezing should be suspected when plaster flakes, crumbles, separates, bursts, crazes, blisters, or peels a year or so after application.

Applying plaster over frozen lath or substrates containing frost can cause the plaster to separate from the lath or substrate after it sets.

Allowing plaster to freeze after it has cured is also harmful. Plaster frozen after curing can sometimes be thawed successfully, but often finish coats will flake off. When the finish coat is damaged by freezing, all of the plaster must be removed. A new finish coat applied over the previously frozen base coats will most likely scale off after it sets.

2. Failing to properly cure plaster coats before the next coat is applied. Failing to prepare installed coats, including providing mechanical keying for the next coat, before applying the next coat.
3. Failing to provide flashing and drips at exterior plaster.
4. Failing to provide proper suction on a base coat. A problem may be caused by not wetting the base coat, thus providing too much suction, or applying too much water, thus providing too little suction. A problem may also be caused by providing different amounts of (not uniform) suction on different parts of the same surface.
5. Permitting foreign particles to fall, blow, or otherwise enter the plaster.
6. Using different finishing tools in different locations.
7. Failing to properly clean or maintain mixing or pumping equipment.
8. Varying overall plaster or individual coat thickness on the same surface.
9. Applying too thin a coat or total thickness.
10. Applying too thick a finish coat.
11. Troweling too little.
12. Troweling too much, especially at joinings.
13. Troweling too soon.
14. Using too much water when troweling.
15. Using bad floating techniques.
16. Using too much water when floating.
17. Failing to prevent plaster base or finish coats from drying too quickly. Unless special precautions are taken, very dry weather and

too much ventilation will each cause either gypsum or Portland cement plaster to cure too quickly. Hot, dry air directed on plaster can also cause too-rapid drying. When a plaster mix dries too quickly, there is insufficient time for the proper chemical reactions to take place and plaster never actually forms. The condition is called dry-out. What remains is not a compound, which is what true plaster is, but just a dry mixture of the original ingredients. Drafts of very dry air, as might pass through an unprotected opening for example, or from a heater, may cause plaster to cure in some spots and just dry out without curing in others. Heating appliances placed too close to plaster, even after the building is occupied, can also cause dry-out if the plaster is not completely cured before the heating device is activated.

Veneer plaster, because it is so thin, is particularly susceptible to dry-out.

18. Allowing too much moisture to occur in a location where gypsum plaster is curing. Very wet weather can prevent gypsum plaster from setting, or make setting very slow, each of which will break gypsum down and make the plaster weak. A similar problem is caused by improper ventilation when plaster is curing. In these conditions, the excess water used to make plaster workable will not evaporate. If gypsum plaster is not permitted to cure due to excess moisture, the plaster will enter a stage called ''rot,'' which is characterized by darkening of the plaster. Rotted plaster is weak and remains moist. The only cure is to remove the bad material and install new plaster. Cement plaster is not subject to rot.

19. Permitting large or rapid temperature fluctuations to occur during application or curing, or to occur between the front and back of plaster.

20. Failing to caulk between plaster and adjacent materials, which permits water to enter the space behind the plaster.

21. Allowing cured gypsum plaster to become wet. This will cause a condition similar to that described in paragraph 18 directly above.

22. Failing to provide a bonding agent where recommended by ASTM, other industry standards, or the plaster manufacturer.

23. Failing to scratch the final coat into the base coat.

24. Leaving the base coat too smooth.

25. Applying cement plaster over gypsum lath.

26. Applying veneer plaster to faded veneer base without using an alum solution treatment or bonding agent to ensure plaster bond. Veneer base will often fade and lose its ability to bond with plaster after exposure to the sun.

Evidence of Failure in Standard Thickness and Veneer Plaster

In the following paragraphs, plaster failures are listed under the headings "Standard Thickness Plaster Failures" and "Veneer Plaster Failures." Those categories are subdivided into failure types, such as "Loose Plaster." Following each failure type are one or more failure sources, such as "Bad Workmanship: Improper Substrate Preparation." After most failure sources, one or more numbers is listed. The numbers represent possible errors associated with that failure source that might cause that failure type to occur.

A description and discussion of the numbered failure causes for failure types: "Structure Failure," "Structure Movement," "Solid Substrate Problems," "Other Building Element Problems," "Wood Framing and Furring Problems," and "Metal Framing and Furring Problems" appear in Chapter 2 under the same headings, and each is listed in the Contents. For example, clarification and explanation of the numbered cause (1) in the example

▪ Metal Framing and Furring Problems: 1 (see Chapter 2).

appears in Chapter 2 under the heading "Metal Framing and Furring Problems," cause 1, which reads

1. Metal framing or furring that is out of alignment.

A description and discussion of the numbered causes that follow failure types: "Bad materials," "Improper System Design," and "Bad Workmanship" appear as subparagraphs and sub-subparagraphs in the part of this chapter titled "Why Standard Thickness and Veneer Plaster Fails," which is listed in the Contents. For example, clarification and explanation of the numbered cause (3) listed in the example

▪ Bad Workmanship: Improper Substrate Preparation: 3.

appears in this chapter under the heading "Why Standard Thickness and Veneer Plaster Fails," subparagraph "Bad Workmanship" sub-subparagraph "Improper Substrate Preparation," cause 3, which reads:

3. Failing to eliminate gloss from an existing surface.

Some failure sources are not followed by numbers. Those titled "Standard Gypsum Board and Veneer Plaster Base Failures" and "Gypsum Plaster Lath Failures" refer to failure types and causes discussed in Chapter 4. Each is a subparagraph in the part of Chapter 4 called "Evidence of Failure in Gypsum Board Systems," which is listed in the Contents. The failure types (such as "Loose or Sagging Ceiling Boards) following each of those failure sources are listed in Chapter 4 as sub-subparagraphs under

"Standard Gypsum Board and Veneer Plaster Base Failures" and "Gypsum Plaster Lath Failures." Note that only the failure types from Chapter 4 are listed here. The failure sources and cause numbers are omitted to prevent repetition. Every potential failure source and cause listed in Chapter 4 for the failure types listed here should be considered as a possible cause for that type of failure.

When more than one failure type is apparent (Fig. 3-10), each must be investigated separately to determine the true cause or causes of the failure.

Standard Thickness Plaster Failures

Loose Plaster. May be caused by:

- Structure Failure: 1 (see Chapter 2).
- Structure Movement: 1, 2, 3, 4, 5, 6, 7, 8, (see Chapter 2).
- Solid Substrate Problems: 1, 2, 3, 4 (see Chapter 2).
- Other Building Element Problems: 1, 2, 3 (see Chapter 2).
- Wood Framing and Furring Problems, 1, 2, 3, 4, 5, 6, 7, 8 (see Chapter 2).
- Metal Framing and Furring Problems: 1, 2, 3, 4 (see Chapter 2).
- Gypsum Plaster Lath Failures: Loose or Sagging Ceiling Boards; Loose or Bowing Wall Boards; Soft or Disintegrating Boards (see Chapter 4).
- Improper System Design: Wrong Plaster Material: 1, 2, 4, 5.
- Improper System Design: Failing to Require Proper Preparation Methods: 1.
- Improper System Design: Selecting an Improper Application: 1, 2, 3, 5, 8, 10.
- Bad Workmanship: Improper Substrate Preparation: 1, 3.
- Bad Workmanship: Improper Wood or Metal Lath Installation: 1, 2, 3, 4, 6, 7, 8.
- Bad Workmanship: Improper Proportioning and Mixing of Plaster: 1, 6, 9.
- Bad Workmanship: Improper Installation and Curing of Plaster: 1, 2, 3, 4, 9, 10, 11, 17, 18, 21, 22, 24, 25.

Soft or Crumbling Plaster. May be caused by:

- Bad Materials: 1, 2, 3, 5.
- Improper System Design: Wrong Plaster Material: 1, 2, 4.

Figure 3-10
This plaster has crumbled, delaminated at the lath, and fallen from the solid substrate, suggesting that several problems, rather than just one, may exist. (*Photo by author.*)

- Improper System Design: Selecting an Improper Application: 2, 3, 8.
- Bad Workmanship: Improper Proportioning and Mixing of Plaster: 1, 2, 4, 6, 8, 9.
- Bad Workmanship: Improper Installation and Curing of Plaster: 1, 2, 3, 5, 17, 18, 19, 20, 21.

Cracking. Cracks may occur only in the finish coat or may be completely through the plaster (Fig. 3-11). Cracks result when a plaster material or bond is not strong enough to withstand the forces imparted to it. Random cracking is usually due to forces produced within the plaster system itself. The cause may be differential movement between different

Figure 3-11 Cracks completely through stucco and so severe that some is about to fall from the wall. (*Photo by author.*)

plaster courses, or between the plaster and its base. Figures 3-12 and 3-13 show two types of plaster cracking that are usually due to forces within the plaster itself.

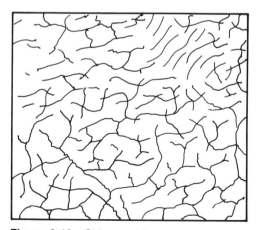

Figure 3-12 Chip cracking.

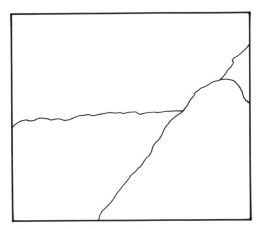

Figure 3-13 Map cracks.

Large cracks that parallel structural or support system elements or which stair-step or emanate from corners of walls, ceilings, or openings are usually caused by movement in the supporting structure. Figure 3-14 shows cracks of the type usually caused by structure or support system movement.

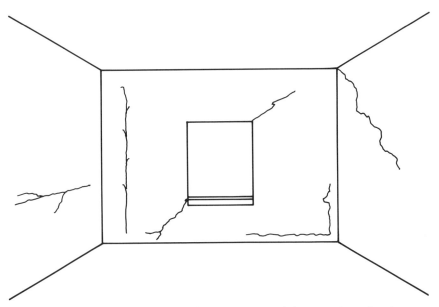

Figure 3-14 Crack types caused by movement of the structure, framing, or furring.

The following defects will cause cracks:

- Structure Failure: 1 (see Chapter 2).
- Structure Movement: 1, 2, 3, 4, 5, 6, 7, 8 (see Chapter 2).
- Solid Substrate Problems: 1, 2, 3, 4 (see Chapter 2).
- Other Building Element Problems: 1, 2, 3 (see Chapter 2).
- Wood Framing and Furring Problems: 1, 2, 3, 4, 5, 6, 7, 8 (see Chapter 2).
- Metal Framing and Furring Problems: 1, 2, 3, 4, 5 (see Chapter 2).
- Gypsum Plaster Lath Failures: Loose or Sagging Ceiling Boards; Wavy Board Surfaces; Loose or Bowing Wall Boards; Soft or Disintegrating Boards; Board Cracks (see Chapter 4).
- Bad Materials: 1, 2, 5.
- Improper System Design: Wrong Accessories or Fasteners: 4.
- Improper System Design: Wrong Plaster Material: 3, 4.
- Improper System Design: Failing to Require Proper Preparation Methods: 1.
- Improper System Design: Selecting an Improper Application: 1, 2, 3, 4, 5, 8, 9.
- Bad Workmanship: Improper Substrate Preparation: 4, 6.
- Bad Workmanship: Improper Wood or Metal Lath Installation: 1, 2, 9.
- Bad Workmanship: Improper Accessory Application: 2, 4.
- Bad Workanship: Improper Proportioning and Mixing of Plaster: 1, 4, 6, 7.
- Bad Workmanship: Improper Installation and Curing of Plaster: 1, 2, 3, 5, 8, 16, 17, 19.

In addition, cracks associated with openings may be caused by:

- Improper System Design: Specifying Improper Application: 7.

In addition, short, fine, nonparallel cracks that form random patterns (known as chip cracks, shrinkage cracks, crazing, and alligatoring) (see Fig. 3-12) may be caused by:

- Bad Workmanship: Improper Substrate Preparation: 7.
- Bad Workmanship: Improper Proportioning and Mixing of Plaster: 2, 8.
- Bad Workmanship: Improper Installation and Curing of Plaster: 4, 9, 11.

In addition, fine cracks resembling the lines on a map (map cracking) (see Fig. 3-13), with cracks 6 inches to 14 inches apart, may be caused by:

- Bad Workmanship: Improper Proportioning and Mixing of Plaster: 9.
- Bad Workmanship: Improper Installation and Curing of Plaster: 10, 13, 18.

In addition, cracks at wall or ceiling angles may be caused by:

- Improper System Design: Specifying an Improper Application: 6.

In addition, wall and ceiling cracks at right angles to the framing, and long cracks in the direction of the main runners, may be caused by:

- Bad Workmanship: Improper Installation and Curing of Plaster: 18.

Fastener Pops.   May be caused by:

- Structure Movement: 6, 7 (see Chapter 2).
- Wood Framing and Furring Problems: 1, 2, 3, 4, 6 (see Chapter 2).
- Metal Framing and Furring Problems: 1, 2 (see Chapter 2).
- Gypsum Plaster Lath Failures: Fastener Pops (see Chapter 4).
- Improper System Design: Wrong Accessories or Fasteners: 1.
- Bad Workmanship: Improper Wood or Metal Lath Installation: 3, 4, 5, 6, 7.
- Bad Workmanship: Improper Accessory Application: 1.

Pitting and Pops Not Associated with Fasteners.   May be caused by:

- Bad Materials: 1, 3, 4, 5.
- Bad Workmanship: Improper Substrate Preparation: 1.
- Bad Workmanship: Improper Proportioning and Mixing of Plaster: 4.
- Bad Workmanship: Improper Installation and Curing of Plaster: 5, 7.

Blisters.   May be caused by:

- Bad Workmanship: Improper Proportioning and Mixing of Plaster: 10.
- Bad Workmanship: Improper Installation and Curing of Plaster: 2, 4, 14.

Stains and Color Variations.   May be caused by:

- Bad Materials: 1, 3, 5.
- Improper System Design: Wrong Accessories or Fasteners: 1.
- Bad Workmanship: Improper Substrate Preparation: 1.
- Bad Workmanship: Improper Wood or Metal Lath Installation: 7.
- Bad Workmanship: Improper Accessory Application: 1.

- Bad Workmanship: Improper Proportioning and Mixing of Plaster: 1, 3, 4, 5, 7.
- Bad Workmanship: Improper Installation and Curing of Plaster: 4, 5, 7, 8, 12, 14, 15, 16, 17, 18, 19, 20, 21.

Texture Variations. May be caused by:

- Bad Workmanship: Improper Installation and Curing of Plaster: 6.

Effloresence. Salts found in plaster, mortar, concrete, and concrete unit masonry will leach out when water is present. When the water bearing the salts evaporates, a white powdery residue is left. Efflorescence on
-

- Solid Substrate Problems: 1 (see Chapter 2).
- Other Building Element Problems: 1, 2 (see Chapter 2).
- Improper System Design: Wrong Accessories or Fasteners: 5.
- Improper System Design: Selecting an Improper Application: 8.
- Bad Workmanship: Improper Installation and Curing of Plaster: 3, 18.

Veneer Plaster Failures

Loose Plaster. May be caused by:

- Standard Gypsum Board and Veneer Plaster Gypsum Base Failures: Soft or Disintegrating Boards; Blisters (see Chapter 4).
- Bad Workmanship: Improper Installation and Curing of Plaster: 2, 23, 24, 26.

Soft or Crumbling Surface. May be caused by:

- Bad Workmanship: Improper Proportioning and Mixing of Plaster: 1, 2.
- Bad Workmanship: Improper Installation and Curing of Plaster: 17.

Cracks. May be caused by:

- Standard Gypsum Board and Veneer Plaster Gypsum Base Failures: Wavy Board Surface; Loose or Sagging Ceiling Boards; Loose or Bowing Wall Boards; Soft or Disintegrating Boards; Board Cracks; Flat Surface and Corner Joint Cracks; Joint Beading or Ridging; Blisters (see Chapter 4).
- Bad Workmanship: Improper Installation and Curing of Plaster: 9, 17.

Ridging and Beading   May be caused by:

- Standard Gypsum Board and Veneer Plaster Gypsum Base Failures: Joint Beading or Ridging (see Chapter 4).
- Bad Workmanship: Improper Installation and Curing Of Plaster: 17.

Fastener Pops.   May be caused by:

- Standard Gypsum Board and Veneer Plaster Gypsum Base Failures: Fastener Pops (see Chapter 4).

Spalling.   May be caused by:

- Improper System design: Wrong Accessories or Fasteners: 2.
- Bad Workmanship: Improper Accessory Application: 2.

Other Failures.   Other failures can be caused by the following:

- Standard Gypsum Board and Veneer Plaster Gypsum Base Failures: Punctures and Board Depressions; Stains and Discolorations; Fastener Depressions: Fastener Bulging; Joint Depressions; Blisters; and Shadowing (see Chapter 4).

Repairing and Extending Existing Standard Thickness Plaster

The nature of plaster makes most minor damage repairable (Fig. 3-15). Loose plaster can be reattached, weak or soft plaster can be cut out and patched, cracks can be filled, spalled areas can be patched, stains can be cut out or painted, nail pops can be repaired, craters can be filled. Most of the time, however, it makes no sense to repair plaster that has suffered severe damage, or when a large portion of the plaster is loose, cracked, spalled, or otherwise damaged (Fig. 3-16). Then, removing the plaster and providing a new finish is often easier and less expensive, and usually results in a better finished surface, than repairing the existing plaster. When the damage is not severe, or covers only a small area, on the other hand, repair is often the right answer. Of course, plaster that has historic significance will often be repaired, even when severely damaged.

In general, repair and extensions of existing plaster should comply with the ASTM Standards listed in the Bibliography. In addition, the part of this chapter "Where to Get More Information" contains a discussion of sources of data about repairing existing plaster. The following paragraphs contain some generally accepted suggestions about repairing existing plaster. In every case, however, where the recommendations of a manufacturer,

Figure 3-15 Ceiling plaster that may be repairable. (*Photo by author.*)

Figure 3-16 There is too much damage to this ceiling plaster to make repair worthwhile. Removing the existing and providing new plaster is probably a better idea here. (*Photo by author.*)

association representing plastering professionals, or plasterer differ with the recommendations here, seriously consider those other recommendations before insisting on the methods or materials discussed here. Because of book space limitations, the recommendations here are necessarily generic. They, therefore, may not apply in a particular case. Often, specific field conditions will dictate different methods or materials.

Materials. Lath and accessories should match those used in the existing installation, but in no case should they be lesser in quality or of designs that are different from those currently recognized as proper for that installation. Sometimes, the existing materials may have contributed to the problem. Errors should not be repeated just to match the existing conditions.

In making extensions and large repairs, it is usually best to use the same plaster materials in the repairs as were used in the original installation. Where existing plaster with a fire rating is to be patched or extended, materials and installations must exactly match the original, or must be identical with assemblies which have been tested and accepted by recognized authorities and are in compliance with the requirements of the building code. Certain plaster materials should not be used in conjunction with other materials. Portland cement plaster is not compatible with gypsum products, for example, and should not be used over gypsum plaster, gypsum lath, gypsum masonry, or any other gypsum product. Usual mixtures of Portland cement stucco should not be used over lime, gypsum, or magnesite stucco.

In making small repairs, sometimes even in making extensions and large repairs, exactly matching existing materials may be inappropriate, or even impossible. An existing mix that was initially inferior should not be duplicated, for example. A lime plaster that contained too much sand in the first place should not be slavishly copied. In fact, lime plaster is seldom used in making repairs, because of its slow setting time. Patches in existing interior lime plaster are often made using a mix of 1 part gypsum neat plaster and 2 parts sand. Sometimes premixed patching plaster is used.

Patches in exterior sand-lime stucco are often made using two equal thickness base coats of 2 to 3 parts Portland cement, 5 parts hydrated lime, and 15 parts of the same aggregate that was used in the material being patched. Often, six pounds per cubic yard of hair or other fiber is added for strength. The finish coat is often 1 part Portland cement and 3 parts of the same aggregate used in the base coat.

Large patches in Portland cement are often made using scratch, brown, and finish coats consisting of 1 part Portland cement, 3 parts sand, and lime equal to about 10 percent of the weight of the cement.

Cracks in Portland cement plaster are usually patched using Portland cement plaster having a fine (100 percent passing a 30 mesh screen) silica sand aggregate. Patching plaster for Portland cement should not be spiked (have gypsum added) to hasten setting. Normal setting times of seven days or more per coat should be observed.

Cracks and small pits and holes in gypsum plaster are usually patched using a mix of 1 part gauging plaster and 2 parts lime putty.

Where the existing plaster material is unknown, tests should be made to determine its contents. It is possible, for example, to determine if an existing stucco is Portland cement-based or is a sand-lime plaster, by applying water to the substrate. Sand-lime plaster will delaminate over three or four days, Portland cement stucco will not. The same test, when applied to a magnesium oxychloride cement (magnesite) plaster surface would probably cause large blisters in the plaster and an active and rapid deterioration of associated metal, even zinc alloy.

Another way to determine if a material is Portland cement or sand-lime plaster is to crush some of the material into a powder, and stir it vigorously in a container of hot water. Sand-lime stucco will dissolve, leaving mostly aggregate in the container. Portland cement stucco powder will remain essentially unchanged.

Where plaster is damaged due to structure settlement, shrinkage, deflection, or creep, it is usually best to wait as long as possible before making repairs, to ensure that the building movement has reached its limits.

Preparation.   The first step in preparing for plaster repairs is to carefully remove soft, broken, or loose plaster back to masonry or lath, and to solid adjacent plaster. The edges should be straight, clean, sharp, and beveled inward (Fig. 3-17) to permit keying repairs into existing materials. Where only the finish coat must be removed, the base coats should be checked to ensure that they are firmly attached and hard. Unsound base coats should be removed. Plaster coats should be removed in step fashion (see Fig. 3-17) so that each new coat in the path will lap over the underlying existing plaster coat. Where part of the lath must be replaced, the first base coat should be cut back so that the new material in that coat will lap over onto the existing lath.

It is important to use great care when removing plaster from wood lath. Plaster adheres to wood lath by penetrating into the spaces between the slats to form keys (see Fig. 3-1), which works quite well so long as the lath, which is very flexible, is not caused to bend. If the lath is bent during plaster removal, the keys on the plaster adjacent to that being removed will break, necessitating removal of the adjacent plaster as well. Before any plaster is removed, each section of plaster that is to be removed from wood lath should be surrounded by a cut that extends completely through the plaster down to the lath, thus isolating the portion to be removed.

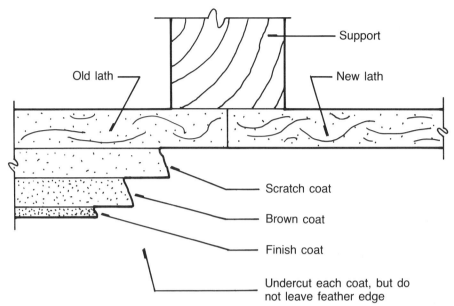

Figure 3-17   Method of making cutouts for plaster repairs.

Existing metal lath that is rusted, broken, or otherwise damaged should be removed, but enough should be left exposed to tie to the new lath.

Damaged existing gypsum lath should be removed. Gypsum lath is particularly susceptible to water damage. Where plaster failure is due to water damage, the gypsum lath will often not be satisfactory as a base for new plaster. A major problem with gypsum lath which has become wet is separation of the surface paper layers from the gypsum core.

Damaged wood lath should be removed.

Where lath is removed, it should be removed from support to support (see Fig. 3-17). Splices between supports are not appropriate.

Lath to be left in place should be repaired where necessary, and re-fastened where loose.

Damaged plaster accessories should be removed.

It may be also necessary to remove existing furring and suspension systems, or to repair the substrate. Refer to Chapter 2 for a discussion of this.

When the framing, furring, or substrate require repair, sufficient plaster, lath, and accessories should be removed to permit repair.

Every trace of paint, dirt, oil, grease, and other foreign matter should be removed from surfaces to receive new lath or plaster.

Small cracks should be opened slightly by running a knife or chisel along them. Cracks 1/16 inch in width and wider should be enlarged by cutting back to solid substrate using a carborundum tipped saw blade. Cuts should be perpendicular to the surface and straight. Cracks should not be further enlarged, except to remove soft, broken, or loose materials, or to permit repairs to back-up materials.

Where cracks are large or caused by substrate movement, and in other locations where appropriate, cracks should be widened to about 6 inches. The plaster should be removed down to the lath or solid substrate. Strip lath should be placed over the substrate, centered at the location of the crack and securely fastened in place.

Except where new lath is to be used, concrete and masonry surfaces to which plaster will be applied should be etched. The surfaces should be wetted, scrubbed with an acid etch solution, and thoroughly rinsed. The process should be repeated if necessary to produce an adequate plaster bond. Old concrete should be roughened by sandblasting, waterblasting, bushhammering, or another appropriate process. Portland Cement Association's "Bonding Concrete or Plaster to Concrete" contains additional recommendations.

Lathing and Accessories.   New metal or gypsum lath should be installed where existing lath of the same type has been removed, and over areas to receive large plaster patches. The lath should be anchored securely to the substrates. Metal lath should be lapped over and tied to existing lath, if any. Where appropriate, cracks should be widened and metal strip lath applied before the plaster is repaired.

Loose wood lath should be renailed to make it tight. Then the entire area to be patched should be covered with metal lath. Plastering over old wood lath without metal lath applied may result in cracked plaster.

New plaster accessories should be installed where existing accessories have been removed, and securely anchored to the substrates. The new accessories should match the lines of the existing accessories. Where the total plaster thickness increases because new plaster is placed over existing plaster, it will be necessary to remove the existing accessories and provide new accessories properly sized for the new conditions.

Plastering—General Requirements.   A bonding agent should be applied to old plaster, patching plaster, and every other surface that will receive new plaster, except that a bonding agent is not usually required on wood lath. Surfaces to which a bonding agent is to be applied should be clean and free from substances that will affect the bond. The bonding agent manufacturer's recommendations should be followed exactly. The bonding agent should be permitted to dry properly before plaster is applied.

Except for finish coats that have blistered due to unhydrated magnesium content (see "Wet Plaster" later in this chapter) the surface of all existing plaster that is to come into contact with new plaster should be wetted, unless the manufacturer of the bonding agent mentioned in the preceding paragraph specifically recommends against wetting.

Concrete, masonry, metal lath, gypsum lath, and existing plaster should be swept clean immediately before plaster is applied, and a bonding agent applied. Surfaces of existing plaster should be dampened, unless the bonding agent manufacturer recommends otherwise.

Wood lath and applied metal lath should be cleaned and the wood lath should be wetted thoroughly. Just before new plaster is applied, existing plaster edges should also be wetted.

Plaster materials should be mechanically mixed at the project site. They should not be hand mixed except where less than one bag of plaster is needed.

Keene's cement and other gypsum plasters should not be retempered.

Portland cement finish coats and patching plaster should not be retempered. Base coat mixes for Portland cement plaster, other than that used for patching cracks and small imperfections, may be retempered before application as frequently as needed to restore the required consistency. Under normal conditions, a Portland cement mix should be placed in its final position within 2-1/2 hours after mixing. Under severe hot or dry conditions, the time between mixing and placing should be reduced to 1 hour.

Retarders should not be used in patching plaster.

At patches and extensions in existing work, new plaster should match the thickness of the existing plaster. Repairs should be built-up using multiple coats. Each base coat should be about 3/8 inch thick. The finish coat should be about 1/8 inch thick. Each coat should be allowed to cure properly before the succeeding coat is applied. Full-thickness patches should be built-up in layers, the same as new work. Most extensions and full-thickness patches should be made using three-coat plaster applications. Two-coat plaster applications should be limited to those recommended by the plaster manufacturer and permitted by applicable ASTM Standards and governing regulations.

The texture of plaster finishes on repairs and extensions should match the existing finishes, unless there is a significant reason for a difference.

Portland cement plaster should be cured by keeping each coat moist until the new plaster is as dry as the surrounding plaster.

After finishing plaster patches, plaster residue and lime should be removed from the plaster surface using clear water. After the water has dried, the area should be wiped with clean dry rags to completely remove plaster dust.

Plastering—Specific Conditions.   The following conditions require some special treatment:

Loose or Bowed Plaster.   Plaster may sag or bulge because the support system fails. Repairing failed support systems is discussed in Chapter 2. Plaster may also sag or bulge because the lath has pulled away from the support system (Fig. 3-18), or because the key between the plaster and the lath has failed (Fig. 3-19). Either of the latter two problems may occur with any lath, of course, but many such failures are related to older plaster which was installed over wood lath.

The easiest separation problem to solve is the case where a wood lath has separated from its supports (see Fig. 3-18) and the supports are sound. The solution requires only the following steps: previously patched cracks, if any, are cleaned out so that the plaster can return to its original position; the plaster is lifted or shoved back into its proper position; holes are drilled through the plaster to the lath; the lath is refastened to the supports using screws placed in the drilled holes; and the screw holes and cracks in the plaster are patched.

The same solution can be used where gypsum lath has separated from its supports, providing that the lath and supports are sound. A word of caution is necessary here, however, since many such failures result from disintegration of the lath due to contact with water. When sagging or bulging plaster results from disintegrated lath, the only solution is to remove the plaster and lath, and start anew.

Metal lath that has separated from a metal support system probably cannot be reconnected through the plaster. It is usually necessary, then, to gain access to the space behind the plaster, and wire tie the lath back in place. The discussion in Chapter 2 about gaining access for repair of the support system applies.

Plaster that has become separated from a solid substrate or lath is usually not repaired. The normal procedure in such cases is to remove the

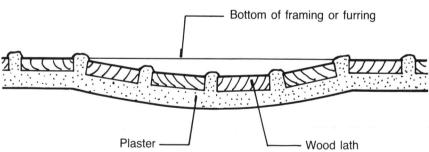

Figure 3-18   Wood lath that has separated from its support system.

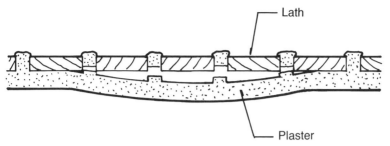

Figure 3-19   Plaster that has separated from its wood lath.

plaster and install new plaster. There are some situations, however, where reattachment of loose or bowed plaster to lath is preferable to removal. They include:

- The plaster is historic and its significance outweighs cost considerations.
- The loose or sagging plaster covers a small area in a large plaster surface.
- Major demolition and renovation would cause great harm to building occupants, and force a major shutdown of essential operations, outweighing the additional cost of the repair.
- Repairs are likely to remain repaired. Often, this requires access to the concealed side of the plaster to permit repair to the substrate or support system.

Usually, when reattachment of plaster to lath is deemed necessary, the plaster has some historic importance. Most such plaster is installed over wood lath. The accepted method for reattaching ceiling plaster to wood lath (see Fig. 3-18) is an injected adhesive bonding technique developed by Morgan W. Phillips and Andrew Ladygo for the Society for the Preservation of New England Antiquities. The technique varies depending on the extent of the problem, the types of plaster involved, and the degree of damage. Some damaged plaster must be stabilized before reattachment can be attempted. Basically, the method includes determining the amount of plaster that has delaminated, cleaning out previously patched cracks so that the plaster can lie flat in its original plane, cleaning the space between the lath and the plaster of loose particles and debris, lifting the plaster back into contact with the lath, and injecting a high-performance liquid adhesive between the lath and the plaster. The preferred method is to inject the adhesive from the back side, which requires drilling holes in the plaster if the back side is not accessible.

Similar methods have been used to reattach bulging plaster on walls.

Generally, reattaching loose plaster is an expensive professional job. Refer to "Where to Get More Information" in this chapter for additional data.

Dry-Out. A common curing problem in which some plaster becomes dried out but not properly cured is called dry-out. The problem can be sometimes solved by rewetting the affected area using a water spray. Sometimes alum is mixed with the sprayed water to aid the wetting action. When rewetting does not solve the problem, it is necessary to remove the dried-out area and place new plaster. Rewetting Portland cement plaster will only work if the setting process is not complete.

Cracks. Repair of cracks should not be attemted until the underlying cause of the cracks has been identified and eliminated. Otherwise, the cracks will often reappear in the repaired surface.

Only a small area of cracking should be repaired at a time. Repairing more cracks than can be finished before the patching plaster has a chance to set should not be attempted.

Wetting is particularly important when repairing cracks due to the small amount of patching plaster used. Dry existing plaster will suck the moisture from the patching plaster and prevent proper curing.

Sometimes, large cracks can be repaired and new cracks prevented by removing a strip of plaster about 6 inches wide down to the lath or solid substrate. Then a strip of lath is placed in the removed portion and fastened to the existing lath or substrate. This will sometimes prevent further cracking.

Small ceiling cracks that reappear after repair, when they are caused by substrate movement, can sometimes be permanently repaired by removing a strip of plaster extending about 15 inches (30 inches total width) on each side of the crack for the entire width of the room or space, then relathing and replastering the removed strip.

When cracks are extensive and are due to seasonal related movement in the substrate, it is sometimes possible to provide a crack-free ceiling by replastering. The existing plaster is furred, covered with metal or gypsum lath, and then plastered as though it were a new installation. The additional furring and lath helps spread the forces generated by substrate movement. The new ceiling should be left free to move at the perimeter so that cracking does not occur there. The capability of the existing structure and suspension system to carry the additional load must be verified, of course.

Usually, plaster with chip cracking must be removed. Sometimes, however, especially if the chip cracking covers only a small area, the cracks may be filled using a trowel with a thin finishing plaster. Wetting of the surface before this patching is essential.

Efflorescence.   The cure for efflorescence differs with the source of the salts and the amount of salts present. Regardless of the source, where the salts causing the efflorescence are small in quantity, repeated washing with a ten percent solution of muriatic acid and clean water rinsing will sometimes alleviate the problem. When the salts have all leached out, the efflorescence will no longer appear.

Sometimes, salts originating in the substrates can be blocked by proper calking and flashing at the plaster level to prevent water from entering the space behind the plaster. Additional measures may be taken to drain any water that does find its way behind the plaster. Where weeps have not been provided, weeps are sometimes drilled or cut as slots into existing plaster, usually at about 12 inches on center.

Most of the time, however, efflorescence cannot be cured simply. Often, it is necessary to completely remove the material containing the salts, and replace it with new material that does not contain salts.

Wet Plaster.   Plaster that has become wet from roof leaks or broken pipes can often be dried out without permanent damage. Where wet conditions persist, however, gypsum plaster may turn dark and crumble or delaminate, and finish surface coats may blister.

Blistering may point out defects in the original application that have remained dormant for years. For example, over-burned dolymetic lime with a high magnesium content may not hydrate completely in the initial cure. Excessive wetting later may cause the magnesium to expand and blister the plaster. The only cure for this condition is to remove the blistered portion of the finish coat to a straight cut line and apply a new finish coat containing completely hydrated magnesium. Care must be taken to prevent the water in the patching finish coat from activating the magnesium in the adjacent material that has been left in place. Some plasterers recommend applying a bonding agent to the existing plaster. Others suggest coating the edge of the existing plaster with a paint or shellac.

Acoustical Plaster.   Plaster used to repair and extend true acoustical plaster seldom has the same acoustical properties as the original material. It may be possible to simulate the original qualities of acoustical plaster. Andrew Ladygo in his 1988 article "New Techniques for Restoring Decorative Plasterwork" describes the methods and materials used to restore acoustical plaster on the Law Library of the Nebraska State Capitol. The solution took much study and experimentation. In most projects, unfortunately, such experimentation and cost are not justified. Acoustical plaster is often simulated using gypsum plaster finished to appear similar to the acoustical plaster.

Textured Finishes. Repairing plaster that has a textured finish requires working the finish into the repair as it is placed. Unfortunately, many repair jobs on textured plaster are visually unsuccessful. There in no substitute for experience, and even an experienced plasterer should practice producing the desired finish immediately before attempting to produce that finish in place on the final surface.

Repairing Existing Veneer Plaster

Repairs to veneer plaster require the same type of materials as used in the initial installation. The method of repair for veneer plaster depends on the extent and cause of the damage. For large cracks along veneer base joints, for example, it may be necessary to remove the plaster and retape the joint properly, then replaster. Small cracks might be repaired using joint compound alone. Cracks that result from too thin a veneer plaster might be repaired using spackling putty. Blistering caused by peeling of the veneer base or a loose paper surface on the base will probably require removing the plaster, repairing or replacing the damaged base, and replastering. It might be possible to repair joint ridging or beading, and dry-out, using joint compound. Using an appropriate primer and painting will cover most stains. Spalling at corners due to using the wrong type corner bead will require removing the wrong bead, installing a proper bead, and refinishing.

Installing New Standard Thickness and Veneer Plaster over Existing Materials

Recommendations and precautions for preparation, lathing, and plastering stated in "Repairing and Extending Existing Standard Thickness Plaster" and "Repairing Existing Veneer Plaster" also apply when plaster is being placed over an existing surface.

Standard Thickness Plaster

New standard thickness plaster may be installed over existing plaster that is too deteriorated to patch, over existing masonry and concrete, and over almost any other existing surface.

Ceilings

Plastered Ceilings. Where the existing structure and suspension systems are adequate to support the additional weight, an entirely new plaster ceiling may be installed over an existing plaster ceiling. First, the existing ceiling is furred with wood or metal, depending on local practices and code requirements, then plastered just as if it were a new installation.

Acoustical Ceilings. It is usually necessary to completely remove existing acoustical ceilings and their support system before installing plaster. Rarely will support systems for acoustical tile or panels be properly sized or spaced to support a plaster ceiling.

Walls

Concrete and Unit Masonry Walls. Where walls are sufficiently rough and not coated with paint or other material that would prevent a bond, plaster may be applied directly to existing concrete and concrete masonry surfaces. Methods used should be the same as for new surfaces.

Where existing surfaces are too slick and cannot be successfully prepared for direct plaster application, metal lath may be used as a base, or the wall may be furred.

Ceramic Tile, Structural Facing Tile, and Other Smooth Surfaces. Smooth surfaces require the use of metal lath. Such surfaces may also be furred out but that application requires more space, and is not usually necessary unless the space is needed for wiring, piping, or some other purpose.

Veneer Plaster

Veneer plaster solves several problems in renovation and remodeling projects. Sometimes, standard thickness plaster finish is too expensive for a project, but gypsum board will not look like the existing plaster. Veneer plaster, though more expensive than gypsum board, is less expensive than standard thickness plaster, and gives a plaster look. In addition, veneer plaster gypsum base can be installed over rough or disintegrating substrates, and many existing surfaces, including plaster, gypsum board, concrete, concrete unit masonry, structural clay tile, and gypsum block.

Veneer plaster can often be installed over existing paint if the paint is sound, washable, firmly adhered, and not glossy. Gloss should be sanded down. The suitability of this application should, however, be verified with the veneer plaster manufacturer in each particular case.

Veneer plaster can be applied over a compatible existing gypsum veneer plaster base after repair. Tape for repairing holes and broken joints should be bedded in veneer plaster, not in standard drywall joint compounds. Compatibility must be verified with the veneer plaster manufacturer, particularly if the base manufacturer is unknown or different from the veneer plaster manufacturer.

Most existing surfaces must be coated with a bonding agent before veneer plaster is applied.

Two-coat systems are usually used over exising surfaces.

Synthetic Stucco Materials

Finish Materials

Synthetic stucco products are so called because they look like stucco. One kind of synthetic stucco consists of Portland cement, and often a fine aggregate, bound with an acrylic bonding agent. These products produce thin, hard coatings. They are sometimes called cementitious coatings, and that is what we will call them here. Cementitious coatings are intended for application over concrete or masonry substrates, usually in a two-coat system, with a total thickness of about 1/8 inch (Fig. 3-20). Besides being decorative, they often also serve as dampproofing or waterproofing. One example of a cementitous coating synthetic stucco is the Thoro Systems product called *Thoroseal*.

Usually, however, when we speak of synthetic stucco, we mean the finishing portion of Exterior Insulation and Finish Systems (EIFS). Most

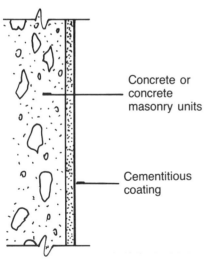

Concrete or concrete masonry units

Cementitious coating

Figure 3-20 Cementitious coating.

EIFS consist of a reinforced finish coat (synthetic stucco) over a layer of insulation, which is fastened to a layer of sheathing applied to furring or framing. But that is not the only configuration possible. There are many EIFS being used today and even more have been used since EIFS were introduced in this country during the 1960s.

The finish (synthetic stucco) portion of most EIFS used today is usually installed in two or more coats and incorporates reinforcement. The Exterior Insulation Manufacturers Association (EIMA) classifies EIFS according to the composition and method of reinforcement of their finish coats.

EIFS Class PB (polymer-based) use a 100 percent acrylic polymer finish coat. They are called thin, soft (flexible) systems in the industry.

EIFS Class PM (polymer modified) use a mixture of Portland cement and acrylic polymer. They are called thick, hard (rigid) systems in the industry.

EIFS Type A finishing coats are externally reinforced with cloth or lath. Type B finishing coats are internally reinforced with fibers. Type C finishing coats are not reinforced.

Base for Synthetic Stucco

Cementitious coatings are applied over concrete or unit masonry.

The base for most EIFS is a two layer system of insulation and gypsum sheathing. Some systems substitute a cement composition board for the gypsum sheathing. Many insulation types are used. Some of them are expanded polystyrene (EPS), extruded polystyrene, polyurethane, and iso-cyanurate foam. Some EIFS substitute a single layer of cement-based insulation plaster board for the insulation and sheathing.

Accessories for Synthetic Stucco

Corner Beads and Trim. Special components are used that are manufactured for the specific purpose.

Reinforcement. Cementitious coatings are not usually reinforced. PB EIFS systems are reinforced with glass fiber mesh. PM EIFS systems are usually reinforced with wire mesh metal lath.

Joint Tape. Each EIFS manufacturer recommends a tape for covering joints in the base material. A commonly used tape is made from open mesh glass fiber cloth.

Synthetic Stucco Installation

Bases for Synthetic Stucco

Concrete and unit masonry to receive cementitious coating should be prepared as suggested earlier in this chapter for solid substrates for standard
thickness plaster, except that surfaces must be smoother because the coating is so thin.

Bases for EIFS should be installed in accordance with the manufacturers recommendations. Some systems require adhesive application. Some
require mechanical fastening. Some require both. Some materials cannot
be installed using adhesives.

Because of gypsum board's susceptibility to water damage, gypsum
sheathing should be covered with a layer of plastic, paper, or felt. Unfortunately, that application is only possible when the insulation is mechanically fastened. Recently, gypsum sheathing has been produced with a glass
fiber mat finish to avoid the problem of disintegration of the paper surface
due to water contact.

Installing Synthetic Stucco

EIFS may be either field constructed from basic components or prefabricated for field installation in panels. Figures 3-21 and 3-22 show a single

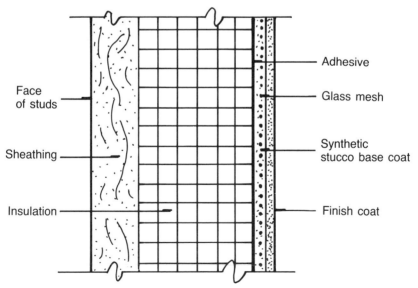

Figure 3-21 Typical polymer-based (PB) EIFS.

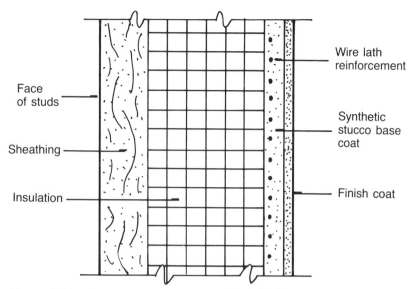

Figure 3-22   Typical polymer-modified (PM) EIFS.

installation configuration each for a PB and a PM system, but product manufacturer's suggested systems differ. In every case, the product manufacturer's instructions should be followed carefully.

Synthetic Stucco Failures and What to Do about Them

Why Synthetic Stucco Fails

At the time of this writing, there are no national product standards applicable to EIFS. While a lack of standards does not, in itself, necessarily lead to failures, that lack makes installation more difficult to monitor, and errors harder to detect during the construction process.

Most synthetic stucco failures are caused either by structure failure; structure movement; solid substrate problems; other building element problems; framing or furring problems; gypsum sheathing problems; bad materials; design errors; or bad workmanship.

Many synthetic stucco failures result from problems with the synthetic stucco itself or its installation, or with the underlying insulation or its installation, which are discussed in this chapter. Other synthetic stucco failures result from problems with the construction underlying the synthetic stucco. These problems include structure failure and movement; and problems associated with solid substrates, other building elements, and wood and metal framing or furring, all of which are discussed in Chapter 2.

Some of the problems discussed in Chapter 2, especially structure movement and solid substrate problems, are as likely to cause synthetic stucco failure as problems with the synthetic stucco or its installation. Consequently, the possibility that the types of problems discussed in Chapter 2 are responsible for a synthetic stucco failure should be investigated and ruled out or, if found to be at fault, rectified before synthetic stucco repairs are attempted. It will do no good to repair synthetic stucco when a failed, uncorrected, or unaccounted-for problem of the types discussed in Chapter 2 is present. The repair will also fail.

Perhaps the major source of EIFS failures is problems with the gypsum sheathing underlying the system. Gypsum sheathing for EIFS and potential reasons for failure in it are discussed in Chapter 4. When EIFS failure is caused by gypsum sheathing problems, the reasons for the sheathing failure should be determined and rectified, and the sheathing repaired or replaced before repairs to the rest of the EIFS are attempted. Repairing an EIFS finish or insulation when the underlying sheathing is damaged will be futile. The original failure is likely to recur.

After the types of problems discussed in Chapter 2 and Chapter 4 have been investigated and found to be not present, or repaired if found, the next step is to discover causes for the synthetic stucco failure that are directly related to the insulation or the synthetic stucco finish, if any are present, and repair them. Possible failure causes include those in the following paragraphs, which contain numbered lists of errors and situations that can cause synthetic stucco failure. Refer to "Evidence of Failure in Synthetic Stucco" later in this chapter for a listing of the types of failure to which the numbered failure causes in this part apply.

Bad Materials.   Improperly manufactured or prepared finishing materials or insulation can result in synthetic stucco failures.

Design Errors.   Design errors often result from not following the manufacturer's instructions. Errors that can lead to failure include:

1. Failing to protect gypsum sheathing by applying a layer of water-resistant plastic, paper, or felt between the sheathing and the insulation. This is, of course, only possible with a mechanically fastened system. Using a water-resistant sheathing might eliminate this failure cause.
2. Failing to require mesh reinforcement at opening corners. This omission can lead to diagonal cracks in the surface.
3. Failing to provide adequate slope on horizontal or sloping surfaces, such as window sills. Standing water will cause finish coats, espe-

cially PB finish coats, to re-emulsify and soften. Sealant will not adhere, joints will open, and finish coats will disintegrate.

4. Selecting foam insulation that is not adequately aged. Shrinkage in such boards as they age can cause cracking in the finish along the joints between boards.

5. Failing to account for structure and thermal movement. A common error is to design the control joint locations based on a flexible system (PB) then switch to a PM system, which is more rigid, and requires more joints.

Bad Workmanship. The common error applicable to every situation is failing to follow the design or the manufacturer's instructions. In addition, the following errors can lead to failure:

1. Applying a coat or the total thickness that is too thin. This is a particular problem on the base coat in PB systems, because the natural thickness that results as the material is applied is only about half of the required 1/16 inch thickness. Particular attention must be paid to double back the base coat to make it the proper thickness.

2. Varying the thickness of the base coat in the same surface.

3. Failing to tightly butt insulation boards. Gaps as small as 1/16 inch can cause cracks.

Evidence of Failure in Synthetic Stucco

The following paragraphs contain synthetic stucco failure types, such as "Loose Material." Following each failure type are one or more failure sources, such as "Bad Workmanship." After most failure sources, one or more numbers is listed. The numbers represent possible errors associated with that failure source that might cause that failure type to occur.

A description and discussion of the numbered failure causes for failure types: "Structure Failure," "Structure Movement," "Solid Substrate Problems," "Other Building Element Problems," "Wood Framing and Furring Problems," and "Metal Framing and Furring Problems" appear in Chapter 2 under the same headings, and each is listed in the Contents. For example, clarification and explanation of the numbered cause (1) in the example

▪ Metal Framing and Furring Problems: 1 (see chapter 2).

appears in Chapter 2 under the heading "Metal Framing and Furring Problems," cause 1, which reads

1. Metal framing or furring that is out of alignment.

A description and discussion of the numbered causes that follow failure types: "Bad Materials," "Design Errors," and "Bad Workmanship" appear as subparagraphs in the part of this chapter titled "Why Synthetic Stucco Fails," which is listed in the Contents. For example, clarification and explanation of the numbered cause (2) listed in the example

▪ Bad Workmanship: 1, 2, 3.

appears in this chapter under the heading "Why Synthetic Stucco Fails," subparagraph "Bad Workmanship," cause 2, which reads:

2. Varying the thickness of the base coat in the same surface.

The failure source titled "Gypsum Sheathing for EIFS Failures" refers to failure types and causes discussed in a subparagraph with that title in the part of Chapter 4 called "Evidence of Failure in Gypsum Board Systems," which is listed in the Contents. Note that only the failure type from Chapter 4 is listed here. The failure sources and cause numbers are omitted to prevent repetition. Every potential failure source and cause listed in Chapter 4 under "Gypsum Sheathing for EIFS Failures" should be considered as a possible cause for that type of failure.

Loose Material.   The synthetic stucco may itself be loose, but the more common problem is insulation that is not solidly fastened to the sheathing. Loose materials may eventually fall off, but earlier than that they will probably result in water leaks through the synthetic stucco. The problem is usually caused by:

▪ Structure Failure: 1 (see Chapter 2).
▪ Structure Movement: 1, 2, 3, 4, 5, 6, 7, 8 (see Chapter 2).
▪ Solid Substrate Problems: 1, 2, 3, 4 (see Chapter 2).
▪ Other Building Element Problems: 1, 2 (see Chapter 2).
▪ Wood Framing and Furring Problems: 1, 2, 3, 4, 5, 6, 7, 8 (see Chapter 2).
▪ Metal Framing and Furring Problems: 1, 2, 3, 4, 5 (see Chapter 2).
▪ Gypsum Sheathing for EIFS Failures (see Chapter 4).
▪ Design Errors: 1, 3. Both will permit water intrusion, destroying the sheathing.

Cracks.   Cracks may affect only the finish material or may go all the way through the system. They may be caused by:

▪ Structure Failure: 1 (see Chapter 2).
▪ Structure Movement: 1, 2, 3, 4, 5, 6, 7, 8 (see Chapter 2).

- Solid Substrate Problems: 2, 3, 4 (see Chapter 2).
- Wood Framing and Furring Problems: 1, 2, 3, 4, 5, 6, 7, 8 (see Chapter 2).
- Metal Framing and Furring Problems: 1, 2, 3, 4, 5 (see Chapter 2).
- Gypsum Sheathing for EIFS Failures (see Chapter 4).
- Design Errors: 2, 4.
- Bad Workmanship: 1, 2, 3.

Sealant Joint Failure. Sealants may fail and permit water to enter the system for the following reasons:

- Structure Failure: 1 (see Chapter 2).
- Structure Movement: 1, 2, 3, 4, 5, 6, 7, 8 (see Chapter 2).
- Solid Substrate Problems: 2, 3, 4 (see Chapter 2).
- Wood Framing and Furring Problems: 1, 2, 3, 4, 5, 6, 7, 8 (see Chapter 2).
- Metal Framing and Furring Problems: 1, 2, 3, 4, 5 (see Chapter 2).
- Gypsum Sheathing for EIFS Failures (see Chapter 4).
- Design Errors: 3.

Repairing Synthetic Stucco

Repairs to synthetic stucco are made using the same materials as those in the initial system. Unfortunately, many problems with EIFS cannot be repaired as such, but rather require removal of the damaged material and the installation of new materials. A good example to illustrate this point is the most common failure, deteriorated sheathing. It is not possible to repair damaged sheathing without removing the EIFS.

Where repairs are possible, they must be made in accordance with the system manufacturer's recommendations, which will vary with the system and the materials used.

Installing New Synthetic Stucco over Existing Materials

Synthetic stucco, particularly EIFS, are effective retrofit materials. They can be installed quite readily over any existing finish to which they can be attached. They have the dual advantage of modernizing the exterior look of an existing building while adding significantly to its energy efficiency. Most EIFS are light enough so that strengthening the existing walls and structural system is not necessary when they are used.

Both prefabricated and field-fabricated EIFS are used over existing materials. Both are installed in the same manner as they would be for new work. Interface methods will depend on the existing materials and surfaces, and the EIFS selected.

Where to Get More Information

The International Institute for Lath and Plaster is a contractor's organization. It has little in print intended to help with existing materials problems, and is not generally a source of information on those problems. An affiliate, however, the Western Lath, Plaster, and Drywall Contractor's Association (formerly California Lathing and Plastering Contractor's Association), is responsible for an excellent 1981 publication called *Plaster/Metal Framing System/Lath Manual*. A new edition was published in late 1988 by McGraw-Hill, but was not available at the time of this writing. While the 1981 edition of *Plaster/Metal Framing System/Lath Manual* does not cover repairing existing materials, it does discuss installing metal lath over existing materials. It is also a good source of information about metal framing, lath, and plaster materials and installation, and covers plaster, including stucco, finishes in detail, with illustrations.

At the time of this writing, Mr. J. R. Gorman, director of the Lath, Plaster, and Drywall Information Bureau (at the address listed in the Appendix for the International Institute for Lath and Plaster) was available to answer questions about existing materials problems. The Lath, Plaster, and Drywall Information Bureau may be also contacted for information about the *Plaster/Metal Framing System/Lath Manual* mentioned in the previous paragraph.

Mr. Walter F. Pruter of W. F. Pruter Associates (see International Institute for Lath and Plaster in the Appendix) would also, at the time of this writing, answer questions about lath and plaster problems on behalf of the International Institute for Lath and Plaster.

John R. Diehl's 1965 *Manual of Lathing and Plastering,* though somewhat dated, remains an excellent reference for all aspects of lathing and plastering. It discusses plaster failures, and includes information about causes, including such subjects as the effect of plaster thickness, plaster quality, substrate type and preparation, environment, and exposure on failure. It includes a good glossary. Unfortunately, many of the entries in its extensive bibliography are too old to be of much help. Mr. Diehl's book may be hard to find today, but is well worth the effort.

The United States Gypsum Company's 1987 *Gypsum Construction Handbook* contains data about veneer plaster and conventional plaster failures, including a discussion of reasons for failure and methods of repair.

The United States Gypsum Company's 1972 *Red Book: Lathing and*

Plastering Handbook includes extensive discussion of plaster failures, including reasons and methods of repair. It is a "must have" document for anyone who is responsible for designing, specifying, installing, or maintaining plaster. It contains much data about failures and their solutions that is only mentioned or not included here. There may be a later edition by now. Other manufacturers may publish similar data.

Van Den Branden/Hartsell's 1971 book, *Plastering Skill and Practice* is a somewhat dated but still good guide for plaster application and maintenance, especially for troubleshooting plaster problems and making repairs. There is an entire chapter dealing with plastering problems.

The Portland Cement Association's "Bonding Concrete or Plaster to Concrete" contains recommendations for preparing old concrete to receive Portland cement plaster, and recommends methods for applying and curing the plaster.

The Portland Cement Association's *Portland Cement Plaster (Stucco) Manual* should be a part of the library of everyone involved in designing, specifying, applying, or maintaining Portland cement plaster. It explains the nature of Portland cement plaster, including its desirable properties. It also lists and describes in detail the materials used in Portland cement plaster, mixes and admixes, lath types, flashing, bonding agents, bases, and methods of applying the plaster. It also includes a discussion of the various tools necessary to apply plaster by hand and by machine, a list of possible problems and their solutions, and an extensive "Glossary of Plastering Terms."

The National Concrete Masonry Association's 1985 *Portland Cement Plaster (Stucco) for Concrete Masonry* is an excellent guide. It contains recommendations for materials, applying Portland cement plaster, control joints, curing plaster, care and maintenance of plaster, and a list of common problems and solutions.

Additional information about reattaching sagging and bowed plaster by the injected adhesive bonding method may be obtained by asking the Society for the Preservation of New England Antiquities (SPNEA) for a copy of the Association for Preservation Technology, Bulletin Vol. XII, No. 2, and any additional information it has available. The individuals responsible for the SPNEA-recommended methods are Morgan W. Phillips and Andrew Ladygo.

John Leek's 1987 article, "Saving Irreplaceable Plaster," contains information about methods and adhesives for reattaching plaster to wood lath where the lath is still fixed to the supports, but the plaster keys have broken, permitting the plaster to sag. The methods suggested are based on the SPNEA methods mentioned, but the proposed adhesives may be less expensive and easier to obtain than those required for the methods developed by SPNEA.

Patricia Poore's 1983 article, "What's Behind Sagging Plaster," contains recommendations for reattaching support systems, lath, and plaster, but is limited to wood supports and wood lath, and reattaching plaster using a new pouring of plaster of paris above the lath. Adhesive reattachment is not covered.

Andrew Ladygo's 1988 "New Techniques for Restoring Decorative Plasterwork" is a technical article by one of the developers of SPNEA recommended injected adhesive bonding method for reattaching plaster. It describes the method and the adhesives used.

Other organizations that may be sources of data about reattaching plaster include The Preservation Institute for the Building Crafts, Greater Portland Landmarks, Campbell Center for Historic Preservation Studies, Eastfield Village, and the Association for Preservation Technology.

The Exterior Insulation Manufacturers Association has produced guides for exterior insulation and finish systems.

Some of AIA Service Corporation's *Masterspec* Basic sections contain excellent descriptions of the materials and installations that are the subject of this chapter. Sections that have applicable data related to plaster are Sections 09200, "Lath and Plaster" and 09215, "Veneer Plaster." Unfortunately, those sections contain little that will help with troubleshooting failed plaster. Sections that have applicable data about synthetic stucco are 07241 "Exterior Insulation and Finish System—Class PB" and 07242 "Exterior Insulation and Finish System—Class PM." They do contain some discussion about potential failure causes, but not about repair.

Every designer should have the full complement of applicable ASTM Standards available for reference, of course, but anyone who needs to understand plaster should definitely own a copy of the following ASTM Standards:

- Standard C 11, "Definition of Terms Relating to Gypsum and Related Building Materials."
- Standard C 841, "Specifications for Installation of Interior Lathing and Furring."
- Standard C 842, "Specifications for Application of Interior Gypsum Plaster."
- Standard C 843, "Specifications for Application of Gypsum Veneer Plaster."
- Standard C 847, "Specifications for Metal Lath."
- Standard C 1063, "Specifications for Installation of Lathing and Furring for Portland Cement-Based Plaster."

ASTM standards for lath, plaster, and accessory materials are listed in the Bibliography and marked with a [3]. They may also be mentioned in this and other chapters.

The Gypsum Association's *Fire Resistance Design Manual: Eleventh Edition (GA-600-84)* is a guide to the fire- and sound-resistance of various wall, ceiling, and furring assemblies containing plaster. Anyone designing or maintaining a building containing fire-rated plaster assemblies should own a copy of the latest version.

Ramsey/Sleeper's *Architectural Graphic Standards* contains data about many plastering conditions.

The Metal Lath/Steel Framing Association's publications *Lightweight Steel Framing Systems Manual* and *Specifications for Metal Lathing and Furring* should be available to everyone responsible for metal lath and plaster.

"Where to Get More Information" in Chapters 2 and 4 and the Bibliography (items followed by [3]) contain additional sources of data about plaster.

Gypsum Board

This chapter includes a discussion of most gypsum board products, including standard gypsum board, veneer plaster gypsum base, gypsum sheathing, gypsum lath for gypsum plaster, and predecorated gypsum board. This chapter also includes a discussion of glass mesh mortar units, which are used as backer board for ceramic tile, though some of those units are not strictly gypsum board products. Gypsum formboard for concrete, and gypsum substrate boards for floors and roof assemblies, are not included. Non-board gypsum products such as structural planking are also not included. Other construction which is associated with the products discussed in this chapter include the building's structural system; solid substrates, such as masonry and concrete; other building elements; and both wood and metal framing and furring. They are discussed in Chapter 2. Metal lath, standard thickness plaster, veneer plaster, and synthetic stucco are discussed in Chapter 3. Ceramic tile applied over gypsum board and glass mesh mortar units is discussed in Chapter 5.

Including all gypsum board types in a single chapter departs from the locations recommended for those products in construction specifications by the Construction Specifications Institute and Construction Specifications Canada's 1983 Edition of *Masterformat*. It is also at odds with most commercial and government agency guide specifications in use today. This deviation is solely for brevity. It does not imply that those other references are wrong. Most products discussed in this chapter are manufactured by single producers and installed in similar ways. Some differences do exist, of course. We will discuss them as we go along. But, for the most part, gypsum board materials, installation techniques, and problems are similar, regardless of the specific board used.

Gypsum Board and Accessory Materials

The term "gypsum board" refers to a variety of products manufactured with a core of gypsum plaster and faced with paper or another material. Gypsum board is also called "drywall," "wallboard," and "plasterboard." In this text, we will refer to all gypsum board products generically as "gypsum board."

The term "gypsum board systems" includes the gypsum board, supporting framing and furring, accessories, and miscellaneous materials used to make the installation complete.

The supporting framing and furring portions of gypsum board systems are discussed in Chapter 2. Boards, accessories, and miscellaneous materials are discussed in this chapter.

The term "standard gypsum board" used in this book refers to: regular, Type X, foil-backed, and water-resistant gypsum board; exterior soffit board; and gypsum backing board, coreboard, and liner board. The term excludes veneer plaster gypsum base, gypsum sheathing, gypsum plaster lath, and predecorated gypsum board, which are here collectively called "special purpose boards." It also does not include glass mesh mortar units, which are discussed separately near the end of this chapter.

Gypsum Board Products

All gypsum board products are manufactured in essentially the same way. The mineral gypsum is crushed, heated to drive off three-quarters of its water content (calcined), ground into a powder, and mixed with water to form a slurry, which is fed between paper sheets on a machine designed for the purpose. The calcined gypsum crystallizes and bonds to the paper. The board is then dried and cut into the proper size.

Many standard gypsum board edge configurations are available. They include square, tapered, rounded, beveled, and tongue and groove long shapes (Fig. 4-1). Ends are square. Some standard boards have long edges

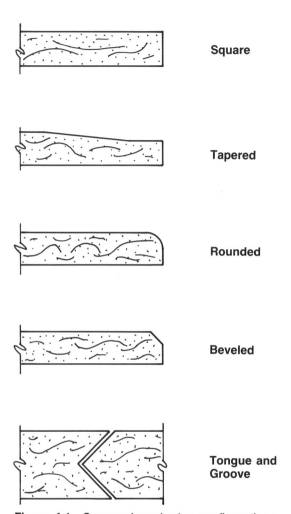

Square

Tapered

Rounded

Beveled

Tongue and
Groove

Figure 4-1   Gypsum board edge configurations.

that are both beveled and tapered. Others are both rounded and tapered. On most standard boards, long edges are finished with paper, while ends are not finished.

Several types of paper covering are used on gypsum boards, depending on the board type and exposure. Surfaces that will be exposed (faces) for field decoration, such as painting, are usually a cream colored, sized, and calendered paper, sometimes called "cream paper." Faces and sides opposite the faces, which are called backs, and which will be covered by other materials, including other gypsum board in multilayered installations, have traditionally been covered with gray, unsized, and uncalendered paper, called "gray paper." Some manufacturers no longer make board with gray paper on both front and back (backer board), but older installations will contain such material. The surfaces of some special-purpose boards are usually covered with tinted green or blue paper to distinguish them from regular boards. Veneer plaster base board, for example, is usually blue, and is often called "blue board." Other types of tinted paper boards are called generically "green board." Some gypsum board types have standard face (cream) and back (gray) papers, but are stamped to designate their special nature. Fire-resistant board, for example, is usually stamped "Type X."

Available gypsum board thicknesses include 1/4, 5/16, 3/8, 1/2, 5/8, 3/4, and 1 inch. As indicated in the text of this chapter, all board types are not available in all standard thicknesses. The 5/16-inch thick boards are used in manufactured housing and, therefore, are of little interest to us here.

Most gypsum boards are 4 feet wide and 8, 10, 12, or 14 feet long. Other sizes are also available in some board types from some manufacturers. Gypsum sheathing and gypsum lath sizes are different, however, as indicated in the discussions of them later in this chapter.

Except where otherwise stated below, gypsum board products should comply with ASTM Standard C 36.

Standard Gypsum Board Types

Regular Gypsum Boards. Regular boards are the type most used as the finish ply on interior ceilings, walls, and partitions. Since some manufacturers stopped making backing board, regular boards have been used also as the base ply in many double-layer applications. Regular boards are available in most standard thicknesses.

Type X (Fire-Rated) Boards. Type X boards are similar to regular gypsum boards, but have fire-resistant cores. They are intended for use where a fire-rated ceiling, wall, or partition is required. Thicknesses are 1/2 and 5/8 inch.

Foil-Backed Gypsum Boards. Regular, Type X, and backing boards may have aluminum foil laminated to the back side. Foil-backed boards are used to face exterior walls where a vapor retarder is required. They are not appropriate as a base for ceramic tile, the interior face ply of a double-layer installation, where radiant heating cables occur, or for adhesive application to any surface. Some manufacturers, however, permit adhesive application to wood studs under special circumstances dictated by the manufacturer.

Water-Resistant Gypsum Boards. Regular or Type X boards with water-resistant cores and water-repellent faces and backs are called water-resistant boards. They are available in 1/2- and 5/8-inch thicknesses. They are appropriate for use on walls and partitions as a base for ceramic tile applied using organic adhesives; plastic tile; plastic tub and shower enclosures; and as a surface to be painted in damp areas. They are not recommended for use painted or as a tile base around tubs or in showers; or in other areas where water will actually contact the surface of the board or its tile, paint, or other covering. Unfortunately, they are often used in such locations anyway. They are never appropriate as a finished surface or tile backing in saunas or in steam rooms, gang showers, or other very wet areas. They also should never be used on ceilings, soffits, or exterior locations. Refer to Chapter 5 for a discussion of tile installation in wet locations.

Water-resistant boards may have been used as sheathing in some buildings, but are seldom used for that purpose.

The facing and backing on water-resistant board is colored, usually green.

Gypsum Backing Boards. Designed for use as concealed plies in multilayer applications, backing boards may have either regular or Type X cores, and may be plain or foil-backed. Backing boards should comply with ASTM Standard C 442, except that water-resistant backing boards should comply with ASTM Standard C 630.

Some manufacturers no longer make backing boards, but existing installations will often have such material in place.

Gypsum Coreboards. As the name implies, coreboards are used as the core portion of shaft walls and laminated gypsum partitions. They are available as a single-ply 1-inch thick material or as a laminated product made from two layers of 1/2-inch thick board. Usual panel width is 24 inches. Coreboards usually have tongue and groove edges, but other edge types are also available. Coreboards should comply with ASTM Standard C 442.

Gypsum Liner Boards. Liner boards are special fire-resistant boards with water-resistant paper faces and backs. They are used as the liner in shaft walls, stairwells, chases, and fire-zone separation walls. They are also used in corridor and other public-space ceilings. They are available in 3/4- and 1-inch thicknesses, and both 24- and 48-inch widths. Edges are usually square, but some are eased.

Exterior Soffit Boards. Soffit boards are especially treated for use on building exteriors where not directly exposed to weather. They are available with either regular or Type X cores, and in either 1/2- or 5/8-inch thicknesses. Soffit boards should comply with ASTM Standard C 931. The paper covering on some soffit boards is beige or another color to distinguish them from other board types.

Special-Purpose Board Types

Veneer Plaster Gypsum Base.   Boards of this type are faced with special paper designed to receive thin plaster veneer. Each manufacturer's boards are made specifically for that manufacturer's veneer plaster, and may not work properly with another veneer plaster formulation. There are two types of veneer plaster gypsum base. The type found in most applications may be regular, foil-faced, or Type X cores. Most are either 1/2 or 5/8 inch thick, but some manufacturers also offer 3/8-inch thick material. Boards are available in 4 feet widths, and from 6 to 16 feet long.

Boards of the second type are specially manufactured for use with radiant heating coils. They are available as either regular or Type X boards, in both 1/2- and 5/8-inch thicknesses.

Both types of veneer plaster gypsum base should comply with ASTM Standard C 588.

Gypsum Sheathing.   Sheathing boards consist of a gypsum core faced on both sides with water-resistant paper or glass cloth. Some gypsum sheathing boards also have a water-resistant core. Type X sheathing is also available. Edges may be either square or tongue and groove. Ends are square. Gypsum sheathing comes in 24 inch and 48 inch widths and in 1/2- and 5/8-inch thicknesses. The 24 inch widths have tongue and groove long edges. Gypsum sheathing is used as a base for exterior insulation and finish systems (EIFS); wood, metal, vinyl, and composition siding; shingles; stucco; and masonry. In some installations, gypsum sheathing adds to the structural stability of the building. Gypsum sheathing should comply with ASTM Standard C 79.

Gypsum Plaster Lath.   Gypsum lath is used as a base for gypsum plaster. Boards are available in regular, Type X, and foil-backed types. Cores may be either regular or water-resistant. Surfaces are water-repellent. Most gypsum lath boards are either 3/8 or 1/2 inch thick, 16 or 24 inches wide, and 48 or 96 inches long, but so-called "long-length" boards up to 12 feet long may also be encountered. Special Type X lath boards are used when radiant heat cables are to be installed. They are 1/2 or 5/8 inches thick, 4 feet wide, and 8, 12, or 14 feet long.

Perforated gypsum lath, which was the mainstay in the lathing business for years, is not generally available today. Existing lath, however, may be either plain or perforated.

Gypsum lath should comply with ASTM Standard C 37.

Predecorated Gypsum Board. Regular or Type X boards to which a finish has been added at the factory are called predecorated boards. The finish material may be vinyl or another plastic film, printed paper, or a factory-applied paint or coating. The finish may be smooth or textured. Long edges are usually finished with the same materials as the facing. Edges are square, beveled, V-grooved, or eased. Decorative board should comply with ASTM Standard C 960.

Other Types of Boards. Many other types of boards are used today or have been used in construction in the past. Included are gypsum sound deadening board, insulating gypsum board, long-length insulating gypsum lath, plastic insulating sheathing, and various fiberboards used for sheathing and other purposes. Some types which were used extensively in the past are not available today. Others are widely used, such as those manufactured by the Homosote Company, but are beyond the scope of this book.

When any of these other board types are encountered and must be dealt with, the best way to approach the problem is to contact the product's manufacturer for advice.

Accessories

Accessories for Standard Gypsum Board. For a general description of gypsum board accessories that might be found in existing construction, refer to ASTM Standard C 1047 and the Gypsum Association publications mentioned in "Where to Get More Information" at the end of this chapter. Figure 4-2 shows the general shapes of gypsum board accessories mentioned in this chapter. Flanges of the shapes shown may be either perforated or expanded mesh when metal. Plastic shapes have solid flanges, as do most U-shaped beads.

In addition to the shapes shown in Figure 4-2, many others are used, including coved interior corners, rounded outside corners, trim with a reveal, plastic trim with flexible fins to form a sound barrier, and many other special shapes, many in plastic (usually vinyl), others in prefinished aluminum or steel.

Corner Beads for Interior Gypsum Board. These are usually formed from galvanized steel, aluminum-coated steel, metal combined with paper, or plastic.

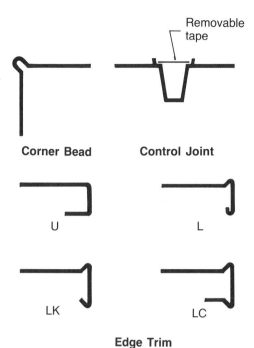

Corner Bead   Control Joint

Edge Trim

Figure 4-2 Standard gypsum board accessories.

Corner Beads for Exterior Gypsum Soffit Board. Since most exterior applications are on flat soffits, corner beads are not usually necessary. When they are needed, exterior corner beads should be formed from zinc.

Edge Trim for Interior Gypsum Board. These are usually formed from galvanized steel, aluminum-coated steel, metal combined with paper, or plastic. Any of the shapes shown in Figure 4-2 (U, L, LK, or LC) may be used.

Edge Trim for Exterior Gypsum Soffit Board. The most normal edge trim is shape LC (see Fig. 4-2) formed from rolled zinc, but batten strips, moldings, and many other accessory types may also be used, and plastic or aluminum accessories may be encountered. Aluminum accessories will often be color anodized, finished with baked enamel, or be otherwise prefinished.

Control Joints for Interior Gypsum Board. Most control joints in interior gypsum board surfaces are fabricated into a shape similar to that shown in Figure 4-2, from galvanized steel or extruded from vinyl. The tape shown covering the slot in Figure 4-2 should have been removed when the joint was installed.

Control Joints for Exterior Gypsum Soffit Board. Control joints in exterior gypsum board soffits should be fabricated into a shape similar to that shown in Figure 4-2 from zinc alloy. The tape shown covering the slot in Figure 4-2 should have been removed when the joint was installed.

Accessories for Veneer Plaster

Corner Beads for Veneer Plaster Base. These are formed from galvanized steel or zinc alloy, and all have fine mesh expanded flanges. The grounds on these beads vary in height depending on whether the veneer plaster is a one-coat or two-coat system. The shape is similar to that shown in Figure 4-2.

Edge Trim for Veneer Plaster. These are also formed from galvanized steel with expanded mesh flanges and varying height grounds depending on the number of coats of veneer plaster to be applied. The shapes are similar to, though not identical with, LC in Figure 4-2.

Control Joints. These are formed from galvanized steel or zinc alloy, too. The shapes are similar to those shown in Figure 4-2.

Accessories for Predecorated Gypsum Board

Trim. These are often aluminum or vinyl, finished to match the board. Those available include, but are not limited to, coved insider corners, rounded outside corners, trim with a reveal, end caps, ceiling trim, bases, and battens for use between panels.

Accessories for Demountable Partitions

Trim. Each partition type will require different trim members. Trim for demountable partitions is usually plastic or prefinished steel or aluminum. Trim types include, but are not limited to, inside and outside corners, end caps, ceiling trim, bases, and battens.

Fasteners

Fasteners for gypsum board products include nails, screws, staples, and clips. Most nails and screws are industry standard types. Clips may differ significantly from manufacturer to manufacturer.

Screws—General Requirements. All screws used with gypsum board products should have a cupped, Phillips-head design intended for use with a power screwdriver designed especially to drive them. The combination of the screw head design and the screwdriver design ensures that the screws will be properly driven to the correct depth to make a uniform depression suitable for finishing without damaging the gypsum board's paper. Three basic and some special screws are used in gypsum board. The basic types are called W, S, and G screws.

Type W screws are used to fasten gypsum board products to wood. They have diamond-shaped points and threads especially designed to penetrate both wood and gypsum board readily.

Type S screws, which are used to fasten gypsum board materials to metal furring and channel studs, include two subtypes: Type S and Type S-12. Type S screws are used for light (25-gage) metal and Type S-12 screws are used for heavier (20-gage and heavier) studs. Both types are self-drilling and self-tapping and are designed to enter the metal easily.

Type G screws are used to fasten gypsum boards to other gypsum boards. They are similar to Type W screws, but have a slightly different thread design.

Fasteners for Standard Gypsum Board and Veneer Plaster Gypsum Base

Nails. Nails for fastening standard gypsum board and veneer plaster gypsum base to wood should be special nails designed for the purpose. They should have heads between 1/4 and 4/16 inch in diameter. Their heads should be flat or concave and thin at the rim. For non-fire-rated assemblies, smooth-shank nails should be long enough to penetrate at least 7/8 inch into the wood supports; annular-ringed nails, however, need only penetrate 3/4 inch. In fire-rated assemblies, nails should be long enough to penetrate the wood substrates the amount dictated by the tested assembly. In one-hour assemblies, the penetration required is often between 1-1/8 and 1-1/4 inches.

Screws. Gypsum board and veneer plaster gypsum base may be fastened to wood or metal using screws. Different screw types are used depending on the substrates.

Type W screws are used to fasten gypsum board and veneer plaster gypsum base to wood. Type W screws should penetrate the supports by 5/8 inch generally, except in some double-layer applications, where 1/2 inch may be enough.

Both Type S and Type S-12 screws are used to fasten gypsum board and veneer plaster gypsum base to metal furring and channel studs, depending on the metal thickness. Type S screws are also sometimes used in double-layer gypsum board construction over wood, in lieu of Type W screws. Type S and S-12 screws should penetrate the supports by at least 3/8 inch.

Type G screws are used to fasten gypsum facing boards to backing boards in solid gypsum assemblies. To be effective, Type G screws must penetrate the backing board by at least 1/2 inch. They should not be used when the backing board is 3/8 inch thick. Then, the facing board should be fastened through the backing board into the supporting framing.

Staples. Staples are used to fasten standard gypsum board in single-ply applications and face plies in double-layer applications in place only in mobile homes, which are beyond the scope of this book.

Staples are used to fasten the base ply of double-layer installations to wood framing or furring, however. Staples for that purpose should be fabricated from 16-gage flattened galvanized wire, and should have a minimum 7/16-inch wide crown and spreading points. Staples should penetrate wood supports by at least 5/8 inch.

Fasteners for Gypsum Sheathing

Nails. Nails for fastening gypsum sheathing to wood should be 11-gage galvanized nails with 7/16-inch diameter heads. They should be 1-1/2 inches long for 1/2-inch thick sheathing and 1-3/4 inches long for 5/8-inch thick sheathing.

Screws. Gypsum sheathing may be fastened to wood or metal using the same type of screws used to install interior gypsum board and veneer plaster base.

Staples. Gypsum sheathing that is 1/2 inch thick may be fastened to wood using staples. The staples should be galvanized 16-gage wire, 7/16 inch wide by 1-1/2 inches long, with divergent points.

Fasteners for Gypsum Lath

Nails. Gypsum lath may be nailed to wood supports using 13-gage, flat-headed, rust-resistant nails with 3/8-inch heads. Nails should be special-purpose, blued gypsum lath nails, which are designed for the purpose. Sometimes, resin-coated, barbed shaft, or screw-type nails are used. Lengths should be sufficient to penetrate supports by at least 3/4 inch.

Screws. Gypsum lath may be fastened to steel studs using Type S or S-12 screws, depending on the stud metal thickness.

Staples. Lath is sometimes applied to wood using staples. Staples should be 16-gage flattened galvanized wire formed with a 7/16-inch wide crown and divergent points. Legs should be long enough to penetrate supports by at least 5/8 inch.

Clips. Gypsum lath may be installed on steel studs using clips designed for the purpose rather than screws.

A second kind of clip is used to stabilize end joints between gypsum lath sheets.

Other Fasteners. Existing gypsum lath may have been secured to metal or wood substrates using wire ties or other methods.

Fasteners for Predecorated Gypsum Board

Nails. Predecorated nails with small heads are used to install predecorated gypsum board, but their use is dictated by the predecorated board manufacturer. Smooth-shank nails should be long enough to penetrate at least 7/8 inch into the wood supports; annular-ringed nails, however, need only penetrate 3/4 inch.

Screws. Screws may also be used to install predecorated boards, where they will be concealed in the complete installation.

Adhesives

Adhesives for Gypsum Board. Two classes of adhesives are used with standard interior gypsum board. They are stud adhesives and laminating adhesives.

Stud adhesives are used to bond single-ply gypsum board to wood or steel supports. Boards adhered to framing with stud adhesive must also be mechanically fastened, but the number of fasteners can usually be reduced. Stud adhesives should comply with ASTM Standard C 557. Stud adhesives are applied in beads with a gun. Standard stud adhesives are solvent based, and should not be used with predecorated gypsum board. There are special adhesives formulated for that purpose.

Laminating adhesives are divided into three types: joint compound adhesives, contact adhesives, and modified contact adhesives.

Joint compound adhesives are made from a dry powder mixed with water. They are used only to laminate gypsum board to solid substrates, including other gypsum board. They are not used to bond gypsum board to framing members. Their use requires that the board also be mechanically fastened. Facing boards also require additional support until the adhesive cures.

Contact and modified contact adhesives are used to laminate boards to each other and to bond boards to metal framing. Modified contact adhesives are also used to bond gypsum board to insulation. Both types require that the boards also be mechanically fastened. Both can be used with predecorated boards.

Contact adhesives are difficult to use. They are thin, and therefore, do not fill in irregularities or bridge gaps. They are also contact-setting, which means that once two adhesive-coated surfaces are brought into contact, they cannot be moved. Contact adhesives do not require the temporary support of facing boards.

Modified contact adhesives are formulated to set more slowly than contact adhesives, which makes them easier to use. They can be moved, for example, for about a half hour or so after contact. They dry fast enough, however, to permit erection with few temporary fasteners. They are also thick enough to bridge small gaps.

Joint Treatment Materials

General Requirements.   Several types of joint treatment materials are used with the various forms of gypsum board products.

Tape.   Joint tape types include paper tape and open-weave glass fiber tape. Glass fiber tape is available in either pressure sensitive, for self-adhering, or plain, for application with compounds or adhesives, forms. Some manufacturers of glass mesh mortar units furnish coated glass fiber tapes for use with their product.

Compounds.   There are two major types of joint treatment compounds used generally. They are drying-type and setting-type joint compounds.

Drying-type compounds are vinyl based. They come either factory mixed, or as a dry powder for mixing in the field with water. They dry by water evaporation.

Setting-type compounds are also a dry powder for field mixing with water, but they dry by a chemical action and are, therefore, said to "set," rather than just dry. The significance is that drying-type compounds dry slowly and shrink until they are completely dry. Setting-type compounds, on the other hand, set chemically and become hard before they dry completely. Thus, the next coat can be added to a setting-type compound much sooner than to a drying-type compound, which speeds up the work.

But, because setting-type compounds are much harder than drying-type compounds, they are not often used for the top coat in a joint finishing system.

There are three different types of drying-type compounds. The first, taping compounds, are used for bedding tape and corner reinforcements. The second, topping compounds, are used as top coats, because they are easy to work with and to sand. The third type, all-purpose compounds, are a compromise between the other two. As usual, the compromise material does neither job as well as the other product, but does do both jobs, which makes it convenient for the installer.

Joint Treatment Materials for Standard Gypsum Board

Tape. Most applications utilize paper tape; others use pressure sensitive or staple-attached open-weave glass fiber tape.

Compounds. Both drying and setting compounds are used, sometimes in the same system. Refer to the "Joint and Fastener Treatment" paragraphs in "Installing Standard Gypsum Board" later in this chapter.

Joint Treatment Materials for Veneer Plaster Gypsum Base

Tape. Both paper and glass fiber tapes are used.

Compounds. Some manufacturers require setting-type compounds. Others require using veneer plaster as the joint compound.

Texture Finishes

There are many textured finishes available. These are proprietary products, and each is a little different from the others. Some texture finish products are the same material as that used to finish joints. Others are completely different formulations. Some have no aggregate. Others have polystyrene, vermiculite, or another aggregate. Some are formulated for spray application. Others are applied using hand tools. Some achieve their texture automatically during the application process itself. Other formulations require stippling, swirling, or some other action during or after application to achieve the texture.

Gypsum Board Installation

Sometimes it is necessary to determine the installation methods used in existing work so that repairs will match and not damage or change the intent of the original application.

The requirements discussed under the various subheadings that follow are offered to help the reader determine the application methods that may have been used in an existing application. They do not contain all the details one needs to know to install new gypsum board.

In every case, installation should have been done in accordance with the applicable ASTM and Gypsum Association standards, and with the recommendations of the manufacturer of the gypsum board product used. Refer to "Where to Get More Information" at the end of this chapter for a discussion of ASTM and Gypsum Association publications that may help.

The data included here is generally applicable to most installation. The requirements for some installations may vary, however. For example, the requirements for fastener size, type, and spacing; adhesive use; joint treatment; and board selection for fire-, smoke-, or sound-rate assemblies may differ significantly from the reqirements presented. When a rated system must be repaired or extended, it is necessary to determine the specific materials, system configuration, and installation methods used. Repairs and extensions of rated assemblies should mimic the existing assembly in all significant particulars.

There are too many possible rated assemblies to describe here. The Gypsum Association's 1984 *Fire Resistance Design Manual* alone contains 63 pages, almost 50 of which are devoted to showing rated assemblies. Some manufacturers list other assemblies. Still other assemblies are required by codes and regulations. When a fire-, sound-, or smoke-rated assembly, or any other significantly different assembly is encountered, the reader should examine the references discussed in "Where to Get More Information" at the end of this chapter, determine the requirements, if any, of applicable codes and regulations, and consult with the manufacturer of the board used.

Substrate Preparation

Solid Substrates. Concrete, masonry, gypsum board, and other solid substrates to which gypsum board will be directly laminated (no furring) must be flat, clean, dry, and smooth. Substrates should not, however, be slick.

Gypsum board should not be directly laminated to the interior surface of exterior concrete or masonry unless those substrates are the inner wythe of a cavity wall. Even cavity walls should not be used as a substrate for direct lamination of gypsum board unless the cavity is properly flashed, insulated, and drained.

Neither concrete nor masonry should ever be used as a substrate for direct lamination of foil-backed standard gypsum board or predecorated gypsum board with an impervious surface, such as vinyl.

Substrates to receive gypsum board by direct lamination should be as smooth as possible without being slick. Protrusions, such as excess joint mortar in masonry constructions and fins on concrete, that would interfere with application or damage the board's surface, should be removed. Depressions should be filled to ensure positive contact with the adhesives used, especially when a contact adhesive is used.

Substrates should be cleaned thoroughly. All traces of dust, dirt, oil, grease, form release compounds, curing compounds, efflorescence, and all other foreign materials should be completely removed.

Masonry materials and joints should be dry, and concretes should be cured for at least 28 days before gypsum board is laminated to them.

Solid substrates that cannot be properly prepared, surfaces of walls that retain earth, and solid (no cavity) exterior concrete and masonry walls should be furred before gypsum board is applied. Chapter 2 contains a discussion of furring.

Framing and Furring.   Framing and furring should be properly installed. Refer to Chapter 2 for a detailed discussion of what constitutes proper installation. Improper installation includes, but is not necessarily limited to, twisted or protruding framing or furring, and framing or furring that is not properly spaced or aligned.

Framing and furring to receive gypsum board must be flat, clean, dry, smooth, and free of projections and foreign matter that would interfere with board placement or damage the board's surface.

Installing Standard Gypsum Board

It is usually possible to determine by examination which materials and methods were used to install standard gypsum board in an existing building. Removing an electrical outlet cover plate will reveal whether the application is single-ply or double-layer, for example. Fewer fasteners than the number recommended by the appropriate ASTM, Gypsum Association, or manufacturer's standards, or fasteners only along board edges and not in the field, may suggest that adhesives have been used in the installation. No visible fasteners may mean that the installation was made using a contact adhesive.

When application methods cannot be determined by observation, it may be possible to ascertain the name of the products used and contact their manufacturers for advice. Where product names cannot be determined, it may be necessary to identify the product types by laboratory analysis and guess at the application methods, based on the recommendations of the manufacturers of similar products or of ASTM or the Gypsum Association.

The requirements presented under this heading apply to most standard gypsum board applications.

General Requirements for Installing Standard Gypsum Board. Installation should be done in accordance with ASTM Standard C 840.

Boards should be installed with the face side out, and butted together at the ends and edges, leaving a joint of not more than 1/16 inch width. They should be installed so that like edges butt. Tapered edges should not abut board ends or cut edges.

Ceiling boards should be applied before wall boards are placed.

Vertical joints should be staggered on opposite sides of partitions so that they do not fall on the same stud.

Neither vertical nor horizontal joints should occur at opening corners.

Joints in the face ply in double-layer applications on ceilings and walls should be offset so that they fall at least 12 inches from joints in the base ply.

On ceilings and walls, in single-ply applications and in the face ply of double-layer applications, the longest available boards should be used in order to minimize the number of end joints, which are hard to finish. Where possible, end joints should be avoided altogether by using facing boards the full width of the ceiling or height of the wall. Unavoidable end joints should be staggered by at least 24 inches, and should fall as far from the center of the ceiling or wall as possible.

Where boards are installed across the framing or furring (see Fig. 2-3), end joints should fall over the framing or furring to make direct attachment possible, and to reinforce the joint. When boards are installed across the framing or furring, the end joints will sometimes not fall over supports. Then, the end joints should be solidly supported with back-blocking.

Where boards are installed with the long edges parallel to the framing or furring (see Fig. 2-2), the edge joints should fall over the framing or furring members to reinforce the joint and make direct attachment possible.

Hollow metal door frames in metal-framed partitions should be spot grouted at each jamb anchor clip before the board is applied.

Unless the partitions are braced independently, as often occurs, for example, in chase walls, studs extending above ceilings should be faced on both sides with gypsum board. Such construction may be made using scraps, except where sound-, fire-, or smoke-ratings are required.

General Requirements for Fasteners in Standard Gypsum Board Installation

Fastener Types. Single-ply applications over wood framing or furring are made using nails or screws.

The first ply of double-layer applications over wood framing or furring are made using either nails, screws, or staples.

Single-ply applications and the first ply of double-layer applications over metal framing or furring are made using screws.

General Rules for Fastener Use. Fasteners should be installed according to the following rules:

Where fasteners are required along board edges parallel to framing or furring members (see Fig. 2-2), they should be placed between 3/8 and 1/2 inch from the board edge.

Where fasteners are required along board edges perpendicular to the framing or furring members (see Fig. 2-3), they should be placed between 3/8 and 1 inch from the board edge.

Fasteners should be driven straight.

Nails and screws should be driven in far enough to produce a slight dimple in the board surface. The paper covering should not be broken, nor the core fractured.

Staples should be driven with the crown perpendicular to the long edge of the board, except that where the long edge falls along a support, staples should be driven with the crown parallel with the long edge. Staples should be tightly in contact with the board. The paper covering should not be cut.

Fasteners should be driven only into board that is being held tightly to the substrate.

Fasteners should be driven into framing or furring members. Nails should penetrate wood not less than 7/8 or more than 1-1/4 inches. Screws should penetrate framing by at least 5/8 inch.

Exceptions occur in some fire-rated assemblies and occasionally in other circumstances, but in most nailed or screwed applications, fastening is not required at the top and bottom of boards placed on walls with the long dimension vertical, and the lack of fasteners there does not signify inferior construction.

Single-ply Standard Gypsum Board Installation without Adhesives

Installing Board.   On ceilings, when the framing or furring spacing is 16 inches on center, most 3/8-inch thick boards will be installed with the long dimension perpendicular to the framing or furring (see Fig. 2-3), 1/2-inch thick board may be installed either with the long edge perpendicular to or parallel (see Fig. 2-2) with the framing or furring, and 5/8-inch thick board will probably be installed with the long dimension parallel with the framing or furring.

On ceilings, when the framing or furring spacing is 24 inches on center, 1/2- and 5/8-inch thick boards will probably be installed with the long dimension perpendicular to the framing or furring (see Fig. 2-3). Where a textured finish occurs, 1/2- and 5/8-inch thick boards will probably be installed with the long dimension perpendicular to the framing or furring. Using 3/8-inch thick boards is not appropriate when the framing or furring spacing is more than 16 inches on center.

On ceilings where a textured finish is to be used, boards should be placed with their long edge perpendicular to the framing or furring (see Fig. 2-3). Boards should be 1/2 inch thick when framing or furring is 16 inches on center and 5/8 inch thick when framing or furring is 24 inches on center. Using 3/8-inch thick boards is not appropriate regardless of the framing or furring spacing.

Boards on walls may be placed with their long edge either perpendicular to or parallel with the framing or furring, depending on which produces the fewest hard-to-finish end joints. On walls that are not taller than the standard length of gypsum board, the boards are usually applied with the long edges vertical. On higher walls, boards are often applied with the long edges horizontal. Where the framing or furring spacing is 16 inches on center, 3/8-inch thick boards may be used. Where the framing or furring is 24 inches on center, either 1/2- or 5/8-inch thick board should be used.

Number and Location of Nails.   Gypsum board may be installed with nails using either the single-nailing or double-nailing method.

In both methods, nails should be spaced 7 inches on center on ceilings and 8 inches on center on walls along each board edge that parallels a framing or furring member.

In the single-nailing method, additional nails should be placed at each intermediate framing or furring member along board edges that are perpendicular to the framing or furring (Fig. 4-3). Nails should also be placed between the edge nails at 7 inches on center on ceilings and 8 inches on center on walls in the field of the board along each intermediate framing or furring member.

In the double-nailing method (Fig. 4-4), two sets of additional nails are

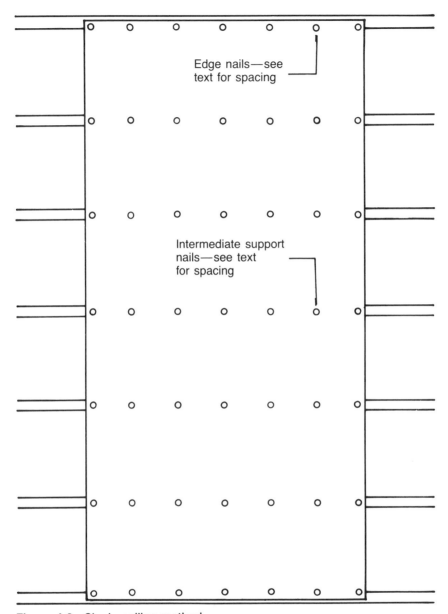

Figure 4-3   Single-nailing method.

placed in the field of the boards along each framing or furring member. In the first set, a nail is placed near each board edge and additional nails are placed at 12-inch centers along the supports between the edge nails. Then

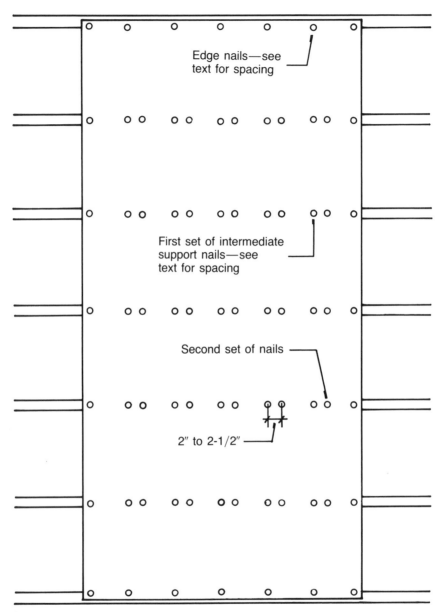

Figure 4-4   Double-nailing method.

the second set of nails is placed 2 to 2-1/2-inches away from the first set of nails, except that second-set nails are not placed along board edges. After the second set of nails has been driven, the first set should be reseated.

Number and Location of Screws (Fig. 4-5). Where wood framing or furring is spaced 16 inches on center, screws in ceilings should be placed at each board edge at, and at 12 inches on center along, each support, and screws in walls should be placed at each board edge at, and at 16 inches on center along, each support.

Where wood framing or furring is spaced 24 inches on center, screws in ceilings and walls should be placed at each board edge at, and at 12 inches on center along, each support.

Where metal framing or furring occurs, screws in ceilings and walls should be placed along at each board edge at, and at 12 inches on center along, each support.

Installing Double-Layer Standard Gypsum Board without Adhesives

Installing Base Ply. On ceilings where the framing or furring spacing is 16 inches on center, 3/8-inch thick boards should be placed with the long edges perpendicular to the framing or furring (see Fig. 2-3), and 1/2-inch thick boards should be placed with the long edges parallel with the framing or furring (see Fig. 2-2). End joints may be located either over or between framing or furring members.

On ceilings where the framing or furring spacing is 24 inches on center, 1/2- and 5/8-inch thick boards should be placed with the long dimension perpendicular to the framing or furring (see Fig. 2-3). Using 3/8-inch thick boards is not appropriate.

On ceilings where a textured finish is to be used, boards should be placed with long edge perpendicular to the framing or furring. Boards should be 1/2 inch thick when framing or furring is 16 inches on center, and 5/8 inch thick when framing or furring is 24 inches on center. Using 3/8-inch thick boards is not appropriate regardless of the framing or furring spacing.

On wood framed or furred walls, the base ply of double-layer applications is usually installed with the long dimension vertical, except where a fire-rating requires horizontal placement.

On metal framed or furred walls, the base ply of double-layer applications may be installed with the long edge either vertical or horizontal, unless a fire-rating requires one or the other.

On walls where the framing or furring is either wood or metal, 3/8-, 1/2-, or 5/8-inch thick boards may be used on framing or furring spacings up to 24 inches on center, except that when the face ply will be 3/8-inch thick board, framing or furring must be spaced at no more than 16 inches on center.

Number and Location of Nails in Base Ply (Fig. 4-6). On ceilings and walls, where the face ply is to be nailed without adhesives, nails in the

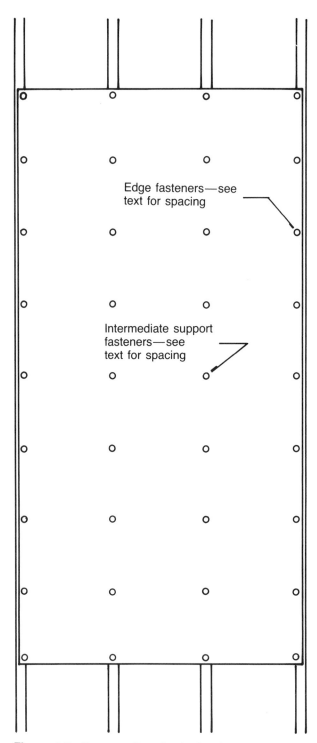

Figure 4-5 Screw pattern in single-ply gypsum board installed without adhesives.

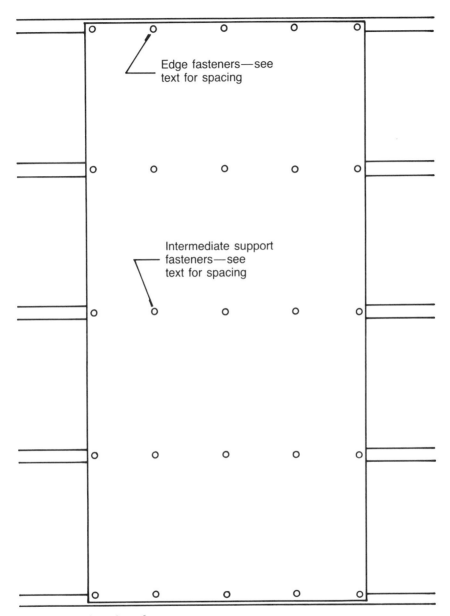

Edge fasteners—see
text for spacing

Intermediate support
fasteners—see
text for spacing

Figure 4-5 (*continued*)

base ply should be placed at each board edge at, and at 16 inches on center along, each support.

Number and Location of Screws in Base Ply (see Fig. 4-6). On wood framed or furred ceilings and walls, where the face ply will be installed

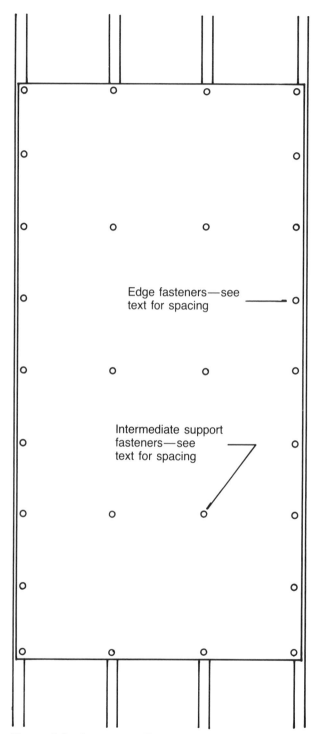

Edge fasteners—see text for spacing

Intermediate support fasteners—see text for spacing

Figure 4-6 Screw or nail pattern in base ply of double-layer gypsum board installed without adhesives.

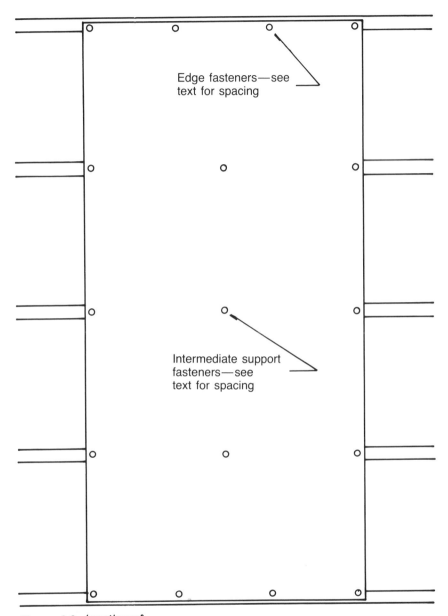

Edge fasteners—see
text for spacing

Intermediate support
fasteners—see
text for spacing

Figure 4-6 (*continued*)

without adhesives, screws in the base ply should be placed at each board edge at, and at 24 inches on center along, each support.

On metal framed or furred ceilings and walls where the face ply is to be installed without adhesives, and the board is applied with the long edge perpendicular to the supports, screws in the base layer should be placed at each board edge at, and at 24 inches on center along, each support.

On metal framed or furred ceilings and walls where the face ply is to be installed without adhesives, and the board is applied with the long edge parallel with the supports, screws in the base layer should be placed at 12 inches on center along the long edge and at each board edge at, and at 24 inches on center along, each intermediate support.

Number and Location of Staples in Base Ply. Double-layer base plies may be attached to wood framing or furring with staples. On walls and ceilings, staples should be placed at 16 inches on center when the face ply will be installed with nails or screws.

Installing Face Ply. On ceilings where the framing or furring spacing is 16 inches on center, 3/8- or 1/2-inch thick boards should be placed with the long dimension perpendicular to the framing or furring (see Fig. 2-3).

On ceilings where the framing or furring spacing is 24 inches on center, 1/2- and 5/8-inch thick boards should be placed with the long dimension perpendicular to the framing or furring (see Fig. 2-3). Using 3/8-inch thick boards is not appropriate.

On ceilings where a textured finish is to be used, boards should be placed with long edge perpendicular to the framing or furring. Boards should be 1/2 inch thick when framing or furring is 16 inches on center and 5/8 inch thick when framing or furring is 24 inches on center. Using 3/8-inch thick boards is not appropriate regardless of the framing or furring spacing.

On walls, the face ply of double-layer applications may be installed with the long edge either vertical or horizontal, unless a fire-rating requires one or the other. Where a fire-rating is not required, the board is usually placed in that direction which will produce the fewest hard-to-finish end joints. On walls that are not taller than the standard length of gypsum board, the boards are usually applied with the long edges vertical. On higher walls, boards are often applied with the long edges horizontal. Either 3/8-, 1/2-, or 5/8-inch thick boards may be used on framing or furring spacings up to 24 inches on center, except that, when the face ply will be 3/8-inch thick board, framing or furring must not be spaced at more than 16 inches on center.

Number and Location of Nails in Face Ply. On ceilings and walls, where the face ply is applied without adhesive, the number and location of nails in the face ply should be the same as those used in single-ply installations as outlined earlier in this chapter (see Fig. 4-3). The double-nailing method (see Fig. 4-4) is seldom used, however, for face plies in double-layer applications.

Number and Location of Screws in Face Ply. On ceilings and walls, where the face ply is applied without adhesive, the number and location of screws in the face ply should be the same as those used in single-ply installations, as outlined earlier in this chapter (see Fig. 4-5).

General Requirements for Adhesives in Standard Gypsum Board Installation. Adhesives are sometimes used to bond single-ply and the first ply of double-layer gypsum board applications to metal studs or to laminate gypsum board to solid substrates, such as concrete, unit masonry, plaster, foam insulation, or other gypsum board.

The adhesive manufacturers' recommendations for installation vary, and should be followed.

Depending on the adhesive used, supplementary fasteners may or may not be needed while the adhesive is curing, and, therefore, may or may not be present in the completed installation.

Even when the adhesive is relied upon completely to hold the work in place, temporary supports may be needed to stabilize the board until the adhesive sets, especially when non-contact adhesives are used, but those temporary supports will probably not be visible in the finished installation.

Installing Single-ply Standard Gypsum Board with Adhesives

Installing Board. Stud adhesives are used to bond gypsum board to wood framing on ceilings and walls. They are applied in beads along each framing member using a caulking gun. Where gypsum boards join, two beads are used, one behind the edge of each board.

On walls, gypsum board is sometimes installed using stud adhesive in a process called pre-bowing, in which the board is deliberately warped before application. After application, the board's tendency to try to straighten holds it tightly to the studs until the adhesive sets.

Adhesives are also used to laminate gypsum board to solid substrates such as concrete or masonry. Gypsum board and adhesive manufacturers' material selection and application instructions vary. Probably the best way to determine what is in place is to ascertain the names of the manufacturers and seek their advice.

Number and Location of Fasteners (Fig. 4-7). When adhesives are used to install gypsum board on wood or metal framing, the number of fasteners needed in some systems may be reduced by as much as 50 percent, but the exact number of fasteners required varies with the manufacturer, adhesives used, and the application method.

On ceilings and walls, where standard gypsum board is installed using stud adhesives, the boards are pressed tight to the framing and fastened in

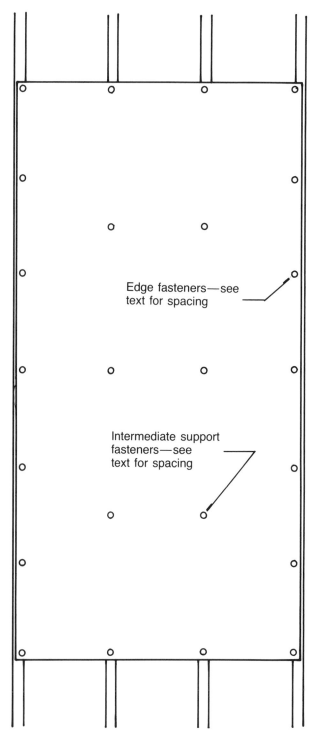

Figure 4-7 Supplementary fasteners in single-ply gypsum board installed using adhesives.

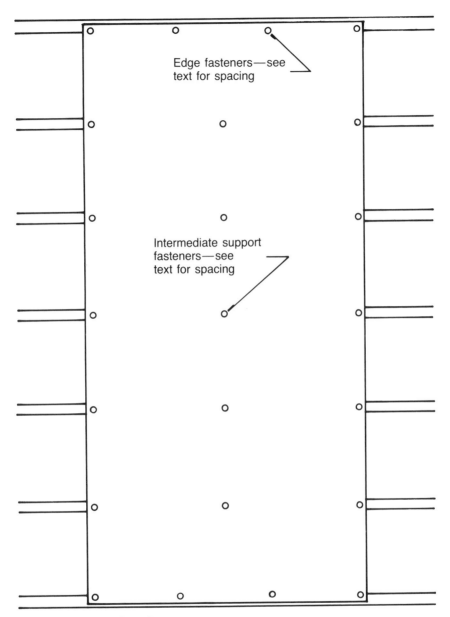

Figure 4-7   (*continued*)

place using nails or screws. Supplementary fasteners should be placed along the entire perimeter of each board at each support. Where an edge or end falls over a framing member or back blocking, the fasteners should be placed at 16 inches on center. Where the edge spans across framing members, a fastener should be placed near the board edge in each framing member.

On ceilings, where standard gypsum board is installed using stud adhesives, additional fasteners should be placed at 24 inches on center in each framing member over the entire field of each board.

On walls, gypsum board installed using stud adhesive and the prebowing process is fastened only at the top and bottom edges, usually at 16 inches on center.

Where adhesives are used to laminate gypsum board to solid substrates such as concrete or masonry, some form of supplementary fastening and temporary bracing is necessary. The methods and number and type of fasteners varies from project to project because the gypsum board and adhesive manufacturers' recommendations vary.

Installing Double-Layer Standard Gypsum Board with Adhesives between Plies

Installing Base Ply. On ceilings where the framing or furring spacing is 16 inches on center, 3/8-inch thick boards should be placed with the long dimension perpendicular to the framing or furring (see Fig. 2-3).

On ceilings where the framing or furring spacing is 16 inches on center, 1/2-inch thick boards should be placed with the long dimension either perpendicular to (see Fig. 2-3) or parallel with (see Fig. 2-2) the framing or furring.

On ceilings where the framing or furring spacing is 24 inches on center, 5/8-inch thick boards should be placed with the long dimension parallel with the framing or furring (see Fig. 2-2) when the face ply is 1/2-inch thick board, and either perpendicular to (see Fig. 2-2) or parallel with the framing or furring, when the face ply is 5/8-inch thick board. Using 3/8- or 1/2-inch thick boards for the base ply here is not appropriate.

On ceilings where a textured finish is to be used, boards should be placed with long edge perpendicular to the framing or furring (see Fig. 2-3). Boards should be 1/2 inch thick when the framing or furring is 16 inches on center, and 5/8 inch thick when the framing or furring is 24 inches on center. Using 3/8-inch thick boards is not appropriate regardless of the framing or furring spacing.

On ceilings, the end joints in a base ply perpendicular to the framing or furring may be located over or between framing or furring members.

On wood framed or furred walls, the base ply of double-layer applications should be installed with the long dimension vertical, unless a fire-rating requires horizontal placement.

On metal framed or furred walls, the base ply of double-layer applications may be installed with the long dimension either vertical or horizontal, unless a fire-rating requires one or the other. Either 3/8-, 1/2-, or 5/8-inch thick boards may be used on framing or furring spacings up to 24 inches on center, except that, when the face ply will be 3/8-inch thick board, framing or furring must not be spaced wider than 16 inches on center.

Number and Location of Nails in Base Ply (see Fig. 4-3). Nails should be spaced 7 inches on center on ceilings and 8 inches on center on walls along each board edge that parallels a framing or furring member.

Additional nails should be placed at each intermediate framing or furring member along board edges that are perpendicular to the framing or furring. Nails should also be placed between the edge nails at 7 inches on center on ceilings and 8 inches on center on walls in the field of the board along each intermediate framing or furring member.

Number and Location of Screws in Base Ply (similar to Fig. 4-5). Where wood framing or furring is spaced 16 inches on center, screws in ceilings should be placed at each board edge at, and at 12 inches on center along, each support, and screws in walls should be placed at each board edge, and at 16 inches on center along, each support.

Where wood framing or furring is spaced 24 inches on center, screws in ceilings and walls should be placed at each board edge at, and at 12 inches on center along, each support.

Where metal framing or furring occurs, screws in ceilings and walls should be placed at each board edge at, and at 24 inches on center along, each support.

Number and Location of Staples in Base Ply. The base ply in double-layer applications may be applied to wood framing or furring with staples. On ceilings and walls, staples should be placed at 7 inches on center when the face ply will be installed with nails or screws.

Installing Face Ply. On ceilings where the framing or furring space is 16 inches on center, 3/8- or 1/2-inch thick boards should be placed with the long dimension either perpendicular to or parallel with the framing or furring.

On ceilings where the framing or furring spacing is 24 inches on center, 1/2- and 5/8-inch thick boards should be placed with the long dimension either perpendicular to or parallel with the framing or furring. Using 3/8-inch thick boards is not appropriate.

On ceilings where a textured finish is to be used, boards should be placed with long edge perpendicular to the framing or furring. Boards should be 1/2 inch thick when the framing or furring is 16 inches on center and

5/8 inch thick when the framing or furring is 24 inches on center. Using 3/8-inch thick boards is not appropriate regardless of the framing or furring spacing.

On walls, the face ply of double-layer applications may be installed with the long edge either vertical or horizontal, unless a fire-rating requires one or the other. Where a fire-rating is not required, the board is usually placed in that direction which will produce the fewest hard-to-finish end joints. On walls that are not taller than the standard length of gypsum board, the boards are usually applied with the long edge vertical. On higher walls, boards are often applied with the long edge horizontal. Either 3/8-, 1/2-, or 5/8-inch thick boards may be used on framing or furring spacings up to 24 inches on center, except that, when the face ply will be 3/8-inch thick boards, framing or furring must not be spaced at more than 16 inches on center.

On ceilings and walls, boards should be offset so that joints fall at least 12 inches from the joints in the base ply.

Adhesive between Plies.   On ceilings and walls, laminated face plies in double-layer installations are installed by sheet, strip, or spot lamination. In sheet lamination, the entire back of the face sheet is covered with adhesive. In strip lamination, the adhesive is applied in ribbons between 16 and 24 inches apart. In spot lamination, spots of adhesive are placed on the back of the facing sheet in a regular pattern. Most sound-rate partitions are installed using strip or spot lamination.

Number and Location of Supplementary Fasteners in Face Ply.   In laminated applications, supplementary fasteners are usually applied.

On ceilings, supplementary fasteners are often placed at 12 inches on center on the perimeter and at 16 inches on center in the field of each board.

On walls, supplementary fasteners are usually placed only along the top and bottom of each board at about 16 inches on center.

Accessories

Control and Isolation Joints.   Control joints should be installed in gypsum board systems where a control or expansion joint occurs in the underlying structure.

Control joints should also be placed in gypsum board surfaces at 30 foot intervals.

Isolation joints should be installed where gypsum board abuts a different material. Isolation joints are often formed by placing a trim edge about 1/4 inch from the different material. The trim edge should not be fastened to the different material or its supports. Perimeter relief is discussed in greater detail in Chapter 2.

Corner Beads.   Every exterior corner should receive a corner bead.

Edge Trim.   Edge trim should be installed in every location where the edge of a gypsum board panel would otherwise be exposed to view.

H-Moldings.   These are sometimes used in exterior gypsum board soffits in lieu of finishing the joints.

Joint and Fastener Treatment.   The following joint treatment is applicable to most gypsum board products. For joint treatment requirements for water-resistant and predecorated gypsum board, refer to the parts of this chapter with those headings.

Interior.   Joints in interior gypsum board are finished using tape and compounds. Tape is placed over the joint in a bed of taping or bedding compound, and covered with the same compound. The compound may be either a drying-type or setting-type compound, but is usually a drying-type taping or all-purpose compound. Topping compounds (some are called finishing compounds) are not appropriate.

After the first coat of compound has dried, a second coat is applied. The second, or fill, coat is usually the same type (drying or setting) compound used to embed and cover the tape. The formulation of this compound may differ from that of the taping or bedding compound, but also should not be a topping compound.

When the fill coat has dried, it is sanded, cleaned, and finished with a thin coat of topping or all-purpose compound. The finish coat is usually a drying-type compound.

Fasteners are also covered with a coat of topping or all-purpose compound, usually of the drying-type.

Exterior.   Joints in gypsum ceiling board on the exterior are finished in a similar fashion to interior joints, except that only setting-type compounds are generally used.

Foil-Backed Board.   Foil-backed board should be applied with the foil toward the framing or furring members. Otherwise, it should be installed in the same manner as other gypsum board products.

Water-Resistant Board. Water-resistant gypsum board application requirements are similar to those for regular gypsum board, with a few exceptions.

Water-resistant board should be installed with the long dimension perpendicular to the wall framing or furring. The bottom row should be held 1/4 inch above a tub, shower receptor, or similar item, and the space caulked with a sealant.

Where a fire-rating is required, two layers should be used, one from floor to ceiling, the other furred out to the face of the tub, shower, or other similar item, and extending from that item to the ceiling.

Boards should be fastened in place with nails or screws, as appropriate, spaced not more than 8 inches on center around the perimeter and in the field of each board. Adhesive application is not appropriate.

Water-resistant board should not be used on ceilings or over a vapor barrier of any kind.

There is some confusion about whether joints and fastener heads in water-resistant gypsum board behind tile should be taped and treated. The 1979 version of ASTM Standard C 840 prohibited taping and treating such joints and fastener heads. The 1984 ASTM Standard C 840, and the applicable current ANSI, Gypsum Association, and Ceramic Tile Institute standards either recommend or require taping and treating joints and treating fastener heads in water-resistant gypsum board behind tile. Some manufacturers require taping and treating, but others do not. Consequently, an existing installation may or may not have had the joints and fasteners behind tile taped or treated.

Floating Interior Angles. Existing gypsum board over wood framing or furring may have floating interior angle construction to help reduce fastener pops and cracking due to structure movement. Care should be taken to not defeat the existing floating construction.

Floating construction is created on ceilings by not fastening the ceiling board at the wall line and supporting the edge of the ceiling board with the wall board (Fig. 4-8).

Floating construction is created on walls by not fastening the board on one wall at the corner and holding the loose edge in place with the board on the other wall (Fig. 4-9). In double-layer construction, the face ply is adhesive-laminated with no fasteners in the corners.

Sound Isolation. Sound-rated and sound-isolated partitions are created by including sound insulation in the partition and sealing the perimeter of all gypsum board with acoustical sealant. Refer to ASTM Standard C 919 and the gypsum board manufacturers' recommendations for the installation of acoustical sealants.

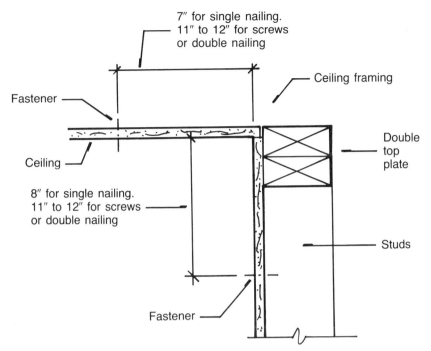

Figure 4-8 Edge of a floating gypsum board ceiling.

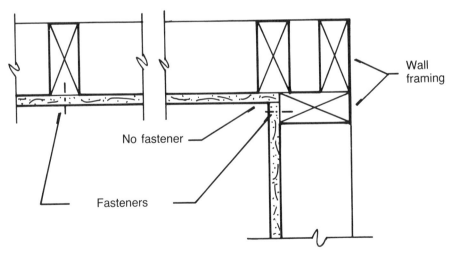

Figure 4-9 Floating gypsum board construction at a wall corner.

Shaftwalls. Shafts may be faced with solid gypsum partitions made up of standard components, but most modern gypsum board shaft enclosures are made with "shaftwall systems," or "cavity shaftwall systems." Shaftwall systems are proprietary systems consisting of framing, panels, and accessories. In general, the components are identical or similar to components used in other gypsum board systems, and their installation and finishing is the same. The framing members, however, are specifically designed for their purpose (refer to Chapter 2).

Solid Partitions. Solid partitions consist of coreboard faced with other gypsum board types. The composite is framed with wood or metal floor and ceiling runners. Plies are laminated using laminating adhesives or joint compound. Face plies are nailed or screwed to the runners at 24 inches on center using screws or nails, as appropriate. The coreboard is also attached to the runners in some systems. Sometimes, the facing boards are screwed or nailed to the core.

Joints of face panels and core should be staggered.

Exterior Soffits. Many exterior soffits are installed using the same methods as for interior ceilings, with boards screwed or nailed to framing or furring and intermediate joints finished with tape and compound. Where framing or furring is spaced at 16 inches on center, 1/2-inch thick soffit board is acceptable. Where spacing is 24 inches on center, 5/8-inch thick board should be used.

Other soffits are installed with boards fastened to supports using screws or nails, but with H-moldings at interior joints.

Some gypsum board soffits consist of gypsum boards laid into suspended ceiling support systems.

In every case, the perimeter of exterior soffits should be finished with a casing or edging member, and protected from the weather by appropriate fascias and drips.

Finishes on Standard Gypsum Board. Gypsum board that is not prefinished may be finished by painting, application of a textured finish (which also may be paint), or by covering with another material, such as ceramic tile (see Chapter 5) or a wallcovering.

Paint. Gypsum board to be painted should have completely finished joints and fastener heads, and all irregularities that would show through the finish should be removed. When the paint will be glossy, additional preparation is necessary. After joints and fastener heads have been finished and irregularities have been removed, the entire surface should be covered with a thin coat of joint compound. The coated surface should then be lightly sanded to remove trowel marks and irregularities. A complete coat of joint compound is sometimes applied to hide irregularities, even when the paint to be used is not glossy, especially on surfaces that will be subjected to strong light.

Textured Finishes. Textured paint finishes are beyond the scope of this book. Surfaces to receive proprietary textured finishes furnished by the gypsum board product manufacturer should be prepared, and the products should be applied, in accordance with the manufacturer's instructions.

The Gypsum Association recommends, and most manufacturers require, limitations on board thickness and direction of installation relative to the framing or furring when textured coatings are to be used. Usually, the board must be applied with the long dimension perpendicular to the framing or furring. Textured finish is usually not recommended for use on 3/8-inch thick board in a single-ply application. For 1/2-inch thick board, the framing or furring usually must be not more than 16 inches on center. For 5/8-inch thick board, the framing or furring may usually be spaced as far apart as 24 inches, but no more. Double-layer installations to receive textured finish usually must be at least 3/4 inch thick. Other restrictions may apply.

In general, whether textured finishes are applied by spray, brush, or roller, joints and fastener heads should be treated, and irregularities that would show through the finish should be removed. Before finish application, the board should be primed, using materials and procedure recommended by the finish manufacturer.

Installing Veneer Plaster Gypsum Base

It is not always possible to determine the exact methods used to install existing veneer plaster gypsum base without removing part of the veneer plaster. Some clues might be gathered, however, by examination. Removing an electrical outlet cover plate will reveal the thickness of the base used and whether the application is a single-ply or double-layer system, for example.

The material thicknesses, installation methods, fastener number and locations, and adhesive application procedures under this heading are useful as general guides only. Actual field conditions may differ significantly from those indicated here.

General Requirements for Installing Veneer Plaster Gypsum Base.

Veneer plaster base should have been installed in accordance with ASTM Standard C 844.

Boards should be installed with the face side out.

Boards should be butted together at the ends and edges, leaving a joint not more than 1/16 inch wide.

Boards should be installed so that like edges butt.

Ceiling boards should be applied before wall boards are placed.

Vertical joints should be staggered on opposite sides of partitions so that they do not fall on the same stud.

Neither vertical nor horizontal joints should occur at opening corners.

On ceilings and walls, in double-layer applications, boards in the face ply should be offset so that the joints fall at least 12 inches from those in the base ply.

On ceilings and walls, in single-ply applications and in the face ply of double-layer applications, the installation should be planned so that the fewest possible number of joints occur. Where possible, end joints should be avoided altogether by using facing boards the full width of the ceiling or height of the wall. Unavoidable end joints should be staggered by at least 24 inches, and should fall as far from the center of the ceiling or wall as possible.

Where panels are installed across framing or furring, end joints should fall over the framing or furring to make direct attachment possible, and to reinforce the joint. Sometimes, when panels are installed across framing or furring, the end joints will not fall over supports. In those cases, the end joints should be supported with back blocking.

Where panels are installed with the long edges parallel to the framing or furring (see Fig. 2-2), the edge joints should fall over the framing or furring members to reinforce the joint and make direct attachment possible.

Hollow metal door frames in metal framed partitions should be spot grouted with joint compound at each jamb anchor clip before the board is applied.

Unless the partitions are braced independently, as often occurs in chase walls, metal studs extending above ceilings should be faced on both sides with veneer plaster gypsum base. Such construction may be made using scraps, except where sound-, fire-, or smoke-ratings are required.

General Requirements for Fasteners in Veneer Plaster Gypsum Base Installations

Fastener Types. Single-ply applications and the base ply of double-layer applications over wood framing or furring are made using either nails or screws.

Single-ply applications and the first ply of double-layer applications over metal framing or furring are made using screws.

General Rules for Fastener Use. Fasteners should be installed according to the following rules:

Fasteners along board ends or edges that are parallel with framing or furring members should be placed between 3/8 and 1/2 inch from the board end or edge.

Fasteners along board ends or edges that are perpendicular to framing or furring members should be placed between 3/8 and 1 inch from the board end or edge.

Fasteners should be driven straight.

Fasteners should be driven in far enough so that the top of the fastener head is flush with the face of the board. The paper covering should not be broken, and the core should not be fractured.

Fasteners should be driven only into board that is being held tightly to the substrate.

Fasteners should be driven into framing or furring members. Nails should penetrate wood not less than 7/8 or more than 1-1/4 inch. Screws should penetrate framing or furring by at least 1/2 inch.

Single-ply Veneer Plaster Gypsum Base Installation without Adhesives

Installing Boards. On ceilings, boards should be applied with the long edge perpendicular to the framing or furring (see Fig. 2-3).

On ceilings where the framing or furring is spaced at 16 inches on center, 3/8-, 1/2-, or 5/8-inch thick boards may be found, depending on the thickness of the veneer plaster.

On ceilings where the framing or furring is spaced at 24 inches on center, 1/2- or 5/8-inch thick boards may be found, depending on the veneer plaster thickness and joint treatment method.

On walls, boards may be placed with the long edge either vertical or horizontal, depending on which direction produces the fewest number of joints, except where a fire-rating requires one direction or the other.

On walls, where the framing or furring is spaced up to 24 inches on center, 3/8-, 1/2-, or 5/8-inch thick boards may be found, depending on the thickness of the veneer plaster and the method of joint treatment.

Number and Location of Nails (see Fig. 4-3). On ceilings, nails should be placed at each board edge at, and at 7 inches on center along, each support.

On walls, nails should be placed at each board edge at, and at 8 inches on center along, each support.

Number and Location of Screws (see Fig. 4-5). On ceilings and walls, screws should be placed at each board edge at, and at 12 inches on center along, each support.

Installing Double-Layer Veneer Plaster Gypsum Base without Adhesives

Installing Base Ply. On ceilings, the base ply of double-layer installations should be installed with the long edge perpendicular to the framing or furring (see Fig. 2-3).

On ceilings where the framing or furring is spaced at 16 inches on center, 3/8-, 1/2-, or 5/8-inch thick boards may be found, depending on the face ply and veneer plaster thicknesses.

On ceilings where the framing or furring is spaced at 24 inches on center, 1/2- or 5/8-inch thick boards may be found, depending on the face ply thicknesses, the veneer plaster thickness, and the joint treatment method used.

On walls, boards should be placed with the long edge parallel with the framing or furring, unless a fire-rating requires placing them with the long edge in the other direction.

On walls, 3/8-, 1/2-, or 5/8-inch thick boards may be used on framing or furring spacings up to 24 inches on center, depending on the face ply thickness, the veneer plaster thickness, and the joint treatment method used.

Number and Location of Nails in Base Ply (see Fig. 4-6). On ceilings and walls, where the face ply is to be nailed without adhesives, nails in the base ply should be placed at each board edge at, and at 16 inches on center along, each support.

Number and Location of Screws in Base Ply (see Fig. 4-6). On ceilings and walls, where the face ply is to be installed without adhesives, screws in the base ply should be placed at each board edge at, and at 24 inches on center along, each support.

Installing Face Ply. On ceilings, boards should be placed with the long dimension perpendicular to the framing or furring.

On ceilings where the framing or furring is spaced at 16 inches on center, 3/8-, 1/2-, or 5/8-inch thick boards may be found, depending on the base ply and veneer plaster thicknesses.

On ceilings where the framing or furring is spaced at 24 inches on center, 1/2- or 5/8-inch thick boards may be found, depending on the base ply thickness, the veneer plaster thickness, and the joint treatment method used.

On walls, the face ply of double-layer applications should be installed with the long edge parallel with the framing or furring, except where a fire-rating requires application perpendicular to the framing or furring.

On walls, either 3/8-, 1/2-, or 5/8-inch thick boards may be used on framing or furring spacings up to 24 inches on center, depending on the base ply thickness, the veneer plaster thickness, and the joint treatment method used.

Number and Location of Nails in Face Ply.   On ceilings and walls, where the face ply is applied without adhesive, the number and location of nails in the face ply should be the same as those used in single-ply installations without adhesives, as outlined earlier in this chapter (see Fig. 4-3).

Number and Location of Screws in Face Ply.   On ceilings and walls, where the face ply is applied without adhesive, screws should be placed at each board edge at, and at 12 inches on center along, each support (see Fig. 4-5).

General Requirements for Adhesives in Veneer Plaster Gypsum Base Installation.   Adhesives are sometimes used to bond single-ply veneer plaster gypsum base installations and the base ply of double-layer veneer plaster gypsum base installations to wood or metal studs or to laminate veneer plaster gypsum base to solid substrates.

The adhesive manufacturers' recommendations for installation vary, and should be followed.

Depending on the adhesive used, supplementary fasteners may or may not be needed while the adhesive is curing, and, therefore, may or may not be present in the completed installation.

Even when the adhesive is relied upon completely to hold the work in place, temporary supports may be needed to stabilize the board until the adhesive sets, especially when non-contact adhesives are used, but those temporary supports will probably not be visible in the finished installation.

Installing Single-ply Veneer Plaster Gypsum Base with Adhesives

Installing Boards.   Stud adhesives are used to bond veneer plaster gypsum base to wood framing on ceilings and walls. Stud adhesive is applied in beads along each framing member using a caulking gun. Where veneer plaster gypsum base panels join, two beads are used, one behind the edge of each board.

Adhesives are also used to laminate veneer plaster gypsum base to metal framing and to solid substrates. Veneer plaster gypsum base and adhesive manufacturers' material selection and application instructions vary. Probably, the best way to determine what is in place is to ascertain the names of the manufacturers and seek their advice.

Number and Location of Fasteners. When adhesives are used to install veneer plaster gypsum base on wood and metal framing, the number of fasteners needed in some systems may be reduced by as much as 50 percent, but the exact number of fasteners required varies with the manufacturer, the adhesives used, and the application method.

On ceilings and walls, where veneer plaster gypsum base is installed using stud adhesives, the boards are pressed tight to the framing and fastened in place using nails or screws. Supplementary fasteners should be placed along the entire perimeter of each board at each support. Where an edge or end falls over a framing member or back blocking, the fasteners should be placed at not more than 16 inches on center. Where the edge spans across framing members, a fastener should be placed near the board edge in each framing member.

On ceilings, where veneer plaster gypsum base is installed using stud adhesives, additional fasteners should be placed at 24 inches on center in each framing member over the entire field of each board (see Fig. 4-7).

Where adhesives are used to laminate gypsum board to solid substrates such as concrete or masonry, some form of supplementary fastening and temporary bracing is necessary. The methods and number and type of fasteners varies from project to project because the gypsum board and adhesive manufacturers' recommendations vary.

Installing Double-Layer Veneer Plaster Gypsum Base with Adhesives between Plies

Placing Boards in Base Ply. On ceilings, veneer plaster gypsum base ply should be placed with the long dimension perpendicular to the framing or furring.

On ceilings where the framing or furring is spaced at 16 inches on center, 3/8-, 1/2-, or 5/8-inch thick boards may be found, depending on the face ply and veneer plaster thicknesses.

On ceilings where the framing or furring is spaced at 24 inches on center, 1/2- or 5/8-inch thick boards may be found, depending on the face ply thickness, the veneer plaster thickness, and the joint treatment method used.

On walls, boards should be placed with the long edge parallel with the framing or furring, unless a fire-rating requires placing them with the long edge in the other direction.

On walls, 3/8-, 1/2-, or 5/8-inch thick boards may be used on framing or furring spacings up to 24 inches on center, depending on the face ply thickness, the veneer plaster thickness, and the joint treatment method used.

Number and Location of Nails in Base Ply (see Fig. 4-3). On ceilings, nails should be placed at each board edge at, and at 7 inches on center along, each support.

On walls, nails should be placed at each board edge at, and at 8 inches on center along, each support.

Number and Location of Screws in Base Ply (similar to Fig. 4-5). On ceilings and walls, screws should be placed at each board edge at, and at 12 inches on center along, each support.

Placing Boards in Face Ply. On ceilings, veneer plaster gypsum base face ply should be placed with the long dimension perpendicular to the framing or furring.

On ceilings where the framing or furring is spaced at 16 inches on center, 3/8-, 1/2-, or 5/8-inch thick boards may be found, depending on the face ply and veneer plaster thicknesses.

On ceilings where the framing or furring is spaced at 24 inches on center, 1/2- or 5/8-inch thick boards may be found, depending on the face ply thickness, the veneer plaster thickness, and the joint treatment method used.

On walls, boards should be placed with the long edge parallel with the framing or furring, unless a fire-rating requires placing them with the long edge in the other direction.

On walls, 3/8-, 1/2-, or 5/8-inch thick boards may be used on framing or furring spacings up to 24 inches on center, depending on the face ply thickness, the veneer plaster thickness, and the joint treatment method used.

Adhesive between Plies. On ceilings and walls, laminated face plies in double-layer installations are installed by sheet, strip, or spot lamination. In sheet lamination, the entire back of the face sheet is covered with adhesive. In strip lamination, the adhesive is applied in ribbons between 16 and 24 inches apart. In spot lamination, spots of adhesive are placed on the back of the facing sheet in a regular pattern.

Number and Location of Supplementary Fasteners in Face Ply. Laminated applications generally require supplementary fasteners.

On ceilings, supplementary fasteners are sometimes placed at 12 inches on center on the perimeter and at 16 inches on center in the field of each board.

On walls, supplementary fasteners are sometimes placed only along the top and bottom of each board, at about 16 inches on center. Some manufacturers recommend using Type G screws as supplementary fasteners in veneer plaster base and fastening the face ply to the base ply in lieu of fastening through the base ply to the framing or furring. The manufacturer should be consulted for fastener spacing recommendations when Type G screws are used. The clue to recognizing Type G screw use is that the screws will be driven three inches or so from the board edges and will protrude through the back of the base ply.

Accessories

Control and Isolation Joints.   Control joints should be installed in veneer plaster systems wherever a control or expansion joint occurs in the underlying structure.

Control joints should also be placed in veneer plaster surfaces at 30 foot intervals.

Isolation joints should be installed where gypsum board abuts a different material. Isolation joints are often formed by placing a trim edge about 1/4 inch from the different material. The trim edge should not be fastened to the different material or its supports. Perimeter relief is discussed in greater detail in Chapter 2.

Corner Beads.   Every exterior corner should receive a corner bead.

Edge Trim.   Edge trim should be installed in every location where the edge of a veneer plaster gypsum base board would otherwise be exposed to view.

Joint Treatment.   Both flat and interior corner joints in veneer plaster gypsum base are reinforced with either paper or glass mesh tape. The tape is placed over the joint and either stapled or bedded in place with a setting-type joint compound or veneer plaster.

Sound Isolation.   Sound-rated and sound-isolated partitions are created in veneer plaster construction in the same way as in standard gypsum board systems.

Shaftwalls and Solid Partitions.   Shaftwalls and solid partitions in veneer plaster systems differ from other shaftwalls only in that the finish material is veneer plaster.

Installing Gypsum Sheathing

Gypsum sheathing is used with many exterior finishes, including exterior insulation and finish systems (EIFS), stucco, masonry, siding, and shingles.

Gypsum sheathing should not be used on exterior ceilings, soffits, or sills, except as a base for stucco.

Panel Application.   It is seldom possible to determine the installation methods used to install gypsum sheathing. It may be difficult even to determine the type and thickness of sheathing that has been used. Often, it will be necessary to first remove a portion of the covering finish to make such determinations.

General Requirements for Gypsum Sheathing Application.   Boards should be butted together at the ends and edges.

Horizontal applications should have tongue-and-groove edges, and should be installed with the tongued edge up.

Long-edge joints in vertical applications and end joints in horizontal applications should fall over the framing to make direct attachment possible, and to reinforce the joint. Where edges cannot fall over framing members, solid blocking should be provided.

Vertical joints should be staggered.

Gypsum sheathing should not be used as a nailing base. Fasteners for finishes should pass through the sheathing into the supports behind.

Gypsum sheathing should not be installed on framing that is spaced more than 24 inches on centers.

Board Placement

Vertical Application.   Boards 48 inches wide should be installed with the long edge vertical. Some codes permit gypsum sheathing to be used as corner bracing in wood-framed structures. Those codes usually require that such sheathing be applied with the long edge vertical.

Horizontal Application.   Boards 24 inches wide are usually applied with the long edge horizontal.

Fasteners

General Requirements for Fasteners.   Fasteners should be installed according to the following rules:

Fasteners should be placed no closer than 3/8 inch from the board edge or end.

Fasteners should be driven straight.

Fasteners should be driven in far enough to bear tightly against the board surface. The paper covering should not be broken, and the core should not be fractured.

Staples should be driven with the crown parallel with the framing.

Fasteners should be driven into framing members. Nails should penetrate wood not less than 7/8 or more than 1-1/4 inch. Screws should penetrate framing by at least 5/8 inch.

Number and Location of Fasteners.   In 48-inch wide sheathing, nails should be spaced 4 inches on center along the edges and 7 inches on center in the field in 5/8-inch thick board. In 1/2-inch thick board, nails should be spaced 4 inches on center along the edges and 8 inches on center in the field.

In 24-inch wide sheathing applied horizontally, nails should be spaced at 4 inches on center at every support. The nail spacing may be increased, however, to 8 inches on center where the finish is wood siding, and where diagonal wood members are used to brace the structure.

Screw spacings should be similar to nail spacing, but some manufacturers may permit wider spacings.

Staples should be spaced 3 inches on center along the edges and 6 inches on center in the field.

Adhesives.   Adhesives may be used to adhere sheathing to the supporting framing. Some codes require using such adhesives in some circumstances where the gypsum sheathing serves a structural function. Sheathing should not, however, be installed with only adhesives and no fasteners. Unless a code specifically permits or requires other spacings, fastener spacing when adhesives are used should be the same as when adhesives are not used.

Finishes should not be applied to gypsum sheathing using adhesives.

Protection.   Neither the Gypsum Association nor most gypsum sheathing manufacturers recommend protecting all gypsum sheathing with a water-repellent covering, such as asphalt-impregnated felt. Most do, however, require such protection in exterior insulation and finish systems (EIFS). Unfortunately, when the insulation in an EIFS is installed using an adhesive, such protective covering is not possible. In spite of sheathing manufacturers' protests, gypsum sheathing has often been installed in EIFS with no protective covering, sometimes with disastrous results. Because there are so many problems associated with using gypsum sheathing in EIFS—even when the gypsum sheathing has a glass mesh fiber facing instead of paper—some manufacturers recommend using glass mesh mortar units with cement cores there instead of gypsum sheathing.

Protection is also recommended where the exterior finish is stucco, where square-edge gypsum sheathing is applied with the long edge horizontal, where the sheathing has a plain (not water-resistant) core, and where the sheathing will be exposed to the weather after application.

Installing Gypsum Plaster Lath

Examination will usually reveal which lathing material type was used in an existing project. Access to the space above ceilings is often possible. Removing an electrical outlet or switch cover plate will usually expose the type of material that was used in walls and partitions.

General Requirements for Gypsum Lath Application. On ceilings where framing or furring spacing is 16 inches on center, either 3/8- or 1/2-inch thick lath may be found; where spacing is 24 inches on center, 1/2-inch thick lath should have been used.

On walls where framing or furring is spaced at 16 inches on center, 3/8-inch thick lath may be found; where spacing is 24 inches on center, 1/2-inch thick lath should have been used.

Boards should be installed with the face side out and butted together without force at the ends and edges.

Hollow metal door frames in metal framed partitions should be grouted solid before the lath is applied.

Board Placement. Gypsum lath should be installed with the long edge perpendicular to the framing or furring. An existing gypsum lath installation may have been installed using either of the two joint alignment methods shown in Figure 4-10. In both methods, end joints should fall over framing or furring members, where the lath is attached by nails, staples, or screws. Where the lath is supported on clips, end joints may fall between supports and be stabilized with clips.

Vertical joints should be staggered on opposite sides of partitions so that they do not fall on the same stud. Neither vertical nor horizontal joints should occur at opening corners. Joints should be staggered, and ceiling joints should not align with wall joints.

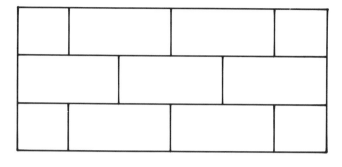

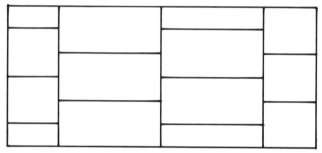

Figure 4-10   Gypsum plaster lath joint alignment methods.

Existing lath on walls may be either perforated or plain. Even when perforated lath was available, it was not recommended for use on ceilings where clip supported, and probably will not be found in such applications.

Fasteners

Fastener Types.   Existing gypsum lath may have been installed over wood using nails, screws, staples, or some other means, and over metal framing or furring using screws, clips, wire ties, clip and rod systems, or some other means.

General Requirements for Fasteners.   Fasteners should be installed according to the following rules:

Nails, staples, and screws should be driven straight.

Driven fasteners along board edges should be placed not closer than 3/8 inch from the board edge.

Nails, staples, and screws should be driven in far enough for the fastener head to contact the lath, but should not break the lath's paper face or fracture its core.

Nails, staples, and screws should be driven only into board that is being held tightly to the substrate.

Nails, staples, and screws should be driven into framing or furring members. Nails should penetrate wood not less than 7/8 inch, or more than 1-1/4 inch. Screws should penetrate framing or furring by at least 5/8 inch. Staples should penetrate not less than 1/2 inch.

Number and Location of Fasteners. Several spacings have been recommended at different times and by different experts for nails, staples, and screws in normal applications. In addition, fire-rating requirements may dictate different spacings from those normally used. As a result, an existing installation may have two, three, four, or five fasteners in each support. Less than four nails or staples is probably inadequate, but where clips are also used, two screws may be sufficient.

The number and spacing of clips varies with the clip type used and from manufacturer to manufacturer. End butt joints usually require at least three clips. Support clips are usually placed one at each support at the top and bottom of each lath board.

Accessories. Accessories for use with gypsum plaster are discussed in Chapter 3.

Foil-Backed Boards. Foil-backed boards should be applied with the foil toward the framing or furring members. Otherwise, they should be installed in the same manner as other gypsum lath.

Installing Predecorated Gypsum Board

It is usually possible to determine the application methods used by examination. Removing an electrical outlet cover plate will reveal whether the application is single-ply or double-layer, for example. A nailed application without adhesives will have visible nails in the surface. No visible fasteners and no battens may mean that the installation was made using a contact adhesive.

General Requirements for Predecorated Gypsum Board Application. Boards should be installed with the face side out and butted together at the ends and edges.

Ceiling boards should be in place before predecorated boards on walls are installed.

Vertical joints should be staggered on opposite sides of partitions so that they do not fall on the same stud.

Neither vertical nor horizontal joints should occur at opening corners.

Hollow metal door frames in metal framed partitions should be spot grouted at each jamb anchor clip before the board is applied.

Unless the partitions are braced independently, as usually occurs, for example, in chase walls, studs extending above ceilings should be faced on both sides with gypsum board. Such construction may be made using scraps, except where sound-, fire-, or smoke-ratings are required.

Board Placement. Predecorated gypsum board panels are almost always installed with the long dimension vertical. Joints should always be located over framing or furring members.

In double-layer applications, the base ply of gypsum board should be installed in the same manner as it would be for standard gypsum board. Refer to requirements included earlier in this chapter.

Fasteners

Fastener Types. The first ply of double-layer applications over wood framing or furring may be installed using either nails, screws, or staples, and over metal framing or furring using screws. Fastener types, spacings, and applications are the same as discussed earlier in this chapter for base ply applications in double-layer systems with regular gypsum board.

Applications of predecorated gypsum board to wood framing or furring may be made using nails with heads colored to match the predecorated boards.

Application of predecorated gypsum board to metal framing or furring may be made using screws. The screws are usually concealed behind edge trim and battens.

General Requirements for Fasteners. Fasteners should be installed according to the following rules:

Fasteners should be driven straight.

Fasteners along board edges should be placed between 3/8 and 1/2 inch from the board edge, to be concealed by trim and battens, where appropriate.

Nails and screws should be driven in far enough to finish flush with the surface of the board's finish. The covering should not be broken, and the core should not be fractured.

Fasteners should be driven only into board that is being held tightly to the substrate.

Fasteners should be driven into framing or furring members. Nails should penetrate wood not less than 3/4 inch. Screws should penetrate wood framing or furring by at least 5/8 inch, and metal framing or furring by at least 3/8 inch.

Fastener spacings may vary with different products. A common spacing for nails is 12 inches on center at every support. Screws are seldom used without adhesives.

Panel Application with Adhesives. Adhesives may be used alone or in conjunction with fasteners. Even when the adhesive is relied upon completely to hold the boards in place, temporary supports and auxiliary fasteners may be needed to stabilize the board until the adhesive sets, especially when non-contact type adhesives are used. Solvent-based contact adhesives should not be used with most predecorated gypsum boards. With every adhesive type, care must be exercised to ensure that adhesive does not contact the exposed face of the boards.

Adhesives Used Alone. Adhesives are sometimes used to bond predecorated gypsum board to wood or metal studs, or to laminate predecorated gypsum board to solid substrates. Predecorated gypsum board with a surface, such as vinyl, which is highly resistant to moisture vapor transmission, should not be laminated directly to concrete, masonry, or other materials which are likely to contain moisture. Those facings will not permit water vapor that evaporates from the substrate to escape. Such moisture will be trapped in the gypsum board, which can aid in mildew formation, damage the board, or cause the facing to delaminate from the board.

Supplementary fasteners may or may not be needed while the adhesive is curing and, therefore, may or may not be present in the completed installation. Adhesive and predecorated gypsum board manufacturers' recommendations for installation vary. Pre-bowing of boards may be required. Pressure-sensitive tape is sometimes used to hold the board in place while the adhesive is curing. Temporary support is often used, but will be removed after the adhesive has set and will not be apparent in the completed work.

Single-ply Installations Using Adhesives. Adhesives are sometimes used to install predecorated gypsum board on wood and metal framing or furring. Using adhesives may eliminate fasteners along the vertical edges and in the field of the board. Fasteners will probably be needed, however, at the top and bottom edges, or at least at the corners of the board. Sometimes pre-bowing is necessary in such installations, but that process should not affect the final work in place.

Double-Layer Applications Using Adhesives. Adhesives are sometimes, though not often, used to laminate the base ply of a double-layer system to framing or furring or a solid substrate. In that application, the base ply is installed in the same manner as described in this chapter for single-ply standard gypsum board applications with adhesives.

Adhesives are also used to laminate predecorated gypsum board to the base ply in double-layer applications. When the predecorated gypsum board is to be laminated, the base ply should be installed exactly as described earlier in this chapter for a single-ply application of standard gypsum board with fasteners and no adhesive.

Laminated predecorated gypsum board is installed by sheet, strip, or spot lamination. In sheet lamination, the entire back of the face sheet is covered with adhesive. In strip lamination, the adhesive is applied in ribbons between 16 and 24 inches apart. In spot lamination, spots of adhesive are placed on the back of the facing sheet in a regular pattern.

In laminated applications, supplementary fasteners are usually applied in corners or only along the top and bottom of each board. Sometimes, pressure-sensitive tape is placed on the back of the board, in lieu of the fasteners.

Other Possible Predecorated Board Installation Methods. Besides the adhesive and nailing methods already discussed, several proprietary systems are also used to install predecorated gypsum board on wood and metal framing or furring, and over concrete or masonry. Such systems employ clips, wire, and plastic components.

Predecorated gypsum board is also used in demountable partitions, where each application method is specific to the proprietary partition system involved.

Accessories

Control and Isolation Joints. Control joints should be installed in predecorated gypsum board systems wherever a control or expansion joint occurs in the underlying structure.

Control joints should also be placed in predecorated gypsum board surfaces at 30 foot intervals.

Isolation joints should be installed where predecorated gypsum boards abut a different material. Isolation joints are often formed by placing a trim edge about 1/4 inch from the different material. The trim edge should not be fastened to the different material or its supports. Perimeter relief is discussed in Chapter 2.

Corner Trim. Every inside and outside corner should receive trim.

End Caps. End caps should be installed in every location where the edge of a predecorated gypsum board panel would otherwise be exposed to view.

Ceiling Trim. Most installations require ceiling trim along each panel.

Base. Prefinished base members are usually required along the floor line of predecorated gypsum board.

Sound Isolation, Shaftwalls, and Solid Partitions. Predecorated gypsum board is seldom used where sound-, fire-, or smoke-ratings are required, due to its open-joint construction.

Gypsum Board System Failures and What to Do about Them

Why Gypsum Board Systems Fail

Most gypsum board system failures are caused by structure failure; structure movement; solid substrate problems; other building element problems; framing or furring problems; bad materials; bad system design; bad workmanship; or failing to protect the gypsum board.

Many gypsum board system failures result from problems with the gypsum board itself or its installation, which are discussed in this chapter. Other gypsum board system failures result from problems with the construction underlying the gypsum board. Those problems include structure failure and movement, and problems associated with solid substrates, other building elements, and wood and metal framing or furring, all of which are discussed in Chapter 2.

Some of the problems discussed in Chapter 2, especially structure movement and solid substrate problems, are as likely to cause gypsum board failure as are problems with the gypsum board or its installation. Consequently, the possibility that the types of problems discussed in Chapter 2 are responsible for a gypsum board failure should be investigated and ruled out or, if found to be at fault, rectified before gypsum board repairs are attempted. It will do no good to repair gypsum board when a failed, uncorrected, or unaccounted-for problem of the types discussed in Chapter 2 is present. The repair will then also fail.

Failures in board products that serve as a base for other finishes, such as veneer plaster gypsum base, gypsum plaster lath, gypsum sheathing, and glass mesh mortar units are likely to be first demonstrated as an apparent failure in the supported finish. Evidence of failure in plaster and synthetic stucco is discussed in Chapter 3. Evidence of tile failure is discussed in Chapter 5. Failures listed in those chapters which are caused by errors related to board products are cross-referenced to this chapter. Potential errors in those board products and the means of repairing them are discussed in this chapter.

After the types of problems discussed in Chapter 2 have been investigated and found to be not present, or repaired if found, the next step is to discover the causes for the gypsum board failure that are directly related to the gypsum board itself, and repair them. Possible failure causes include those in the following paragraphs, which contain numbered lists of errors and situations that can cause gypsum board failure. The numbered failure causes apply to standard gypsum board, veneer plaster gypsum base, gypsum sheathing, gypsum plaster lath, and predecorated gypsum board. Refer to "Evidence of Failure in Gypsum Board Systems" later in this chapter for a listing of the types of failure to which the numbered failure causes in this part apply.

Glass mesh mortar units are discussed separately near the end of this chapter.

Bad Materials. Improperly manufactured materials are not unheard of, but are far less common than improper system design or bad workmanship. Some problems that can cause failure are:

1. Boards that are not square.
2. Boards that are covered with the wrong paper type. This could be caused by mislabeling.
3. Water that is to be used in joint compounds containing enough dirt, iron, or other impurities to produce discoloration.
4. Materials that have become contaminated either before delivery or in the field.
5. Board materials that have become wet before application.
6. Boards that are manufactured with too soft a core. Soft board will compress unduly when fasteners are driven.
7. Boards that have face paper that is not completely bonded to the core.
8. Improperly manufactured boards.

Bad System Design. In addition to the types of errors discussed in Chapter 2, design errors that affect gypsum board system performance include selecting the wrong gypsum board, accessories, or fasteners; and not selecting the proper preparation for, and application of, the materials selected.

Wrong Gypsum Board Material. The gypsum board selected must be suitable for the substrates and conditions to be encountered. Errors in selecting the proper gypsum board include:

1. Selecting gypsum lath for use in exterior work where it will be exposed to high humidities.
2. Selecting gypsum lath for use with Portland cement plaster.
3. Selecting gypsum lath for application directly on the interior face of exterior masonry or concrete.
4. Selecting gypsum sheathing for use in an exterior insulation and finish system (EIFS) where the insulation must be applied using an adhesive. Gypsum sheathing must be protected from wetting by a layer of felt or other impervious material, which is not possible in EIFS where the insulation is applied using an adhesive. Wet sheathing is the largest single evidence of EIFS failure. Refer to Chapter 3 under "Synthetic Stucco Failures and What to Do about Them" for additional discussion.

Wrong Accessories or Fasteners. Accessories and fasteners must be appropriate. Errors include:

1. Selecting accessories or fasteners that can rust for use in exterior or wet areas.
2. Selecting the wrong types of nails or screws for a particular installation. Specifying Type W screws for use in metal supports, for example. Specifying nails with heads that are too large or small can also be a problem. When heads are too large, even a slight offset can drive the head through the board's paper face. Casing, common, and other nails whose heads are small relative to their shank diameter will not hold gypsum board in place.
3. Selecting the wrong size or length nails or screws. The fastener length and size recommendations of the Gypsum Association and the gypsum board manufacturers are more important than they appear to be. It is obvious that fasteners that are too short will not properly hold the board in place. It is not so apparent, however, that using nails that are too long will usually leave loose boards if wood supports shrink, while proper length nails probably will not.
4. Selecting the wrong accessories for the material or application. Selecting plastic edge trim where taping is required is a commonly occuring example.

Failing to Require Proper Preparation Methods. Proper preparation is essential if gypsum board failure is to be prevented. The following error will cause problems:

1. Failing to require proper preparation of substrate surfaces and surfaces within the gypsum board system. Specific requirements should be given. Requiring that preparation be in accord with the manufacturer's recommendations is not usually sufficient, especially where existing construction is involved.

Selecting Improper Application Methods.   This category includes the following types of problems:

1. Failing to take normal structure movement into account. Preparation should be made in the design to take care of settlement, shrinkage, expansion, warping, and deflection.
2. Failing to design to accommodate differential structural or thermal movement between two different framing, furring, or other support members. This is a particular problem in corners, especially at ceiling and wall intersections.
3. Failing to provide flashing and drips to prevent water from getting into or behind exterior gypsum soffit board, sheathing, or lath.
4. Failing to require separate support for insulation above a gypsum board ceiling, thus permitting the weight of the insulation to bear directly on the gypsum board. This is more of a problem when the ceiling board is thin.
5. Requiring the use of a board material that is too thin for the support spacings or other structural requirements.
6. Requiring that gypsum board be applied directly (without furring) on an exterior wall or another wall that is likely to become damp or wet. Dampness will cause mildew or staining and may cause the board to bow, sag, loosen, or even disintegrate.
7. Requiring that any gypsum board be applied directly (without furring) to uncured concrete or still-wet unit masonry where the board can become damp or wet.
8. Requiring that predecorated board with a moisture-resistant face, such as vinyl, be applied directly to concrete, masonry, or another surface where even minor amounts of moisture escaping from the substrate can become trapped in the gypsum board by the board's impervious facing. Predecorated board should never be applied directly to the interior face of exterior walls, regardless of how dry they may appear to be. The board's manufacturer should be consulted before any predecorated board is applied directly to concrete or masonry, regardless of location. Water or water vapor trapped in the board can cause the finish to blister, delaminate, or become discolored.

9. Requiring that gypsum board be attached to the wide face of wood framing, such as joists and headers, as often occurs in stairwells. When the lumber shrinks, the attached board will crack.
10. Failing to require the necessary expansion, control, and isolation joints; spacing expansion joints too far apart. Long runs of board and large board areas, particularly on ceilings, require expansion joints. Control joints are needed in most locations where gypsum board or its supports abut materials other than gypsum board. Isolation joints are needed where the abutting material is likely to move differentially from the gypsum board or its supports. This latter is a particularly serious problem in high-rise buildings where the gypsum board system abuts an exterior wall or structural element.
11. Failing to require that opening corners be reinforced.

Bad Workmanship.   Good workmanship is essential if gypsum board system failures are to be prevented. The installer not following the recommendations of recognized authorities, such as ASTM and the Gypsum Association, is a major cause of problems. Problems are also caused by the installer ignoring the manufacturer's recommendations or the designer's requirements, which are often presented in the form of architect's drawings and specifications. Specific reasons for failure due to bad workmanship include improper substrate preparation; improper storage and handling of materials; improper board placement; improper fastener, accessory, and adhesive application; and improper joint and fastener finishing.

Improper Substrate Preparation.   Examples of improper substrate preparation include:

1. Failing to remove dust, dirt, oil, tar, grease, efflorescence, loose particles, and other foreign substances, especially where adhesives are used in the application. This requirement also applies to surfaces within gypsum board systems. For example, gypsum board must be cleaned before joint treatment begins and again before finishing begins.
2. Failing to achieve the correct surface tolerance.
3. Failing to eliminate gloss from the existing surface where the board is to be directly applied using adhesives.
4. Failing to cut back and clean out cracks and holes, especially where the board is to be directly applied using adhesives.
5. Failing to fill depressions deeper than 1/4 inch, especially where the board is to be directly applied using adhesives.
6. Failing to remove protrusions.

Improper Storage and Handling of Materials. Examples include:

1. Allowing board to warp excessively before application.
2. Improperly cutting gypsum board.
3. Permitting board to become damaged during storage or handling.
4. Careless handling of the board.

Improper Board Placement. Examples include:

1. Installing the support system and boards too soon after structure erection. This is a particular problem in buildings with concrete frames and slabs, where the structure goes through a process known as "creep," in which the structure slowly settles into a new shape. Creep is a one-time event, not cyclic as some other forms of building movement are. Therefore, if the construction of interior finishes is delayed until most creep has taken place, forces generated by the creep will be less of a factor in finish failures.
2. Installing gypsum board on framing or furring that is misaligned, twisted, or protruding.
3. Installing gypsum board on wood framing or furring that is too hard or flexible, where nails cannot be driven properly.
4. Attaching gypsum board on the wide face of wood framing, such as joists and headers, as often occurs in stairwells.
5. Applying any gypsum board directly (without furring) on an exterior concrete, masonry, or other wall that is likely to become wet or damp, regardless of how dry the wall is at the time of application.
6. Applying any gypsum board directly (without furring) on wet materials such as fresh concrete or new masonry walls or on materials that may later become wet, regardless of location.
7. Applying predecorated board with a moisture-resistant face, such as vinyl, directly (without furring) on concrete, masonry, or another surface where moisture escaping from the substrate can become trapped in the gypsum board, regardless of location.
8. Applying gypsum board over wood supports that have a high moisture content.
9. Applying gypsum board to wet or damp substrates.
10. Using boards that are too thin for the support spacings or other structural requirements.
11. Placing gypsum board on studs with the leading edge of the board facing in the same direction as the stud flanges. To prevent misaligned panel edges and other failures, board must be placed with the leading edge toward the closed side of a channel stud (opposite the open flanges, as shown in Fig. 4-11). Misaligned joints and other failures will also result when all stud flanges are not pointed in the

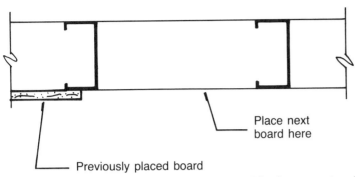

Place next
board here

Previously placed board

Figure 4-11   Gypsum boards must be placed in the correct order.

same direction. Either cause can result in joint beading or ridging, fastener pops, or plaster cracks.

12. Improperly fitting boards, which includes jamming boards together too tightly and forcing boards into spaces too small for them. Both will bow the boards and place them under stress, which prevents board contact with the framing.

13. Leaving too wide a gap between boards, thus creating a weak joint.

14. Applying boards with unlike adjacent edges in contact. Tapered factory edges should not be placed against cut edges, for example.

15. Extending gypsum board across an expansion or control joint.

16. Installing boards on walls before boards on ceilings have been placed, especially where the ceiling is floating at its juncture with the walls. When this is done, the ceiling board is left unsupported.

17. Placing the nailed board first at floating corners. This leaves the unnailed board without support.

18. Installing boards with unsupported ends. This may result from failing to locate ends over supports and not providing back blocking, or failing to fasten the ends to the supports.

19. Installing boards with unsupported edges, which can result from failing to locate the edges over supports when the board is applied parallel to the supports or from failing to fasten the edges to the supports.

20. Installing boards having damaged edges or ends or leaving boards with damaged edges or ends in place. Boards experiencing edge or end damage either before or during application should not be left in place with the damage concealed by joint treatment materials. Damaged edges will not remain concealed over the life of the installation.

21. Scoring or cutting the board's paper face beyond the edge of a cutout.

22. Failing to remove burrs from cut ends and edges of boards.

23. Failing to stagger end joints, which makes them more visible and weakens the system.
24. Locating end joints in the center of walls and ceilings, which makes them move visible.
25. Failing to close joints in gypsum sheathing.
26. Failing to use large sheathing boards where structural performance is required; failing to place such boards with the long edge vertical.
27. Locating joints—other than expansion or control joints—at opening corners.

Improper Fastener, Accessory, or Adhesive Application. Examples include:

1. Using the wrong nail type. Ring-shank nails are less likely to pop than plain-shank nails, for example.
2. Using the wrong screw type, which may cause the screws to loosen.
3. Using fasteners that will rust in locations where they will become wet.
4. Using defective fasteners. Fasteners with deformed heads can penetrate the board's paper facing, for example.
5. Using fasteners that are too large in diameter.
6. Using fasteners that are too small in diameter.
7. Using fasteners that are too short to properly engage the supports.
8. Using nails that are too long. Nails should be the shortest that will adequately support the board. Nails that are too long contribute to loose boards, nail popping, and other failures.
9. Using nails with heads that are too large. When heads are large, even a slight offset during driving will tear the paper facing.
10. Using nails with heads that are too small. Common nails and other nails whose heads are small relative to their shank diameter will not hold the board in place.
11. Using the wrong kind of hammer. Hammers should be a crown-headed type that produce a uniform dimple (depression) around the nail heads.
12. Failing to hold the board firmly against the framing or furring while driving fasteners. Failing to place initial fasteners near the center of the boards and succeeding fasteners in a progressively outward direction toward the edges will often cause panels not to be held tightly to the supports during fastening. Driving fasteners will not pull loosely held boards into tight contact with the framing or furring.
13. Using an improperly adjusted screwdriver. This may cause screws to be left loose.

14. Using too few fasteners, which will leave the boards loose and able to sag, bow, or flex. Flexing will force fasteners deeper into the board, which will depress the fill over the fastener heads.

15. Underdriving fasteners (not driving them in far enough). Fasteners should be driven into proper contact with the board, creating the correct depth and size of dimple in the surface, while not damaging the paper or crushing the core.

16. Overdriving fasteners (driving them in too far) and not driving fasteners straight. Overdriven and crooked fasteners will probably penetrate the paper surface or crush the board's core, or both, and will not support the board properly. Fasteners driven using the wrong type of hammer or an improperly adjusted screwdriver can puncture the board's paper face and damage the board's core. When wet joint compound is applied to broken surface paper, the board may swell and bulge.

17. Missing the framing or furring with the fasteners. Such fasteners cannot support the boards.

18. Driving fasteners into flexible or extremely hard wood framing or furring. These fasteners may not penetrate the correct amount or may twist or break off.

19. Failing to redrive fasteners loosened by pounding adjacent to the fasteners or on the opposite side of the partition. Loosened fasteners should be redriven at the time the gypsum board is installed, but often are not.

20. Failing to properly fasten sheathing.

21. Using accessories of the wrong type. Using plastic edge beads where joints must be taped is an example; using accessories that will rust in exterior locations is another.

22. Using accessories of the wrong size.

23. Failing to install proper control, expansion, and isolation joints in correct locations.

24. Failing to properly attach edge trim or corner bead flanges.

25. Failing to properly support adhesive-applied gypsum board until the adhesive has set.

26. Failing to force the entire surface of gypsum board installed using contact adhesives into contact with the supports until the adhesive has set. The board should be pounded into place over its entire surface with a rubber mallet or other suitable tool.

27. Using contact adhesives on irregular surfaces so that gaps remain.

Improper Joint or Fastener Finishing.   Examples include:

1. Failing to provide the correct ratio of water to dry compound.

2. Using too much water in the joint compound.

3. Using dirty water in the joint compound.
4. Using old joint compound.
5. Overmixing the joint compound, trapping air bubbles in it.
6. Using the wrong compound (taping instead of topping, for example).
7. Using topping compound instead of bedding compound to bed tape.
8. Failing to properly apply the joint compound, including (but not limited to) using too little pressure when applying the compound.
9. Applying too much joint compound beneath the tape.
10. Applying too little joint compound beneath the tape.
11. Applying too much joint compound either beneath or over the tape.
12. Applying too little joint compound over the tape.
13. Applying too much joint compound over the tape. This is a failure symptom only when the tape is still intact.
14. Failing to pre-wet the paper tape before installing it. Tape that is not pre-wet will absorb too much moisture from the topping compound, which will cause the compound to shrink into the tape's configuration.
15. Applying too much water to the tape, which can cause loss of bond between the joint compound and the tape.
16. Not properly bedding the tape. Failing to press tape into the compound, for example.
17. Applying too much pressure to the tape, thereby forcing too much compound out from beneath the tape.
18. Failing to cover embedded tape with a skim coat of joint compound.
19. Applying too little joint compound to finish the fastener heads.
20. Bad finishing technique.
21. Sanding joint compound too much, which leaves visible depressions.
22. Finishing the joint too high. Joints should finish just slightly higher than the surface of the board. Anything higher will result in shadowing. High joints are caused by applying too much joint compound or by not feathering the compound out onto the gypsum board.
23. Permitting significant differences to occur in the porosity of the board and the joint compounds, which affects the final appearance of the board after it has been painted, because the paint does not adhere equally to all surfaces.
24. Scoring or slitting the tape during application or finishing. Joint tape is sometimes damaged when the finisher uses the wrong tool, but more often the tape is deliberately split or scored to make the joint easier to finish when the tape has been improperly installed.
25. Failing to allow sufficient time for joint compound coats at joints and fastener heads to properly dry before applying the next compound coat or the board finish, such as paint.

26. Permitting the joint compound to dry too rapidly.
27. Permitting large or rapid temperature fluctuations to occur during the application or curing of joint compounds.
28. Failing to caulk between gypsum board and adjacent materials, which permits water to enter the space behind the gypsum board.
29. Failing to tape or improperly taping veneer plaster gypsum base joints.

Failing to Protect the Gypsum Board.   Reasons for failure include:

1. Allowing gypsum board or joint finishing materials to freeze.
2. Permitting water to contact the board (Fig. 4-12).
3. Permitting high humidity conditions to exist during gypsum board storage or installation; during or after joint treatment application or curing; during finish application or curing; or after the gypsum board system has been installed and finished. Hygrometric expansion due to the gypsum board absorbing water when high humidity is present,

Figure 4-12   Water entering from the exterior caused the damage shown in this photograph. (*Photo by author.*)

and later contraction when the air becomes dry, will cause cracks, board sag, bowed or wavy board surfaces, and joint treatment problems. Too much humidity during application and curing can cause loss of the bond between joint compounds and tape.

4. Permitting humidity to become too low in the application area permits boards to dry out excessively, which can make the paper covering brittle and lead to its tearing during fastening. Low humidity can also cause joint compounds to dry out too rapidly, which will make them shrink and crack.

5. Permitting temperatures to get excessively high or low or fluctuate too much in the installation area, either during or after board application and finishing, or during joint compound application or curing. Fluctuations often result from poor heat distribution. High temperatures can cause joint compounds to dry out too fast and crack, especially when the humidity is low. Extreme temperature fluctuations cause excessive thermal expansion and contraction in wood framing and furring and in gypsum board, and lead to joint treatment failures.

6. Permitting large temperature variations to occur after gypsum board finishing. This may be caused by poor building ventilation or inadequate heating. Large variations cause excessive expansion and contraction cycles, which can cause nails to work loose and pop.

7. Permitting the building's framing or walls to transmit cold outdoor temperatures to interior surfaces. Airborne dust collects on colder areas along gypsum board supports, especially at fasteners, and darkens the surface at those locations.

8. Permitting excessive ventilation or drafts to occur during joint finishing or compound curing, which causes joint compounds to dry too rapidly.

9. Permitting cold, wet conditions to occur in the area where joints are being finished or cured.

10. Permitting impacts to damage edge trim or corner beads.

11. Permitting the board's paper finish to be exposed to sunlight before painting, which can darken the paper.

12. Using cheap paint or improperly painting the gypsum board.

13. Permitting abuse to occur after the board has been installed.

14. Permitting sheathing to become wet.

15. Not applying felt or other impervious material over gypsum sheathing where stucco or the insulation portion of an EIFS occurs; where square edge sheathing is applied with the long edge horizontal; where sheathing with a plain (not water-resistant) core is to be exposed to the weather after application; and in other locations where such covering is recommended.

16. Leaving gypsum plaster lath exposed on the exterior with no plaster covering.

Evidence of Failure in Gypsum Board Systems

Gypsum board system failures, where the gypsum board is exposed, may appear as wavy, loose, sagged, bowed, soft, disintegrated, cracked, punctured, stained, or discolored gypsum board; beaded or ridged joints; nail pops; bulged or depressed fasteners; tape or fastener photographing; blisters; debonded compound; or shadowing.

Failure of gypsum board that is covered by other materials, such as plaster or ceramic tile, may be apparent only when the covering material fails. The evidence of the failure will vary, depending on the covering material.

In the following paragraphs, gypsum board failures are divided into: "Standard Gypsum Board and Veneer Plaster Gypsum Base Failures" which includes all applications of regular, Type X, foil-faced, water-resistant, and exterior gypsum board, and veneer plaster gypsum base; "Gypsum Sheathing for EIFS Failures"; "Other Gypsum Sheathing Failures"; "Gypsum Plaster Lath Failures"; and "Predecorated Gypsum Board Failures." These categories are further subdivided into failure types, such as "Loose or Sagging Ceiling Boards." Under each failure type heading, one or more numbers is listed. The numbers represent possible causes for that failure type.

A description of the numbered failure causes that follow "Structure Failure," "Structure Movement," "Solid Substrate Problems," "Other Building Element Problems," "Wood Framing and Furring Problems," and "Metal Framing and Furring Problems" appear in Chapter 2 under these headings, each of which is listed in the Contents. For example, clarification and explanation of the numbered cause (1) listed in the example

▪ Metal Framing and Furring Problems: 1 (see Chapter 2).

appears in Chapter 2 under the heading "Metal Framing and Furring Problems," cause 1, which reads

1. Metal framing or furring that is out of alignment.

A description and discussion of the numbered causes that follow "Bad Materials," "Bad System Design," and "Bad Workmanship" appear as subparagraphs and sub-subparagraphs in the part of this chapter titled "Why Gypsum Board Systems Fail," which is listed in the Contents. For example, clarification of the numbered cause (2) listed in the example

▪ Bad Workmanship: Improper Substrate Preparation: 2.

appears in this chapter under the heading "Why Gypsum Board Systems Fail," subparagraph "Bad Workmanship," sub-subparagraph "Improper Substrate Preparation," cause 2, which reads

2. Failing to achieve the correct surface tolerance.

Glass mesh mortar units are covered separately later in this chapter.

Standard Gypsum Board and Veneer Plaster Gypsum Base Failures

Unusual Sounds, Such as Grinding or Squeaking Noises. Such sounds often increase in loudness or occur only when additional load or pressure is applied. A person walking across a floor above a gypsum board ceiling can generate squeaks or popping sounds, for example. Such sounds are caused by one of the following:

- Structure Failure: 1 (see Chapter 2).
- Structure Movement: 1, 2, 3, 4, 6, 7 (see Chapter 2).
- Wood Framing and Furring Problems: 2, 7, 8 (see Chapter 2).
- Metal Framing and Furring Problems: 3, 4 (see Chapter 2).

Wavy Board Surfaces. This problem may be caused by one of the following:

- Structure Failure: 1 (see Chapter 2).
- Structure Movement: 2, 3, 4, 5, 7, 8 (see Chapter 2).
- Solid Substrate Problems: 1, 2, 3, 4 (see Chapter 2).
- Other Building Element Problems: 1, 2, 3 (see Chapter 2).
- Wood Framing and Furring Problems: 1, 2, 5, 7, 8 (see Chapter 2).
- Metal Framing and Furring Problems: 1, 3, 4 (see Chapter 2).
- Bad System Design: Failing to Require Proper Preparation Methods: 1.
- Bad System Design: Selecting Improper Application Methods: 1, 2, 4, 5, 6, 7, 10.
- Bad Workmanship: Improper Substrate Preparation: 1, 2, 3, 4, 5, 6.
- Bad Workmanship: Improper Storage and Handling of Materials: 1.
- Bad Workmanship: Improper Board Placement: 1, 2, 3, 5, 6, 9, 10, 12, 15.
- Bad Workmanship: Improper Fastener, Accessory, or Adhesive Application: 12, 14, 19.
- Bad Workmanship: Failing to Protect the Gypsum Board: 3, 5, 6.

Loose or Sagging Ceiling Boards. This failure may be caused by one of the following:

- Structure Failure: 1 (see Chapter 2).
- Structure Movement: 1, 2, 3, 4, 5, 6, 7, 8 (see Chapter 2).
- Other Building Element Problems: 1, 2, 3 (see Chapter 2).
- Wood Framing and Furring Problems: 1, 2, 3, 5, 6, 7 (see Chapter 2).
- Metal Framing and Furring Problems: 1, 2, 3 (see Chapter 2).
- Bad System Design: Wrong Accessories or Fasteners: 2, 3.
- Bad System Design: Failing to Require Proper Preparation Methods: 1.
- Bad System Design: Selecting Improper Application Methods: 1, 2, 3, 4, 5, 10.
- Bad Workmanship: Improper Substrate Preparation: 1, 2, 3, 4, 5, 6.
- Bad Workmanship: Improper Storage and Handling of Materials: 1.
- Bad Workmanship: Improper Board Placement: 1, 2, 3, 9, 10, 12, 15, 16, 18, 19.
- Bad Workmanship: Improper Fastener, Accessory, or Adhesive Application: 1, 2, 4, 6, 7, 8, 9, 10, 12, 13, 14, 16, 17, 18, 19, 23, 25, 26, 27.
- Bad Workmanship: Failing to Protect the Gypsum Board: 2, 3.

Loose or Bowing Wall Boards. May be caused by one of the following:

- Structure Failure: 1 (see Chapter 2).
- Structure Movement: 1, 2, 3, 4, 5, 6, 7, 8 (see Chapter 2).
- Solid Substrate Problems: 1, 2, 3, 4 (see Chapter 2).
- Other Building Element Problems: 1, 2 (see Chapter 2).
- Wood Framing and Furring Problems: 1, 2, 3, 5, 6, 7, 8 (see Chapter 2).
- Metal Framing and Furring Problems: 1, 2, 3, 4 (see Chapter 2).
- Bad System Design: Wrong Accessories or Fasteners: 2, 3.
- Bad System Design: Failing to Require Proper Preparation Methods: 1.
- Bad System Design: Selecting Improper Application Methods: 1, 2, 5, 6, 7, 10.
- Bad Workmanship: Improper Substrate Preparation: 1, 2, 3, 4, 5, 6.
- Bad Workmanship: Improper Storage and Handling of Materials: 1.
- Bad Workmanship: Improper Board Placement: 1, 2, 3, 5, 6, 9, 10, 12, 15, 17, 18, 19.
- Bad Workmanship: Improper Fastener, Accessory, or Adhesive Application: 1, 2, 4, 6, 7, 8, 9, 10, 12, 13, 14, 16, 17, 18, 19, 25, 26, 27.
- Bad Workmanship: Failing to Protect the Gypsum Board: 2, 3.

Soft or Disintegrating Boards.   May be caused by one of the following:

- Solid Substrate Problems: 1 (see Chapter 2).
- Other Building Element Problems: 1, 2 (see Chapter 2).
- Bad Materials: 2, 5, 6.
- Bad System Design: Wrong Gypsum Board Material: 1, 3.
- Bad System Design: Selecting Improper Application Methods: 3, 6, 7.
- Bad Workmanship: Improper Storage and Handling of Materials: 3, 4.
- Bad Workmanship: Improper Board Placement: 5, 6, 9.
- Bad Workmanship: Failing to Protect the Gypsum Board: 2, 3, 4, 9, 13, 28.

Board Cracks.   Cracks in the board itself often appear as diagonal cracks which start in a room corner, or where the gypsum board contacts a structural element, or at the corner of an opening (Fig. 4-13). Cracks may penetrate only the surface of the board or extend completely through. Cracks extending completely through the board are sometimes called fractures. Board cracks are caused by one of the following:

- Structure Failure: 1 (see Chapter 2).
- Structure Movement: 1, 2, 3, 4, 5, 6, 7, 8 (see Chapter 2).
- Solid Substrate Problems: 2, 3, 4 (see Chapter 2).
- Wood Framing and Furring Problems: 1, 2, 7, 8 (see Chapter 2).
- Metal Framing and Furring Problems: 1, 2, 4 (see Chaper 2).
- Bad System Design: Selecting Improper Application Methods: 1, 9, 10, 11.
- Bad Workmanship: Improper Storage and Handling of Materials: 2, 3, 4.
- Bad Workmanship: Improper Board Placement: 1, 2, 4, 8, 15, 21, 23.
- Bad Workmanship: Failing to Protect the Gypsum Board: 13.

Flat-Surface and Corner Joint Cracks.   Cracks may appear along the edge of the tape over a joint, along the edge of edge trim or corner beads, or along the center of the joint itself.

Cracks occurring along the center of a joint may be caused by one of the following:

- Structure Failure: 1 (see Chapter 2).
- Structure Movement: 1, 2, 3, 4, 5, 6, 7, 8 (see Chapter 2).
- Solid Substrate Problems: 2, 3, 4 (see Chapter 2).
- Wood Framing and Furring Problems: 1, 2, 4, 7, 8 (see Chapter 2).
- Metal Framing and Furring Problems: 1, 3, 4 (see Chapter 2).

Figure 4-13
Crack at the
corner of an
opening. (*Photo
by author.*)

- Bad System Design: Selecting Improper Application Methods: 1, 2, 9, 10.
- Bad Workmanship: Improper Board Placement: 1, 2, 4, 8, 11, 12, 13, 15, 16, 17, 18, 19, 27.
- Bad Workmanship: Improper Fastener, Accessory, or Adhesive Application: 23.
- Bad Workmanship: Improper Joint or Fastener Finishing: 1, 2, 3, 4, 6, 8, 11, 12, 20, 24, 25, 26, 27.
- Bad Workmanship: Failing to Protect the Gypsum Board: 2, 3, 5, 6, 8, 9, 13.

Cracks along the edge of joint tape, edge trim, or corner beads are caused by one of the following:

- Bad Materials: 4.
- Bad System Design: Wrong Accessories or Fasteners: 1.
- Bad Workmanship: Improper Substrate Preparation: 1.
- Bad Workmanship: Improper Fastener, Accessory, or Adhesive Application: 21, 22, 24.
- Bad Workmanship: Improper Joint or Fastener Finishing: 1, 2, 3, 4, 6, 7, 8, 9, 15, 18, 25, 26, 27.
- Bad Workmanship: Failing to Protect the Gypsum Board: 1, 3, 4, 5, 8, 9, 10.

Punctures and Board Surface Depressions. Holes in gypsum board surfaces may extend partly (depressions) or completely (punctures) through the board. Such holes may be caused by the following:

- Failing to Protect the Gypsum Board: 13.

Stains and Discolorations. Stains may be caused by fungus, such as mildew, or may be chemical stains. Board may be discolored by water (Fig. 4-14) or other materials. Staining and discolorations may be caused by:

- Solid Substrate Problems: 1 (see Chapter 2).
- Other Building Element Problems: 1, 2 (see Chapter 2).
- Bad Materials: 3, 4, 5.
- Bad System Design: Wrong Accessories or Fasteners: 1.
- Bad System Design: Failing to Require Proper Preparation Methods: 1.
- Bad System Design: Selecting Improper Application Methods: 3, 6, 7.
- Bad Workmanship: Improper Substrate Preparation: 1.
- Bad Workmanship: Improper Board Placement: 5, 6, 9.
- Bad Workmanship: Improper Fastener, Accessory, or Adhesive Application: 3, 21.
- Bad Workmanship: Improper Joint or Fastener Finishing: 3, 20, 23, 25.
- Bad Workmanship: Failing to Protect the Gypsum Board: 2, 9, 11, 12.

Joint Beading or Ridging. Beading or ridging is a condition in which the finished surface of the joint topping compound raises, forming a bead or ridge (Fig. 4-15). Beading or ridging results from:

- Structure Failure: 1 (see Chapter 2).
- Structure Movement: 1, 2, 3, 4, 5, 6, 7 (see Chapter 2).

Figure 4-14   Water from cleaning the floor above stained this gypsum board ceiling. (*Photo by author.*)

- Solid Substrate Problems: 2, 3, 4 (see Chapter 2).
- Wood Framing and Furring Problems: 1, 4, 6, 8 (see Chapter 2).
- Metal Framing and Furring Problems: 1, 2, 4 (see Chapter 2).
- Bad System Design: Selecting Improper Application Methods: 1, 2, 10.
- Bad Workmanship: Improper Storage and Handling of Materials: 2, 3, 4.
- Bad Workmanship: Improper Board Placement: 2, 8, 11, 13, 18, 19, 20, 22.

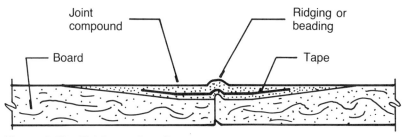

Figure 4-15   Ridging or beading.

■ Bad Workmanship: Improper Joint or Fastener Finishing: 11.
■ Bad Workmanship: Failing to Protect the Gypsum Board: 3, 5.

Fastener Pops.   A condition in which the joint finishing compound over a fastener raises or pops out, leaving the fastener head exposed (Fig. 4-16). Nail pops are much more common than screw pops, because screws have a larger holding capacity than nails. Nail pops, which are affected by gravity, are caused by one of the following:

■ Structure Movement: 6, 7 (see Chapter 2).
■ Wood Framing and Furring Problems: 1, 2, 3, 4, 6 (see Chapter 2).
■ Metal Framing and Furring Problems: 1, 2 (see Chapter 2).
■ Bad System Design: Wrong Accessories or Fasteners: 1, 2, 3.
■ Bad Workmanship: Improper Board Placement: 2, 3, 8, 12.
■ Bad Workmanship: Improper Fastener, Accessory, or Adhesive Application: 1, 3, 5, 7, 8, 11, 12, 15, 18, 19.
■ Bad Workmanship: Improper Joint or Fastener Finishing: 19, 20.
■ Bad Workmanship: Failing to Protect the Gypsum Board: 5, 6.

Figure 4-16   A nail pop. (*Photo by author.*)

Screws may also raise up or pop out for many of the same reasons nails pop, or for one of the following reasons:

■ Bad System Design: Wrong Accessories or Fasteners: 2, 3.
■ Bad Workmanship: Improper Fastener, Accessory, or Adhesive Application: 2, 13.

Fastener Depressions. Depressed areas over fasteners are caused by:

■ Wood Framing and Furring Problems: 1, 3, 5 (see Chapter 2).
■ Metal Framing and Furring Problems: 1 (see Chapter 2).
■ Bad Materials: 6.
■ Bad System Design: Wrong Accessories or Fasteners: 2, 3.
■ Bad Workmanship: Improper Board Placement: 2, 3, 12.
■ Bad Workmanship: Improper Fastener, Accessory, or Adhesive Application: 1, 2, 4, 9, 11, 12, 14, 16, 18.
■ Bad Workmanship: Improper Joint or Fastener Finishing: 8, 19, 20, 21.
■ Bad Workmanship: Failing to Protect the Gypsum Board: 4, 5, 8.

Fastener Bulging. Bulges around fasteners may be the first sign of impending fastener pops, but not necessarily so. They may also be caused by:

■ Bad Workmanship: Improper Fastener, Accessory, or Adhesive Application: 4, 9, 11, 12, 13, 16.

Joint Depressions. A depressed line occurring at joints can be caused by one of the following:

■ Wood Framing and Furring Problems: 1 (see Chapter 2).
■ Metal Framing and Furring Problems: 1 (see Chapter 2).
■ Bad Workmanship: Improper Board Placement: 2.
■ Bad Workmanship: Improper Joint or Fastener Finishing: 12, 21.

Tape and Fastener Photographing. Tape or fasteners may be apparent (Fig. 4-17) after joints or fasteners are finished for the following reasons:

■ Bad Workmanship: Improper Joint or Fastener Finishing: 9, 12, 14, 19, 25.

Blisters. Two types of blisters affect gypsum board work.

One type, tape blisters, occur at joints and range in size from very small to several inches long. They happen when the bond is broken between

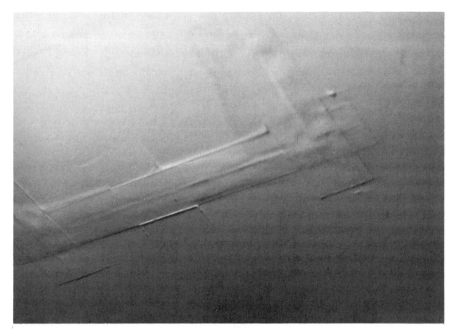

Figure 4-17   A really bad case of tape photographing. There is no topping compound here at all. (*Photo by author.*)

the tape and the bedding compound, usually for one of the following reasons:

- Bad Workmanship: Improper Board Placement: 13.
- Bad Workmanship: Improper Joint or Fastener Finishing: 2, 7, 10, 14, 16, 17.

The second type of blisters that affect gypsum board occur in the gypsum board panels themselves. They are caused by:

- Solid Substrate Problems: 1 (see Chapter 2).
- Other Building Element Problems: 1, 2 (see Chapter 2).
- Bad Materials: 2, 7.
- Bad System Design: Selecting Improper Application Methods: 6, 7.
- Bad Workmanship: Improper Storage and Handling of Materials: 4.
- Bad Workmanship: Improper Board Placement: 5, 6, 9.
- Bad Workmanship: Failing to Protect the Gypsum Board: 2, 3, 9.

Compound Debonding.   The reasons that topping compound will not bond to the gypsum board or to the joint tape include the following:

- Bad Materials: 4.
- Bad System Design: Failing to Require Proper Preparation Methods: 1.
- Bad Workmanship: Improper Substrate Preparation: 1.
- Bad Workmanship: Improper Joint or Fastener Finishing: 1, 3, 4, 12, 18, 25.

Pitting.   There are several reasons that small pits might appear in finished joint compound, including:

- Bad Workmanship: Improper Joint or Fastener Finishing: 2, 5, 8.

Shadowing.   The condition in which joints are apparent in the completed work for reasons other than joint discoloration, beading or ridging, joint depressions, nail pops, fastener depressions, tape and fastener photographing, or tape blisters is called shadowing. There are several reasons for shadowing, including:

- Wood Framing and Furring Problems: 1 (see Chapter 2).
- Metal Framing and Furring Problems: 1 (see Chapter 2).
- Bad System Design: Wrong Accessories or Fasteners: 2, 3.
- Bad Workmanship: Improper Board Placement: 2, 14, 23, 24.
- Bad Workmanship: Improper Fastener, Accessory, or Adhesive Application: 1, 2, 12, 13.
- Bad Workmanship: Improper Joint or Fastener Finishing: 16, 22, 23, 25.
- Bad Workmanship: Failing to Protect the Gypsum Board: 7.

Gypsum Sheathing for EIFS Failures.   Failures of gypsum sheathing that lead to EIFS failures are also discussed in Chapter 3. Reasons for failure include the following:

- Structure Failure: 1 (see Chapter 2).
- Structure Movement: 1, 2, 3, 4, 5, 6, 7 (see Chapter 2).
- Solid Substrate Problems: 1, 2, 3, 4 (see Chapter 2).
- Other Building Element Problems: 1, 2 (see Chapter 2).
- Wood Framing and Furring Problems: 1, 2, 3, 4, 5, 6, 7, 8 (see Chapter 2).
- Metal Framing and Furring Problems: 1, 2, 3, 4 (see Chapter 2).
- Bad Materials: 1, 2, 5, 6.
- Bad System Design: Wrong Gypsum Board Material: 4.
- Bad System Design: Wrong Accessories or Fasteners: 1, 2, 3.

- Bad System Design: Failing to Require Proper Preparation Methods: 1.
- Bad System Design: Selecting Improper Application Methods: 1, 2, 3, 5, 10.
- Bad Workmanship: Improper Substrate Preparation: 1, 2, 6.
- Bad Workmanship: Improper Storage and Handling of Materials: 1, 2, 3, 4.
- Bad Workmanship: Improper Board Placement: 1, 2, 3, 8, 9, 10, 11, 12, 13, 15, 18, 19, 23, 25, 26.
- Bad Workmanship: Improper Fastener, Accessory, or Adhesive Application: 1, 2, 3, 4, 5, 6, 7, 8, 9, 10, 12, 13, 14, 15, 16, 17, 18, 19, 20, 23.
- Bad Workmanship: Failing to Protect the Gypsum Board: 13, 14, 15.

Other Gypsum Sheathing Failures

Structural Failure. Most structural failures are caused by design or workmanship errors in the structure itself. Sheathing that serves a structural function can, however, contribute to structural failure. Gypsum sheathing problems that can cause structure failure include the following:

- Bad Materials: 1, 2, 5, 6, 7.
- Bad System Design: Wrong Accessories or Fasteners. 1, 2, 3.
- Bad System Design: Failing to Require Proper Preparation Methods: 1.
- Bad System Design: Selecting Improper Application Methods: 3, 5, 10.
- Bad Workmanship: Improper Substrate Preparation: 1, 2, 6.
- Bad Workmanship: Improper Storage and Handling of Materials: 1, 2, 3, 4.
- Bad Workmanship: Improper Board Placement: 2, 3, 8, 9, 10, 11, 12, 13, 15, 18, 19, 23, 25, 26.
- Bad Workmanship: Improper Fastener, Accessory, or Adhesive Application: 1, 2, 3, 4, 5, 6, 7, 8, 9, 10, 12, 13, 14, 15, 16, 17, 18, 19, 20, 23.
- Bad Workmanship: Failing to Protect the Gypsum Board: 13, 14, 15.

Other Sheathing Failures. Unfortunately, damaged sheathing will seldom be apparent until something else fails. Air leaking into interior spaces is a common symptom of gypsum sheathing problems, for example. Many sheathing failures result from one of the following:

- Structure Failure: 1 (see Chapter 2).
- Structure Movement: 1, 2, 3, 4, 5, 6, 7 (see Chapter 2).

- Solid Substrate Problems: 1, 2, 3, 4 (see Chapter 2).
- Other Building Element Problems: 1 (see Chapter 2).
- Wood Framing and Furring Problems: 1, 2, 3, 4, 5, 6, 7, 8 (see Chapter 2).
- Metal Framing and Furring Problems: 1, 2, 3, 4 (see Chapter 2).
- Bad Materials: 1, 2, 5, 6, 7.
- Bad System Design: Wrong Accessories or Fasteners: 1, 2, 3.
- Bad System Design: Failing to Require Proper Preparation Methods: 1.
- Bad System Design: Selecting Improper Application Methods: 1, 2, 3, 5, 10.
- Bad Workmanship: Improper Substrate Preparation: 1, 2, 6.
- Bad Workmanship: Improper Storage and Handling of Materials: 1, 2, 3, 4.
- Bad Workmanship: Improper Board Placement: 1, 2, 3, 8, 9, 10, 11, 12, 13, 15, 18, 19, 23, 25.
- Bad Workmanship: Improper Fastener, Accessory, or Adhesive Application: 1, 2, 3, 4, 5, 6, 7, 8, 9, 10, 12, 13, 14, 15, 16, 17, 18, 19, 20, 23.
- Bad Workmanship: Failing to Protect the Gypsum Board: 13, 14, 15.

Gypsum Plaster Lath Failures.   Failure in the lath will be visible in the plaster. Evidence of standard thickness plaster over gypsum lath failures, and the possible reasons for these failures, are discussed in Chapter 3. Among the reasons that plaster fails is a failure of gypsum plaster lath. The reasons that gypsum lath fails include the following:

Wavy Surfaces.   May be caused by one of the following:

- Structure Failures: 1 (see Chapter 2).
- Structure Movement: 2, 3, 4, 5, 7, 8 (see Chapter 2).
- Solid Substrate Problems: 1, 2, 3, 4 (see Chapter 2).
- Other Building Element Problems: 1, 2, 3 (see Chapter 2).
- Wood Framing and Furring Problems: 1, 2, 5, 7, 8 (see Chapter 2).
- Metal Framing and Furring Problems: 1, 3, 4 (see Chapter 2).
- Bad System Design: Failing to Require Proper Preparation Methods: 1.
- Bad System Design: Selecting Improper Application Methods: 1, 2, 4, 5, 6, 7, 10.
- Bad Workmanship: Improper Substrate Preparation: 1, 2, 3, 4, 5, 6.
- Bad Workmanship: Improper Storage and Handling of Materials: 1.

- Bad Workmanship: Improper Board Placement: 1, 2, 3, 5, 6, 9, 10, 12, 15.
- Bad Workmanship: Improper Fastener, Accessory, or Adhesive Application: 12, 14, 19.
- Bad Workmanship: Failing to Protect the Gypsum Board: 3, 5, 6.

Loose or Sagging Ceiling Surfaces. May be caused by one of the following:

- Structure Failure: 1 (see Chapter 2).
- Structure Movement: 1, 2, 3, 4, 5, 6, 7, 8 (see Chapter 2).
- Other Building Element Problems: 1, 2, 3 (see Chapter 2).
- Wood Framing and Furring Problems: 1, 2, 3, 5, 6, 7 (see Chapter 2).
- Metal Framing and Furring Problems: 1, 2, 3 (see Chapter 2).
- Bad System Design: Wrong Gypsum Board Materials: 1.
- Bad System Design: Wrong Accessories or Fasteners: 2, 3.
- Bad System Design: Failing to Require Proper Preparation Methods: 1.
- Bad System Design: Selecting Improper Application Methods: 1, 2, 3, 4, 5, 10.
- Bad Workmanship: Improper Substrate Preparation: 1, 2, 3, 4, 5, 6.
- Bad Workmanship: Improper Storage and Handling of Materials: 1.
- Bad Workmanship: Improper Board Placement: 1, 2, 3, 9, 10, 12, 15, 16, 17, 18, 19.
- Bad Workmanship: Improper Fastener, Accessory, or Adhesive Application: 1, 2, 4, 6, 7, 8, 9, 10, 12, 13, 14, 16, 17, 18, 19, 23, 25, 26, 27.
- Bad Workmanship: Failing to Protect the Gypsum Board: 2, 3.

Loose or Bowing Wall Surfaces: May be caused by one of the following:

- Structure Failure: 1 (see Chapter 2).
- Structure Movement: 1, 2, 3, 4, 5, 6, 7, 8 (see Chapter 2).
- Solid Substrate Problems: 1, 2, 3, 4 (see Chapter 2).
- Other Building Element Problems: 1, 2 (see Chapter 2).
- Wood Framing and Furring Problems: 1, 2, 3, 5, 6, 7, 8 (see Chapter 2).
- Metal Framing and Furring Problems: 1, 2, 3, 4 (see Chapter 2).
- Bad System Design: Wrong Gypsum Board Materials: 1, 3.
- Bad System Design: Wrong Accessories or Fasteners: 2, 3.
- Bad System Design: Failing to Require Proper Preparation Methods: 1.

- Bad System Design: Selecting Improper Application Methods: 1, 2, 5, 6, 7, 10.
- Bad Workmanship: Improper Substrate Preparation: 1, 2, 3, 4, 5, 6.
- Bad Workmanship: Improper Storage and Handling of Materials: 1.
- Bad Workmanship: Improper Board Placement: 1, 2, 3, 5, 6, 9, 10, 12, 15, 17, 18, 19.
- Bad Workmanship: Improper Fastener, Accessory, or Adhesive Application: 1, 2, 4, 6, 7, 8, 9, 10, 12, 13, 14, 16, 17, 18, 19, 25, 26, 27.
- Bad Workmanship: Failing to Protect the Gypsum Board: 2, 3.

Soft or Disintegrating Lath

- Solid Substrate Problems: 1 (see Chapter 2).
- Other Building Element Problems: 1, 2 (see Chapter 2).
- Bad Materials: 2, 5, 6.
- Bad System Design: Wrong Gypsum Board Materials: 1, 2, 3.
- Bad System Design: Selecting Improper Application Methods: 3, 6, 7.
- Bad Workmanship: Improper Storage and Handling of Materials: 3, 4.
- Bad Workmanship: Improper Board Placement: 5, 6, 9.
- Bad Workmanship: Failing to Protect the Gypsum Board: 2, 3, 4, 9, 13, 28.

Lath Cracks.   Lath cracks often appear as diagonal cracks in the plaster, starting in a room corner where the gypsum lath contacts a structural element, or at the corner of an opening. Lath cracks are caused by one of the following:

- Structure Failure: 1 (see Chapter 2).
- Structure Movement: 1, 2, 3, 4, 5, 6, 7, 8 (see Chapter 2).
- Solid Substrate Problems: 2, 3, 4 (see Chapter 2).
- Wood Framing and Furring Problems: 1, 2, 7, 8 (see Chapter 2).
- Metal Framing and Furring Problems: 1, 3, 4 (see Chapter 2).
- Bad System Design: Selecting Improper Application Methods: 1, 9, 10, 11.
- Bad Workmanship: Improper Storage and Handling of Materials: 2, 3, 4.
- Bad Workmanship: Improper Board Placement: 1, 2, 4, 8, 15, 21, 23.
- Bad Workmanship: Failing to Protect the Gypsum Board: 13.

Fastener Pops. Nail pops are caused by one of the following:

- Structure Movement: 6, 7 (see Chapter 2).
- Wood Framing and Furring Problems: 1, 2, 3, 4, 6 (see Chapter 2).
- Metal Framing and Furring Problems: 1, 2 (see Chapter 2).
- Bad System Design: Wrong Accessories or Fasteners: 1, 2, 3.
- Bad Workmanship: Improper Board Placement: 2, 3, 8, 12.
- Bad Workmanship: Improper Fastener, Accessory, or Adhesive Application: 1, 3, 5, 7, 8, 11, 12, 15, 18, 19.
- Bad Workmanship: Improper Joint or Fastener Finishing: 19, 20.
- Bad Workmanship: Failing to Protect the Gypsum Board: 5, 6.

Screws may also raise up or pop out for many of the same reasons nails pop, or for one of the following reasons:

- Bad System Design: Wrong Accessories or Fasteners: 2, 3.
- Bad Workmanship: Improper Fastener, Accessory, or Adhesive Application: 2, 13.

Fastener Depressions. Depressed areas over fasteners are caused by:

- Wood Framing and Furring Problems: 1, 3, 5 (see Chapter 2).
- Metal Framing and Furring Problems: 1 (see Chapter 2).
- Bad Materials: 6.
- Bad System Design: Wrong Accessories or Fasteners: 2, 3.
- Bad Workmanship: Improper Board Placement: 2, 3, 12.
- Bad Workmanship: Improper Fastener, Accessory, or Adhesive Application: 1, 2, 4, 9, 11, 12, 14, 16, 18.
- Bad Workmanship: Improper Joint or Fastener Finishing: 8, 19, 20, 21.
- Bad Workmanship: Failing to Protect the Gypsum Board: 4, 5, 8.

Predecorated Gypsum Board Failures. Evidence of failure in predecorated gypsum board is generally the same as that for standard gypsum board, and the reasons given earlier in this chapter for failures in standard gypsum board apply. Damage may be more apparent in predecorated boards, however, particularly if the facing material is smooth or glossy. In addition, predecorated board is subject to damage due to the following:

- Bad System Design: Selecting Improper Application Methods: 8.
- Bad Workmanship: Improper Board Placement: 7.

Repairing and Extending Existing Gypsum Board

Most gypsum board products can be repaired (Fig. 4-18). When the damage is extensive or severe, however, it may make more sense to remove the existing gypsum board and install new materials. When the damage is less severe, but still significant, it may be better to leave the existing material in place and cover it with a new layer of gypsum board. When the damage is slight or covers only a small area, repairs are usually made.

In general, repair and extension of existing gypsum board should comply with the ASTM standards listed in "Where to Get More Information" near the end of this chapter, and in the Bibliography. The following paragraphs contain some generally accepted suggestions about repairing gypsum board. In every case, the recommendations of the ASTM and Gypsum Association standards cited and the gypsum board product's manufacturer should be followed when they differ from the data here. Because of book space

Figure 4-18 As bad as the gypsum board partitions in this photograph look, they are repairable. (*Photo by Stewart Bros., courtesy of Mid-City Financial Corporation.*)

limitations, the recommendations here are necessarily generic and, therefore, may not apply in a particular case. Specific field conditions will often dictate different methods or materials. In addition, the special requirements of the hundreds of possible fire-rated gypsum board assemblies are not discussed in detail here. For conditions not addressed here, the cited sources should be searched for guidance. Even when the data here seem to address a specific case, it is still a good idea to consult the cited references, because, in many subject areas, they contain more detail than is presented here.

Materials. Gypsum board, accessories, and finishing materials should match those used in the existing work, but in no case should they be lesser in quality or design than those currently recognized in the industry as proper for the installation at hand. Sometimes, the existing materials may have contributed to the problem. Errors should not be repeated just to match the existing material.

When extending an existing surface or making large repairs, it is usually best to use the same gypsum board that was used in the original installation. Where an existing fire- or sound-rate assembly is to be patched or extended, the new materials and installation must exactly match the existing, or must be identical with equivalent, assemblies which have been tested and accepted by recognized authorities for the ratings required.

When making small repairs—sometimes even when making large repairs or extending existing surfaces—exactly matching the existing materials may be inappropriate or even impossible.

Some materials are incompatible and should not be used together. Care must be exercised, for example, to ensure that the veneer plaster base used in a repair is made by the same manufacturer as the veneer plaster, and that the same products are used in making repairs that were used in the original work. Veneer plaster gypsum base made by one manufacturer will probably not be compatible with veneer plaster made by a different manufacturer.

Preparation for Gypsum Board Repairs. The first step in preparing damaged gypsum board surfaces to be repaired is to remove loose soft gypsum board surface and core materials and to cut the remaining board off in straight lines. The next step is to check the supports and substrates to ensure that they are sound.

Damaged substrates, if any are found, should then be repaired.

Framing and furring should also be repaired when it is found to be damaged, out of alignment, twisted, not properly located, loose, or otherwise not appropriate for the repairs to be made. Refer to Chapter 2 for discussion.

Dirt, oil, grease, loose paint, loose wall coverings, and foreign material should be removed from surfaces that new gypsum board will contact, and the surfaces should be left clean and dry.

Repairs

General Requirements.   Each of the following requirements is applicable to several different types of repairs.

When it is obvious that simply repairing failed gypsum board will not prevent future failures of the same or related types because of excessive structure movement or excessive differential movement in the substrates, the course of action necessary to solve the problem is dictated by the cause of the damage. When the failure is due to improper structural design, the design must be corrected if gypsum board repairs are to be successful. Where the structural movement is insufficient to cause other problems and the only problem is failing gypsum board, or where the structure movement is planned—as it might be in some high-rise structures—it may be necessary to make changes in the gypsum board systems. It may be necessary, for example, to increase the width of isolation joints between the gypsum board systems and adjacent structural elements. The following paragraphs assume that any structural defects encountered have been corrected.

Where the failure is due to not providing a means to accommodate structure or support system movement, including differential movement, repairs to the gypsum board will be futile until the underlying cause has been corrected or the movement has been provided for the gypsum board system. The correct number of expansion, control, and isolation joints must be properly located, for example. With a few exceptions, which will be clear to the reader, the following paragraphs assume that such problems have been effectively dealt with.

When structure movement or differential movement between supports is the cause of cracking, seeking the recommendation of a knowledgeable representative of the gypsum board manufacturer is in order. Sometimes, seeking the advice of a knowledgeable architect, structural engineer, or other professional may be advisable.

When the failure is connected with a failure to eliminate condensation or to provide proper flashing and caulking to prevent water from entering the board, the following paragraphs assume that such deficiencies have been corrected.

When the failure is linked to stresses resulting from excessively high or low humidities or temperatures, repair of the gypsum board will be unsuccessful until the cause of the problem has been eliminated.

When there is not enough framing or furring; the framing or furring is improperly located or missing (Fig. 4-19); or the framing or furring is mis-

Figure 4-19
This nail pop and the long crack occurred because there is no framing member behind the edge bead at this location. (*Photo by author.*)

aligned, twisted, or protruding sufficiently to cause gypsum board failure, it is often necessary to correct these conditions before effective repairs can be made. Refer to Chapter 2 for a discussion about repairing framing and furring. The following paragraphs assume, for the most part, that the condition being discussed can be repaired without removing the board and repairing the underlying framing and furring.

When gypsum board failure is due to improperly fitting boards, usually the only solution is to remove the boards, cut them to the proper size, and reinstall them, or discard the removed boards and install new, properly fitted boards. Refastening oversized boards without resizing them will probably not be a permanent solution to the problem. This is, of course, a major operation, which may not be worth the effort and expense unless the damage is extensive, the appearance of the condition is totally unacceptable, or the boards are in imminent danger of falling.

When the failure is caused by too thin a gypsum board having been used, the problem might be solved by installing another layer of thicker board over the existing board. The gypsum board manufacturer should be consulted about the proper board thickness and installation methods. There are also specific applicable references in the following paragraphs.

When the failure is due to bad materials, such as improperly manufactured or severely damaged boards, it is often necessary to remove the damaged boards and provide new boards.

When the failure is due to applying gypsum board directly to the interior face of an exterior wall, or to the face of fresh concrete or wet masonry, or over another wet material, the proper solution is to remove the existing material and install a new finish using furring. In some cases, it may be possible to leave part of the existing material in place. It is not advisable, however, to apply furring over the existing material, even when fasteners penetrate into the substrate. Existing material that is sound at the time the new furring is applied may deteriorate later when additional moisture enters it from the substrate and may leave the furring loosely attached.

When the failure occurs because the fasteners have penetrated the board's surface and no longer offer support, the solution is to remove the existing fasteners and drive new fasteners—preferably screws—adjacent to the existing fastener locations.

Fasteners that offer too little support because they are too small, too short, or have heads that are too small can sometimes be left in place and the problem solved by driving new fasteners—preferably screws—adjacent to the existing fasteners.

When the failure occurs because the fasteners are not driven in far enough, are loose, are the wrong type, or missed the supports when they were driven, the safest solution is to remove the existing fasteners and drive new fasteners. Simply driving the existing fasteners down tight may not be adequate, depending on the reason that the fasteners are not tight. The new fasteners should be screws.

When there are not enough fasteners or fasteners were driven in the wrong locations, driving the proper number of additional fasteners—preferably screws—in the correct locations may solve the problem.

When the failure is due to failed adhesives or failing to adequately hold the board in place until the adhesive had cured, it might be possible to rebond the board using injected adhesives. The gypsum board manufacturer should be consulted before adhesive injection is attempted, however. In most cases, it will be necessary to either remove the installed gypsum board and properly install new board or fur the wall and apply new gypsum board.

Removing partly adhered gypsum board with its backing intact is difficult, and probably impossible.

Loose, Sagging, Bowed, or Wavy Boards.   Repairs depend on the cause of the damage. Where framing members are out of alignment, the fasteners in the vicinity of the loose, sagging, bowed, or wavy boards should be removed or driven into the board and new fasteners driven into the supports while the boards are held tightly against the supports and in proper alignment. New fasteners should be driven only into supports that are in contact with the boards. Where insufficient members are in proper contact, it may be necessary to remove a portion of the board and correct the underlying problem.

When framing members are misaligned, twisted, or protruding, after the lumber has properly dried, improperly driven and loose fasteners and fasteners that have damaged the board should be removed and the boards refastened using screws.

Where ceiling boards are sagging or wavy because they are too thin, support the weight of insulation, or have become wet, there are two possible solutions. The ceiling board may be removed and new board installed. Alternatively, the ceiling board may be left in place, furred with resilient furring channels, and another layer of gypsum board installed. Wet board must, of course, be permitted to dry after the cause of the wetting has been removed or controlled. The new furring must be attached through the existing gypsum board to the underlying support system members.

Soft or Disintegrating Boards.   Here, the only reasonable solution is to remove the damaged boards and install new boards (Fig. 4-20). In some rare cases, it may be possible to install new board over the damaged board using furring, but such installations should only be tried after consultation with the gypsum board manufacturer.

Cracking.   Before cracks are repaired, it is first necessary to remove the cause of the cracking. If cracks are caused by structure movement or hygrometric expansion of the board, and the cause is not corrected or accounted for in the gypsum board system, the cracks will simply reappear.

When cracks appear in relatively new construction, it is best to wait until a full heating cycle has passed before attempting to make repairs.

When cracks occur along the edges of the joint tape, it is usually necessary to cut back the edges of the tape that are not bonded and bed any loose tape before attempting crack repair. It is sometimes necessary to completely remove the existing tape and refinish the joint using tape and joint compounds as if it were a new joint.

Figure 4-20   The gypsum board in this photograph has absorbed water and begun to disintegrate. The condition is occurring in a shower. The dark material is mildew. (*Photo by author.*)

Where joint cracks, whether in flat surfaces or corners, extend completely through the existing joint tape, it is necessary to remove the tape and retape and refinish the joint.

Where cracks occur along the flanges of edge trim or corner beads, it is necessary to remove the joint compound from the flange and refinish the joint. Where the cracks have been contributed to by improper fastening of the edge trim or corner bead, proper fastening is required to keep the cracks from recurring.

Cracks in corners may generally be repaired and refinished in the same manner as flat joints. Where the corner has not been constructed using a floating method, fasteners closer than 6 inches to the angle should be removed before retaping and refinishing.

Where cracks are due to differential movement in supporting framing or furring, imposition of additional control joints may help solve the problem. When, for example, corner cracks are due to differential movement in supports, it may be necessary to remove the existing joint-finishing materials and install a control joint at that location. The control joint might consist of two edge trim members separated by a joint that is filled with an elastomeric sealant.

Most cracks smaller than 1/8 inch wide can usually be repaired using joint compounds. Sanding before refinishing with paint or other decoration is usually sufficient to hide the repair. Some sources recommend covering small cracks with latex emulsion. Others suggest that hairline cracks be repaired using shellac and that the board surfaces near larger cracks be coated with shellac before joint compounds are applied.

Most cracks that are more than 1/8 inch wide, including cracks caused by extending face paper cuts beyond the edge of cutouts, can be repaired by taping over the crack and finishing with joint compound exactly as though it were a new joint between boards. Since there will be no depression along the board edges, the joint finishing compound should be feathered wider than normal to reduce shadowing.

Some cracks that are wider than 1/8 inch can be repaired by gouging out some of the existing compound and finishing with new compound. Torn tape should be removed, however, and the joint should then be retaped and finished in a manner similar to that which is appropriate for new joints.

Board Surface Punctures and Depressions. Holes in boards may be repaired by cutting out the broken or punctured board section and installing a new section of board as a plug. Large sections of damaged boards (Fig. 4-21) should be cut away to the lines of the supports. Cut-out portions should be square or rectangular. The edges should be sloped inward at a 45 degree angle. A piece of matching gypsum board should be cut and fitted into the opening. The joint surrounding the new piece should be finished as a butt joint would be finished. Sometimes, it is necessary to bond a strip of gypsum board to the back face of the existing in-place board to act as a brace for the new plug.

Stains and Discolorations. Repair of stained or discolored gypsum board is primarily a finishing problem. Many such problems can be solved by applying paint having a high solids content.

Joint Beading or Ridging. Repairing joint beading and ridging defects should be done during warm weather, but not until after a complete heating cycle has passed.

When humidity or temperature fluctuations have caused the beading or ridging, repairs should not be made until these conditions have been corrected.

In most cases, and especially where the beading or ridging was caused by a minor problem, such as the applicator using too much joint compound, beading or ridging can be alleviated by simply sanding down the ridges

Figure 4-21   A gypsum board ceiling with major damage. The broken boards should be cut and removed, and new pieces of board installed. (*Photo by Stewart Bros., courtesy of Mid-City Financial Corporation.*)

without repairing the underlying condition. Sanding should continue down to the tape, but care should be taken to ensure that the tape is not damaged. The sanded surface should be filled with several layers of joint compound. Each layer should be permitted to dry before the next layer is applied. The completed repair should be sanded or wiped with a damp sponge after 24 hours to feather the edges. If the ridges are still not concealed after that, it may be necessary to apply, sand down, and feather out additional joint compound layers. Sometimes the beading or ridging will recur, necessitating further repairs.

Where the beading or ridging is the result of the gypsum board being installed with the leading edge in the wrong direction (see Fig. 4-11) or of the studs being placed with the flanges not all pointing in the same direction, and it recurs after the simple repairs described in the preceding paragraph have been made, it may be necessary to remove the boards and reinstall them, or install new boards, this time placing the boards in the correct order. Where the studs are not placed with the flanges all in the same direction, the beading or ridging may again recur unless the studs are removed and properly reinstalled.

When beading or ridging recurs after the simple repairs described above, and the underlying cause of the problem is a weak or open joint or failure to back-block unsupported edges, it may be necessary to cut out a portion of the gypsum board and properly install a new piece of gypsum board with proper support and fastening. Where the recurring beading or ridging results from damaged board edges, removal of the damaged board and placing new board may be necessary. In either case, the joint should then be refinished as if it were a new joint.

Where the cause of the recurring beading or ridging is improperly placed boards or boards that were forced too tightly together, it may be possible to prevent a further recurrence by cutting a wider joint between the boards, removing the old fasteners or driving them through the boards, placing new fasteners, and refinishing the joints. In really severe cases, it may be necessary to remove the boards and place new boards, or overlay the boards with furring and place new boards.

Nail Pops. Nail pops that appear immediately after installation should be repaired immediately. Nail pops that occur later should not be repaired until after at least one full heating season.

Some experts believe that when the nail head is not visible, a popped nail may be simply tapped back into place or just left alone. Care should be taken to ensure that such nails are not overdriven, however. Others believe that if nail pops are repaired at all they should be handled in the same way whether exposed or concealed.

Some experts believe that visible popped nails can be successfully tapped below the board's surface and not removed. Others disagree, especially when the nails have rusted (Fig. 4-22). They believe that popped nails should be removed.

Most agree, however, that when a nail head is visible, a new fastener should be driven between 1-1/2 and 2 inches away from the removed nail's location. The new fastener may be a longer nail than that originally used, but a gypsum board screw is preferable.

After the new fasteners have been placed, the depression left by the removed nail and the depression created when driving the new fastener should be filled with joint compound and finished to match the adjacent surface.

Fastener Depressions. Before repairs are made, the underlying cause should be determined and corrected. If too few fasteners were used, additional fasteners should be installed. In every case the depressions should be filled with joint compound and sanded flush with the adjacent surface.

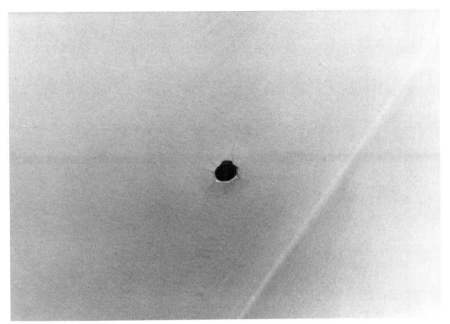

Figure 4-22   A rusted nail pop. *(Photo by author.)*

Fastener Bulging.   Repairing bulges requires driving another fastener, preferably a screw, adjacent to the bulge while holding the board tightly against the supports, removing the bulged materials, including swollen board core and scuffed paper, removing the existing fastener or driving it into the board, filling the depressions with joint compound, and finishing to match the adjacent surface.

Joint Depressions.   It will usually be possible to repair joint depressions by filling the depression flush with the adjacent surface using joint compound and feathering out the edges. The new joint topping should be sanded smooth.

Tape and Fastener Photographing.   When joint tape that is covered by joint compound is apparent in the finished work, it may be possible to diminish its visibility by sanding the tape edges to feather them out. The sanded edges should be then sealed with a primer and covered with several thin coats of joint compound which is feathered out onto the board surface.

Fasteners that are visible in the completed work should be given additional coats of joint compound, which should be feathered out to conceal the fastener location.

Tape Blisters.   Small blisters may be repaired by slitting the blister with a knife and removing enough dried compound to permit placing new compound. New joint compound should then be forced beneath the existing tape, filling the blister. The tape should then be forced into the compound, squeezing out excess compound, and left smooth and level. When the compound is dry, a skim coat of compound should be applied over the tape. When that it dry, the joint should be finished with joint compound and sanded smooth.

Large blisters can be repaired by slitting the blister and removing the blistered tape. After enough dried compound has been removed to permit placing new tape, a new section of tape should be bedded into a layer of bedding compound. When the bedding compound is dry, a skim coat of compound should be applied over the tape. When that is dry, the joint should be finished using joint compound and sanded smooth.

Drywall Blisters.   The appropriate repair method depends on the size of the blister. Small blisters may be repaired by injecting an adhesive such as wood glue into the blister and pressing the paper back flat against the board's core.

Large blisters require cutting out the blistered area and finishing with tape and joint compound. More than one width of tape may be needed. The work should be done in a similar manner to that used in finishing new joints.

Compound Debonding.   Tape that has debonded from the joint compound should be removed along with enough dried compound to permit the application of new tape and compound. New tape should be applied, bedded in bedding compound, and finished as for a new joint.

Compound Pitting.   Repair requires filling in the pits with joint compound by applying another topping coat over the joint. The topping coats should be feathered out as far as necessary to make the joint less apparent.

Shadowing.   The methods used to repair shadowing problems differ depending on the cause of the shadowing.

Shadowing due to crowning joints too high can be reduced or alleviated by sanding the joint as low as possible without damaging the tape, applying additional coats of joint finishing compound, and feathering it to a width of 14 to 16 inches.

Shadowing due to a significant difference between the porosity of board and joint finishes can sometimes be reduced by applying the right type of primer-sealer to the joint material as well as over the entire surface of the board before painting. Sometimes, additional coats of primer-sealer on the joint compound will help. When shadowing caused by porosity differences is still present in spite of extra painting procedures, the shadowing may be reduced by applying a textured finish.

Shadowing caused by cold outdoor temperatures being transferred to indoor surfaces can be corrected by cleaning and repainting the area. Future incidents may be reduced by insulating the interior surface from the exterior temperature, which can be fairly easily accomplished during initial construction. Correcting an existing condition, however, may require constructing a new wall finish inside the existing one, and properly separating the new from the old. Insulation should be placed in the new void to reduce temperature differentials between the supports and the finish.

Predecorated Gypsum Board. Repairing the surface of a damaged predecorated board may sometimes be possible, but usually the only solution to such a problem is to remove the board and install new board. Since each predecorated board product is different, the manufacturer should be consulted for repair instructions.

It may be possible to improve loose or bowed predecorated board by removing the fasteners, correcting the cause of the loose or bowed condition, and reinstalling the removed board. Where nails having small heads were used in the original installation, it may be relatively simple to drive them through the board without much damage to the surface. Unfortunately, many applications where small-headed nails are used also contain adhesives. Only part of the adhesive may have failed to hold, but the remaining adhesive may make removal of the boards impossible without damaging the boards so much that they are unusable.

It may be possible to reattach adhesive-applied predecorated board by injecting adhesives behind the boards and pushing them back in place. Most likely, however, this method will not work or will result in visible damage to the board's surface.

Textured Finish. The type of textured finish discussed in the following paragraphs is the proprietary type furnished by gypsum board manufacturers.

When an existing textured finish is damaged or deemed undesirable, there are several possible methods for solving the problem. One method is to remove the texture by sanding, and apply a new texture. Spot repairs, however, are unlikely to exactly match the existing finish. It may be necessary to remove the finish from the entire surface before a good match can be achieved.

Another method is to cover the damaged or undesired finish with a wall covering. Before a wall covering can be applied, however, it will be necessary to make the wall smooth. Satisfactory smoothness may be achieved by sanding the surface down to the gypsum board, removing all texture. Another, quicker method is to sand only the high spots and fill the rest with layers of joint compound until the wall is smooth. A single heavy coat is not a good idea, because thick layers of joint compound shrink and crack.

The most drastic method is to cover the existing wall with a layer of gypsum board. Refer to "Installing New Gypsum Board over Existing Materials," immediately following, for a discussion.

Installing New Gypsum Board over Existing Materials

In addition to the obvious reasons for installing new gypsum board over unsound or damaged existing surfaces, and for using a gypsum board finish over existing materials, such as concrete, to improve their appearance, gypsum board is also sometimes selected to solve the problem, prevalent in some older buildings, of the existence of lead-based paint. Sometimes a thin (usually 1/4 inch thick) gypsum board layer is used to conceal an existing, unwanted, or damaged textured finish.

Every type of gypsum board discussed in this chapter is suitable for installation over existing masonry, concrete, plaster, gypsum board, tile, and other materials. Methods differ depending on the gypsum board product to be installed, the existing material, and the condition of the existing surface. Restrictions discussed earlier apply to gypsum board products when they are installed over existing surfaces, of course. Predecorated gypsum board with a vinyl surface, for example, should not be directly applied using adhesives over concrete or masonry that is still damp, or that is likely to become wet in the future. If the errors discussed earlier are committed, the same failures will occur.

Installation of gypsum sheathing in Exterior Insulation and Finish Systems (EIFS) is discussed in Chapter 3.

Gypsum board may be installed over existing surfaces by direct lamination or by covering the existing surface with new framing or furring.

Installing New Gypsum Board by Lamination

It is often possible to directly laminate gypsum board products to existing surfaces that are sufficiently stable, structurally sound, in plane, and smooth but not too slick. Thinner gypsum board products are often the choice for direct lamination. Where a painted or otherwise decorated board is preferred, 1/4-inch thick board is often used.

When adhesives are used for the direct lamination of gypsum board to existing substrates, screws or nails are often necessary as supplementary support while the adhesive is setting. Sometimes, removable bracing is used for the same purpose. It is customary to use pressure-sensitive tape on the back side of some board types, including predecorated board, to hold them in place while the adhesive sets.

Fasteners used as supplementary supports should be long enough to penetrate the wood framing or furring behind the existing finish. Nails should penetrate the supports by at least 7/8 inch. Screws should penetrate by at least 5/8 inch into wood and 3/8 inch into metal. The new finish should not be fastened to the existing finish.

Installing New Gypsum Board over New Framing or Furring

All gypsum board products can be installed over framing or furring, when existing surfaces are not satisfactory for direct lamination. Where surfaces are too irregular even for direct furring application, shimming may be necessary. Sometimes conditions are so bad that the existing construction cannot be used as a substrate for the new gypsum board. It may be appropriate to remove an existing wall or partition entirely and provide a completely new construction. When complete removal is not appropriate, it may be necessary to construct an entirely new partition that faces the existing wall or partition.

Care must be exercised when dealing with existing fire-resistant assemblies to ensure that the rating is not voided. Sometimes, adding a layer of gypsum board can change the rating of an assembly. Improperly attaching a new layer may destroy the effectiveness of the assembly, decreasing rather than increasing its fire resistance.

Gypsum Board and Accessory Materials. Gypsum board products, accessories, fasteners, adhesives, joint treatment materials, and textured finishes should be the same as for new gypsum board over new supports, as outlined earlier in this chapter, and should comply with the applicable standards mentioned.

Substrate Preparation. The requirements stipulated earlier in this chapter for the preparation of surfaces to receive gypsum board apply here as well. The following are additional requirements.

Unrepairable Existing Construction. Where the existing surface is extremely uneven, unsound, contains large voids, or has framing or furring members that are unsound, not rigid, or improperly aligned, it may be necessary to remove the existing construction entirely.

Sometimes, it is possible to leave such construction in place and face it with new framing or furring. Refer to Chapter 2 for a discussion of placing framing and furring over existing work.

Preparation for Application Using Both Adhesives and Fasteners. Surfaces must be in generally good condition to permit board installation using adhesives. They must be smooth but not slick, clean, complete, and dry. Large voids should be filled completely and left flush with the adjacent surface.

Good adhesion is essential. Loose paint and paper must be removed. Surfaces should be tested to ensure a good adhesive bond. Tests may consist of installing 8-inch square pieces of the gypsum board to be applied in several locations using the adhesive that is best. After the adhesive cures, removal should tear off the gypsum board's paper backing.

Preparation for Direct Attachment Using Fasteners and No Adhesives. Where new gypsum board will be applied using fasteners without adhesives, the substrates must be smooth, clean, and dry.

Small voids must be filled solid and flush with the adjacent surface using the same materials as presently exist. Larger voids must be either filled solid or have shims placed in them to provide backing for the new board. Shims may be gypsum board, where appropriate, or wood. Wood shims should be 1-1/2 inches wide and the thickness of the void being filled so that the face of the shim finishes flush with the adjacent existing finish. Gypsum board shims may be used when the void to be filled is the proper thickness so that they will finish flush with the adjacent finish. Gypsum board shims should be at least 2 inches wide. Shims should be fastened in place using masonry nails to masonry, nails or screws to wood, and screws to metal framing or furring. Fasteners should be placed at 6 inches on center along the entire length of each shim.

Fire Resistance. Where fire-resistant assemblies are to be faced with gypsum board, voids less than 16 inches across should be filled with fire-resistant materials that are consistent with the assembly. Larger voids should be covered with Type X gypsum board of a thickness consistent with the framing spacing and rating required. The Gypsum Association or the gypsum board manufacturer should be consulted for advice.

Installing Gypsum Board. The requirements stipulated earlier in this chapter for the installation of all types of standard gypsum board, veneer plaster gypsum base, and predecorated gypsum board, including general requirements for board application and requirements for fasteners, adhesives accessories, joint and fastener treatment, floating angles, sound isolation, special applications such as shaftwalls and solid partitions, and finishing, also apply here, except where those requirements are specifically modified in the following discussion.

General Requirements for Installing Gypsum Board. The following requirements modify or add to earlier requirements.

Existing framing must be located before gypsum board application. Nailing or screwing new gypsum board directly to existing finishes is not acceptable. Where framing or furring exists, fasteners must enter the existing framing or furring. Where the existing material is applied directly to a solid substrate, such as masonry, the new board must be fastened through the existing finish to the substrate.

Fastener penetration into supports should be the same as stipulated earlier for new work. All finish material thicknesses must, of course, be taken into account when selecting fastener length. Only that portion of a fastener that actually penetrates the support should be counted in penetration calculations.

Direct Application of Standard Gypsum Board or Veneer Plaster Gypsum Base without Adhesives. On ceilings, where existing supports are spaced at 16 inches on center, 3/8- or 1/2-inch thick board may be used. Where existing supports are spaced at 24 inches on center, 1/2- or 5/8-inch thick board may be used. Thinner (1/4- and 3/16-inch thick) boards should be used only with the concurrence of their manufacturer.

On walls, 3/8-, 1/2-, or 5/8-inch thick boards may be used. Thinner (1/4- and 3/16-inch thick) boards should be used only with the concurrence of their manufacturer.

Fastener number and location should be as stipulated earlier for new single-ply gypsum board installed without adhesive.

Direct Application of Standard Gypsum Board or Veneer Plaster Gypsum Base with Adhesive. For existing surfaces that are sound, flat, and level, and that have no void spaces, the thinnest board available should be considered. Standard board, for example, may be 1/4 inch or 3/16 inch thick. The board manufacturer should be consulted, however, before board selection is made. A specific application may have peculiarities which precludes the use of thinner boards.

Adhesives should be selected in accordance with the recommendations of the Gypsum Association and the adhesive and board manufacturers.

In walls and ceilings, supplementary fasteners should be placed at board edges at, and not more than 24 inches on center along, each support. Additional bracing and support may also be necessary until the adhesive has set.

Application of New Gypsum Board to New Framing or Furring. Installation of the framing and furring is discussed in Chapter 2. Application of standard gypsum board, veneer plaster gypsum base, and predecorated gypsum board to the new furring should be done essentially as stipulated earlier in this chapter for application of the same type new gypsum board.

Glass Mesh Mortar Unit Materials and Installation

Materials

Glass Mesh Mortar Units. Glass mesh mortar units are a family of products that are also called "tile backer boards," "cementitious tile backer boards," or "tile base." There are at least three different products in general use at the time of this writing (late 1988) that fit into this category. In the past, there were others also, but they are either not manufactured today or are no longer generally recommended as a backing for ceramic tile. Occasionally, one of those earlier products will be encountered in an existing building, but many of them failed so miserably that they were replaced long ago. By the time you read this, there may be new products available for the purpose.

The products in general use in 1988 are similar in purpose and use, but otherwise different in significant ways. They also differ significantly from the water-resistant gypsum board products that they are intended to replace.

Each manufacturer, of course, claims that its product is superior, and we will not argue the point here. The differences and similarities in these products are important when one is trying to recognize an existing material.

Available Products. Two of the available products have cores based on Portland cement. Wonderboard by Modulars, Incorporated has a lightweight concrete core. Durock Tile Backer Board, by Durabond Division, United States Gypsum Company, has an aggregate Portland cement core. The third product, Dens-Shield, by Georgia Pacific Corporation, has a water-resistant gypsum core.

One advantage that all available glass mesh mortar units have over water-resistant gypsum board is that the glass mesh mortar units can be used as a backing for tile applied using organic adhesives, dry-set mortar, or latex cement mortar. Water-resistant gypsum board is usable as a tile base only when the tile is applied using organic adhesive. The difference is due to the board facing. Water-resistant gypsum board has a water-resistant paper face. Glass mesh mortar units have coated glass mesh fabric faces. The facing on Wonderboard has a high-density Portland cement coating. Durock Tile Backer Board has a polymer coating. Dens-Shield is treated with a proprietary product for water resistance.

Another advantage of glass mesh mortar units over water-resistant gypsum board is that the glass mesh mortar units can be used on ceilings as well as walls. The two products with Portland cement-based cores can also be used as floor underlayment and as tile underlayment on countertops. Water-resistant gypsum board is usable only on walls. Units with Portland cement-based cores have also been used in exterior applications. Units with gypsum cores are not suitable for exterior use.

Size and Thickness.   Panel sizes and thicknesses are not the same for all available glass mesh mortar units. Wonderboard is 7/16 inch thick, 36 inches wide, and 48, 60, 64, or 72 inches long.

Durock Tile Backer Board is 1/2 inch thick, 36 inches wide, and 48, 60, or 72 inches long.

Dens-Shield is 1/2 inch thick, 48 inches wide, and 96 inches long.

Fasteners for Glass Mesh Mortar Units.   Fasteners are generally industry standard types.

Nails.   Glass mesh mortar units may be fastened to wood studs using 1-1/2 inch, screw-type, galvanized roofing nails.

Screws.   Glass mesh mortar units may be fastened to wood or metal using screws. Different screw types are used depending on the substrates.

Rust-resistant Type W screws are used to fasten glass mesh mortar units to wood framing, and to wood subflooring. Screw length is usually 1-1/2 inches.

Either Type S or Type S-12 rust-resistant screws are used to fasten glass mesh mortar units to metal furring and channel studs, depending on the metal thickness. Screw length is usually 1-1/4 inches.

Joint Treatment Materials for Glass Mesh Mortar Units

Tape.   The three product manufacturers mentioned in this chapter all require a 2-inch wide coated glass fiber mesh tape.

Compounds.   Where tile occurs, tape is embedded in the same material used to set the tile. Where a glass mesh mortar unit is to be painted (no tile), joint finishing compounds are the same or similar to those for standard interior gypsum board.

Installing Glass Mesh Mortar Units

Panel Application

General Requirements.   Installation methods for glass mesh mortar units differ somewhat depending on the product. The manufacturer's instructions should be followed in every case.

Glass mesh mortar units that have cores based on Portland cement may be used as tile floor underlayment over a wood subfloor. The panels must be laid in a bed of dry-set or latex-Portland cement mortar.

Panel Direction.   Glass mesh mortar units on ceilings are installed with the long edge perpendicular to the framing. Panels on walls are installed either vertically or horizontally.

Joint Locations.   End joints in boards applied across framing and long edge joints in boards applied parallel with framing should fall over framing members. Edges and ends that are parallel to framing should be continuously supported.

Fasteners.   In wall and ceiling applications, glass mesh mortar units should be nailed or screwed to the framing. Either nails or screws may be used to fasten units to wood. Screws are used to fasten units to metal framing. Staples or adhesive attachment are not appropriate.

At walls and ceilings, fasteners should penetrate the boards at intermediate supports. Where panels join at a support, fasteners are installed through the panels or between the panels with a washer to lock the panels in place. Where glass mesh mortar units are installed over a solid backing, such as plywood, gypsum board, or plaster, the fasteners should penetrate the backing and anchor the glass mesh mortar units to the underlying framing.

Manufacturers usually require that nails be placed about 8 inches on center on walls and 6 inches on center on ceilings, but some manufacturers require a 6 inch spacing on both. Screws should be placed about 6 inches on center on both walls and ceilings.

Glass mesh mortar units on floors should be fastened in place with nails or screws at about 6 to 8 inches on center in each direction. Fasteners should pass through the finish flooring and subflooring and anchor the glass mesh mortar units to the joists below.

Joint Treatment.   Some product's manufacturers require that joints between panels be left open. Some require that the joints be filled with dry-set or latex-Portland cement mortar. All require that joints on walls and ceilings be covered with glass mesh tape. When tile is to be installed, the tape should be embedded in a thin layer of dry-set or latex-Portland cement mortar. When tile does not occur, the tape should be embedded in joint compound.

Some manufacturers require taping joints between panels on floors, but others do not. Tape should be bedded in mortar.

Finishing. Glass mesh mortar units are usually covered with ceramic tile. Refer to Chapter 5 for a discussion of tile application methods.

Glass mesh mortar units that occur without tile covering may be painted after a joint finishing compound has been applied over the entire face of the board. This may not be an appropriate procedure, however, with all products or under all circumstances. The suitability of finishing glass mesh mortar units in this manner should be verified with the manufacturer.

Glass Mesh Mortar Unit Failures and What to Do about Them

Why Glass Mesh Mortar Units Fail

Glass mesh mortar units fail for many of the same reasons that gypsum board fails. These reasons are listed in "Gypsum Board System Failures and What to Do about Them" earlier in this chapter and are not repeated here. As is true for gypsum board, a glass mesh mortar unit's failure may be caused by structure failure; structure movement; solid substrate problems; other building element problems; framing and furring problems; bad materials; bad system design; bad workmanship; or failure to protect the glass mesh mortar units. The failure causes listed here are in addition to those listed in this chapter under "Gypsum Board System Failures and What to Do about Them."

Structure Failure, Structure Movement, Solid Substrate Problems, other Building Elements Problems, Wood Framing and Furring Problems, and Metal Framing and Furring Problems. There are no failure causes in any of these categories that are not listed in Chapter 2. Each time "gypsum board" or just "board" appears in the referenced material, substitute "glass mesh mortar units."

Bad Materials. There are no failure causes in this category which are not listed in "Gypsum Board System Failures and What to Do about Them." Each time "gypsum board" or just "board" appears in the referenced material, substitute "glass mesh mortar units."

Bad System Design. Properly designing the installation is essential if tile failures are to be prevented. The designer should closely follow the glass mesh mortar unit manufacturer's recommendations. Most design errors that can lead to failure are listed in "Gypsum Board System Failures and What to Do about Them." Each time "gypsum board" or just "board" appears in the referenced material, substitute "glass mesh mortar units." Additional causes include the following:

GMMU1.   Using glass mesh mortar units with gypsum cores as floor underlayment.

Bad Workmanship. Good workmanship is essential to a successful tile installation. The installer should closely follow the glass mesh mortar unit manufacturer's recommendations. Most workmanship errors that can cause failures are listed in "Gypsum Board System Failures and What to Do about Them." Each time "gypsum board" or just "board" appears in the referenced material, substitute "glass mesh mortar units." The following is an additional failure cause:

GMMU2.   Failing to use joint tape where the manufacturer recommends such use. Failing to properly attach or embed tape in accordance with the glass mesh mortar unit manufacturer's recommendations.

Evidence of Failure in Glass Mesh Mortar Units

Glass mesh mortar unit failure appears as tile failure. Refer to Chapter 5 for a discussion of tile failure. When tile failure has been determined to have resulted from a failure in a glass mesh mortar unit substrate, look for one of the possible causes listed below. In the following paragraphs, glass mesh mortar unit failures are listed by failure source, such as "Structure Failure." Each failure source is followed by one or more numbers representing possible failure causes.

A description of the numbered failure causes that follow "Structure Failure," "Structure Movement," "Solid Substrate Problems," "Other Building Element Problems" "Wood Framing and Furring Problems," and "Metal Framing and Furring Problems" appear in Chapter 2 under these headings and are listed in the Contents. For example, clarification and explanation of the numbered cause (1) listed in the example

■ Metal Framing and Furring Problems: 1 (see Chapter 2).

appears in Chapter 2 under the heading "Metal Framing and Furring Problems," cause 1, which reads

1. Metal Framing or furring that is out of alignment.

A description and discussion of the numbered causes that follow "Bad Materials," "Bad System Design," and "Bad Workmanship" appear as subparagraphs and sub-subparagraphs in the part of this chapter titled "Why Gypsum Board Systems Fail," which is listed in the Contents. For example, clarification of the numbered cause (2) listed in the example

- Bad Workmanship: Improper Substrate Preparation: 2.

appears in this chapter under the heading "Why Gypsum Board Systems Fail," subparagraph "Bad Workmanship," sub-subparagraph "Improper Substrate Preparation," cause 2, which reads

2. Failing to achieve the correct surface tolerance.

Each time "gypsum board" or just "board" appears in the referenced material, substitute "glass mesh mortar units."

Clarification of the alphanumeric (GMMU1) failure causes appears in this chapter under "Why Glass Mesh Mortar Units Fail," which is listed in the Contents.

Glass Mesh Mortar Unit Failures. Glass mesh mortar units fail for the following reasons:

- Structure Failure: 1 (see Chapter 2).
- Structure Movement: 1, 2, 3, 4, 5, 6, 7, 8 (see Chapter 2).
- Solid Substrate Problems: 2, 3, 4 (see Chapter 2).
- Other Building Element Problems: 1, 2, 3 (see Chapter 2).
- Wood Framing and Furring Problems: 1, 2, 3, 4, 5, 6, 7, 8 (see Chapter 2).
- Metal Framing and Furring Problems: 1, 2, 3, 4 (see Chapter 2).
- Bad Materials: 1, 8.
- Bad System Design: Wrong Board Material: GMMU1.
- Bad System Design: Wrong Accessories or Fasteners: 1, 2, 3.
- Bad System Design: Failing to Require Proper Preparation Methods: 1.
- Bad System Design: Selecting Improper Application Methods: 1, 2, 4, 10.
- Bad Workmanship: Improper Substrate Preparation: 1, 2, 6.
- Bad Workmanship: Improper Storage and Handling of Materials: 1, 2, 3, 4.
- Bad Workmanship: Improper Board Placement: 1, 2, 3, 8, 9, 11, 12, 13, 15, 18, 19, 20, 23.
- Bad Workmanship: Improper Fastener, Accessory, or Adhesive Application: 1, 2, 3, 4, 5, 6, 7, 8, 9, 10, 12, 13, 14, 15, 16, 17, 18, 19, 23.
- Bad Workmanship: Improper Joint or Fastener Finishing: GMMU2.

■ Bad Workmanship: Failing to Protect the Gypsum Board Units: 3, 5, 6, 13.

Installing Glass Mesh Mortar Units over Existing Construction

Floors

When room and door height is adequate, glass mesh mortar units with Portland cement-based cores can be applied as a tile base over many existing finish materials when the substrates are wood or plywood. For example, with a few exceptions such as cushion-back vinyl, glass mesh mortar units may be installed without removing existing resilient flooring. The installation is made in a manner similar to that for installing glass mesh mortar units in new construction. Installation instructions should be obtained from the manufacturer.

Walls

Glass mesh mortar units may be used over existing wall finish materials that are sufficiently in plane and have not disintegrated enough to form an improper base. Glass mesh mortar units installed over existing wall materials must be fastened through the existing finishes to the supports. They should not be installed using adhesives or be fastened to the existing finish materials.

Where to Get More Information

Some of AIA Service Corporation's *Masterspec* Basic sections contain excellent descriptions of the materials and installations that are the subject of this chapter. Unfortunately, those sections contain little that will help with troubleshooting failed gypsum board systems. Sections that have applicable data are:

■ Section 09200, Lath and Plaster, 2/85 Edition.

■ Section 09215, Veneer Plaster, 2/88 Edition.

■ Section 09250, Gypsum Drywall, 8/87 Edition.

■ Section 09270, Gypsum Board Shaft Wall Systems, 2/88 Edition.

Every designer should have the full complement of applicable ASTM Standards available for reference, of course, but anyone who needs to understand gypsum board systems should definitely own a copy of the following ASTM Standards:

■ Standard C 11, Definition of Terms Relating to Gypsum and Related Building Materials.

■ Standard C 645, Specifications for Non-Load (Axial) Bearing Steel Studs, Runners (Track), and Rigid Furring Channels for Screw Application of Gypsum Board.

■ Standard C 754, Specifications for Installation of Steel Framing Members to Receive Screw-Attached Gypsum Wallboard, Backing Board, or Water-Resistant Backing Board.

■ Standard C 840, Specifications for Application and Finishing of Gypsum Board.

■ Standard D 955, Specifications for Load-Bearing (Transverse and Axial) Steel Studs, Runners (Track), and Bracing or Bridging, for Screw Application of Gypsum Board and Metal Plaster Bases.

■ Standard C 1007, Installation of Load-Bearing (Transverse and Axial) Steel Studs and Accessories.

ASTM standards for gypsum board materials and for fasteners, accessories, joint materials, and other devices used in installing gypsum board, and other ASTM Standards that are of use to anyone interested in gypsum board, are listed in the Bibliography and marked with a [4]. They may also be mentioned in this and other chapters.

The following Gypsum Association documents are applicable to the subjects discussed in this chapter:

■ The 1984 *Fire Resistance Design Manual: Eleventh Edition (GA-600-84* is a guide to the fire resistance and sound resistance of various wall, ceiling, and furring assemblies containing gypsum board. Anyone designing or maintaining a building containing fire-rated gypsum board installations should own a copy.

■ The 1985 *Recommended Specifications for Application and Finishing of Gypsum Board (GA-216-85)* contains illustrated specifications. The information contained is excellent. Unfortunately, the specifications are not in the CSI three-part format, which makes them unusable directly by many specifiers.

■ The 1985 *Gypsum Board Products Glossary of Terminology (GA-505-85)* is excellent.

■ The 1985 *Using Gypsum Board for Walls and Ceilings (GA-201-85)* is another excellent source of data about installing and finishing gypsum board products. It covers gypsum board products; supporting construction; furring; application of gypsum board, including predecorated boards; attachments and fasteners; joint treatment; decorating; and special construction such as sound isolation, application over foam insulation, and application in bath and shower areas, on exterior soffits, and in electric radiant heat installations. It also discusses resurfacing existing construction using gypsum board, and gypsum board problems and remedies.

- The 1986 *Recommended Specifications: Gypsum Board Types, Uses, Sizes and Standards (GA-223-86)* is a one-page capsule look at the subject. It is a handy reference.

- The 1986 *Recommendations for Covering Existing Interior Walls and Ceilings with Gypsum Board (GA-650-86)* goes directly to one of the subjects in this book. It is a "must have" for anyone responsible for installing new gypsum board over existing surfaces.

- The 1986 *Fire Resistant Gypsum Sheathing (GA-252-86)* is a definitive guide to gypsum sheathing materials and installation.

- The 1988 *Recommended Specifications: Recommendations for Installation of Steel Fire Door Frames in Steel Stud-Gypsum Board Fire-Rated Partitions (GA-219-86)* is self-explanatory.

The Gypsum Association publications mentioned above may be obtained from the Gypsum Association at the address listed in the Appendix.

James T. Frane's 1987 book, *Drywall Contracting,* talks about the drywall applicator, and such subjects as estimating drywall work and starting and organizing a drywall contracting business, but it also covers gypsum board application, tools, installation methods, joint treatment, surface treatments, and solving common drywall problems. In the problem-solving chapter it covers fastener, joint, and joint compound problems and problems with the boards themselves, such as damaged edges and bowing. It also offers a method for refinishing a textured wall. Check with the publisher at the address listed in the Appendix for price and availability.

The United States Gypsum Company's 1972 *Red Book: Lathing and Plastering Handbook, 28th Edition* contains data about veneer plaster gypsum base and gypsum plaster lath, including a discussion of failures and remedies. There may be a later edition by now. Other manufacturers may publish similar data.

The United States Gypsum Company's 1987 *Gypsum Construction Handbook, Third Edition* contains data about gypsum board materials, installation, and finishing and problems affecting gypsum board and their remedies. It is a "must have" for anyone who is responsible for designing, specifying, installing, or maintaining gypsum board. There may be a later edition by now. Other manufacturers may publish similar data.

The Exterior Insulation Manufacturers Association has produced guides for exterior insulation and finish systems.

Ramsey/Sleeper's *Architectural Graphic Standards* contains data about gypsum board systems.

Also refer to items in the Bibliography followed by [4].

Ceramic Tile

This chapter includes all forms of ceramic tile and related setting beds and joint grout. Other associated construction that affects tile, such as the building's structural system; solid substrates such as masonry and concrete; other building elements; and both wood and metal framing and furring are addressed in Chapter 2. Plaster substrates are discussed in Chapter 3; gypsum board and glass mesh mortar units are examined in Chapter 4.

The phrase "ceramic tile" is generic. It includes glazed wall tile, ceramic mosaic tile, quarry tile, and paver tile. The listing and descriptions in this chapter are general in nature only. Other tile types may be encountered in existing construction, and other names may be used by various producers.

Ceramic tile products are used on floors, walls, and overhead surfaces and on both the interior and exterior of buildings.

Ceramic Tile Types and Their Uses

Most ceramic tile produced in this country complies with ANSI Standard A137.1-1980, but as much as fifty percent of the tile installed here may have been manufactured in another country. As discussed later in this chapter, even some special-purpose and faience (glaze-decorated earthenware) tile produced in this country may not comply with ANSI Standard A137.1.

Some foreign-made tile may comply with ANSI Standard A137.1, but much will not have been tested for compliance. The untested tile may comply with a standard applicable in its country of origin. When a tile is encountered which does not comply with ANSI Standard A137.1, it may be necessary to obtain the standard with which it complies in order to diagnose whatever problem has been encountered. Unfortunately, there is no current international standard for ceramic tile. Foreign standards are included in building codes and are generally enforceable or recognized in the United States. Requirements in foreign standards may not, however, be equivalent to those of ANSI standards.

In addition, there are a limited number of trim shapes available in some foreign-made tiles.

Glazed Wall Tile

Glazed wall tile is glazed with either a semi-matt, matt, high gloss (bright), or crystalline (crackled-appearing) finish. Edges are usually cushioned (slightly rounded). Most wall tile is 4-1/4 inches square, 4-1/4 by 6-1/2 inches, or 6-1/2 inches square and about 1/4 or 5/16 inch thick. Some wall tile is sheet mounted. Some sheet-mounted tile is pregrouted with an elastomeric material.

Matching trim is available for use with wall tile. Shapes include beads, coved surface units with square tops, coved bases with square tops, coved bases with bullnosed tops, bullnosed returns, surface bullnoses, double bullnoses, and other shapes, all in various sizes (Fig. 5-1).

Glazed wall tile is intended for use only on walls and other vertical surfaces. Some heavy duty glazed tiles may be used in residential applications on countertops, and even on floors.

Decorative thin wall tile is a separate category of wall tile intended for decorative use in residential applications. It is thinner than standard wall tile and will not withstand impact loads.

Accessories are available to match the wall tile. They include soap holders, tumbler holders, toothbrush holders, towel bars, robe hooks, roll paper holders, and others.

Ceramic Mosaic Tile

Ceramic mosaic tile may be either glazed or unglazed, and either porcelain or natural clay based. Edges are usually cushioned (slightly rounded). ANSI

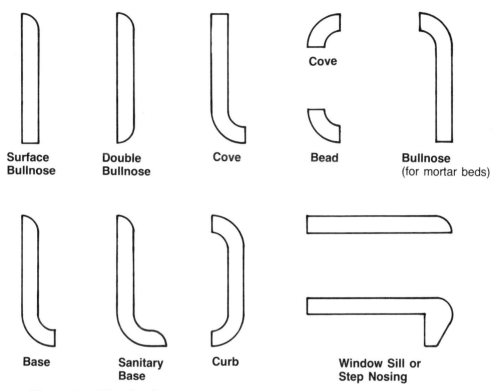

Surface Bullnose   **Double Bullnose**   **Cove**   **Bead**   **Bullnose** (for mortar beds)

Base   **Sanitary Base**   **Curb**   **Window Sill or Step Nosing**

Figure 5-1   Tile trim shapes.

Standard A137.1 requires ceramic mosaic tile to have less than six square inches of face area. It is available in a variety of sizes and shapes including 1 by 1 inch, 1 by 2 inches, and 2 by 2 inches. Usual thickness is 1/4 inch, but some thicker ceramic mosaic tile may be found. Slip-resistant surfaces are available. Conductive ceramic mosaic tile is also available, but only from a limited number of manufacturers. Ceramic mosaic tile is usually sheet mounted for application. Some is pregrouted with elastomeric materials.

Matching trim is available in ceramic mosaic tile. Shapes include beads, coves, and surface bullnoses in various sizes (see Fig. 5-1). Trim edges may be square or cushioned.

Ceramic mosaic tile is used on either walls or floors and on both interior and exterior surfaces. Floor tile is usually, but not always, unglazed. Ceramic mosaic tile is also used on countertops and as a decorative finish on cabinets and built-in furniture.

Quarry Tile

Quarry tile is made from shale or natural clay. It may be either glazed or unglazed. Edges are usually square. Faces may be plain, grooved, or figured. Backs may be plain or have a depressed or raised pattern. Tiles are available in a variety of sizes, including, but not limited to, 3 by 3 inches, 4 by 4 inches, 4 by 6 inches, 4 by 8 inches, 6 by 3 inches, 6 by 6 inches, 8 by 8 inches, and 12 by 12 inches. Thicknesses vary from 1/2 to 3/4 inch, but 3/4-inch thick materials are available only from a limited number of manufacturers. Slip-resistant surfaces are available.

Matching trim is available in quarry tile. Shapes include coves, bases, surface bullnoses, double bullnoses, and window sill or step nosings in various sizes.

Quarry tile is suitable for both interior and exterior surfaces. It is generally used on floors and other horizontal traffic-bearing surfaces, but may also appear on window stools or vertical surfaces.

Paver Tile

Paver tile is made from natural clay or porcelain. It may be either glazed or unglazed. Edges may be square or cushioned. Faces are usually plain. Backs may be plain or have a depressed or raised pattern. Tiles are available in a variety of sizes, from 4 by 4 inches up to 24 by 24 inches. Thicknesses vary from 5/16 inch to 1/2 inch.

Matching trim is available in paver tile. Shapes include coves, bases, bullnoses, surface bullnoses, double bullnoses, and window sill or step nosings in various sizes.

Paver tile is generally used on floors, but may also appear on window stools or vertical surfaces.

Special-Purpose Tile

Special-purpose tile may have physical or appearance characteristics that are different from normal tile, and that are usually agreed on by the manufacturer and the buyer. It may be stain- or chemical-resistant, frost-proof, particularly resistant to thermal shock, or have some other characteristic that makes it different from ordinary ceramic tile. It may also be of a special or unusual shape or configuration, or have a pattern intended to create an unusual architectural effect. It may be glazed or unglazed.

Additional Definitions

Producers use many terms to sell their products. Some of them include:

Impervious: Tile with a water absorption rate of 0.5 percent or less.

Vitreous: Tile with a water absorption rate of between 0.5 percent and 3.0 percent.

Semi-Vitreous: Tile with a water absorption rate between 3.0 percent and 7.0 percent.

Non-Vitreous: Tile with a water absorption rate exceeding 7.0 percent.

Slip-Resistant: Tile containing an embedded or applied abrasive to make it less slippery.

Monocottura: Some Italian manufacturers use this term to describe their paver tile. It simply means "single-fired."

Mortar and Adhesive Types and Their Uses

Portland Cement Mortar

Portland cement mortar is a mixture of Portland cement, sand, and a liquid. The liquid may be either water or liquid latex. The ingredients in Portland cement mortar are mixed at the installation site.

Portland cement mortar is used as thick setting beds, sometimes called "conventional," or "mud" beds. It is used on both vertical and horizontal surfaces.

Dry-Set Mortar

Dry-set mortar is a factory-made mixture of Portland cement, sand, and water-retentive additives. Only water is added at the construction site. Some older existing dry-set mortar may have been field mixed, which can sometimes result in inconsistent mortar. Current ANSI standards do not permit field mixing of dry-set mortar.

Dry-set mortar is a bond coat. It is used over a cured Portland cement setting bed and, in thin-set installation systems, directly on substrates.

Latex-Portland Cement Mortar

Latex-Portland cement mortar is a mixture of Portland cement, sand, and a polymer (liquid latex such as SBR or acrylic). In most cases, the Portland cement and sand are factory-mixed and the polymer is added at the construction site. Some latex producers, however, permit mixing the sand, cement, and their latex at the construction site, but such systems do not conform with ANSI standards. In yet another type of latex-Portland cement mortar, the sand, cement, and latex in dry-powder form are factory-mixed. This type requires the addition of water only at the construction site.

Latex-Portland cement mortar is a bond coat. It is used over a cured Portland cement setting bed and, in thin-set installation systems, directly on substrates.

Chemical-Resistant Epoxy Mortar

Chemical-resistant epoxy mortar is a mixture of epoxy resins, hardeners, and silica sand or another filler. The epoxy parts are shipped separately and blended at the construction site.

Chemical-resistant epoxy mortar is a thin-set material for use where chemical resistance is needed. It is normally used only on horizontal interior surfaces.

Modified Epoxy-Emulsion Mortar

Modified epoxy-emulsion mortar is a mixture of emulsified epoxy resin, hardener, Portland cement, and silica sand. The Portland cement and sand are factory blended. The other parts of the mixture are shipped separately and blended at the construction site with the cement and sand mixture.

Modified epoxy-emulsion mortar is intended for use where good bond strength is required, but chemical resistance is not. It is normally used on horizontal interior surfaces.

Furan Mortar

Furan mortar is a chemical-resistant mortar created by mixing furan resin, hardener, fillers, and an acid catalyst.

Furan mortar is a thin-set material for use where chemical resistance is needed. It is usually used on floors. The tile must be waxed when furan mortar is used to permit tile cleaning.

Organic Adhesives

Organic adhesives are factory-prepared organic materials which are applied in the field without the addition of other materials. The adhesive material in organic adhesives is suspended in a solvent which evaporates after installation. ANSI A136.1 lists two types of organic adhesives, but Type I is more water-resistant than Type II, and is the type normally used in commercial structures.

Organic adhesives are best used to install tile on walls in dry, low-heat areas, over smooth substrates, such as plaster or gypsum board, where they are not subject to impact loads. Organic adhesives may also have been used in an existing building to install tile on floors and counters; in wet areas, such as tubs, showers, and kitchens; and over masonry and concrete. In fact, The Tile Council of America's *Handbook* recommends using organic adhesives in these kinds of wet areas, even over water-resistant gypsum board. But such installations will often fail unless proper precautions are taken and the workmanship is excellent. See "Tile Failures and What to Do about Them" later in this chapter.

Epoxy Adhesives

Epoxy adhesives are two-part adhesives with a high bond strength. They are used to install tile in thin-set applications on floors, counters, walls, and similar installations. A typical use is to install a tile base on the exterior surface of a metal walk-in freezer. Epoxy adhesives are not specifically formulated to be chemical resistant, but do offer more resistance to chemicals than do organic adhesives.

Grout Types and Their Uses

Portland Cement Grout

Portland cement grout may be either factory premixed (Commercial grout) or field mixed (sand-Portland cement grout). Commercial Portland cement grout contains Portland cement and other ingredients. Sand-Portland cement grout is made up of equal parts of Portland cement and fine sand.

Portland cement grout is used in all tile types except glazed wall tile, in both interior and exterior applications, and on both vertical and horizontal surfaces. Portland cement grout on vertical surfaces is usually white. On floors it should be gray, so that stains and dirt are not as apparent. Unfortunately, in too many cases, white or light colored grout is used on floors, leading to problems which are discussed later in this chapter.

Both Portland cement grout types require wetting of tile surfaces before application and damp curing.

Dry-set Grout

Dry-set grouts are made at the factory from Portland cement and additives, which provide water retention during curing.

Dry-set grout is used in all types of tile, in both interior and exterior applications, and on both vertical and horizontal surfaces. Dry-set grout on vertical surfaces is usually white. Dry-set grout on floors should be gray. The comments in the "Portland Cement Grout" section earlier about using white grout on floors also apply to dry-set grout.

Dry-set grout does not require wetting of tile surfaces before application, except under some very dry conditions. Damp curing, however, is usually recommended by dry-set grout manufacturers.

Latex-Portland Cement Grout

Latex-Portland cement grouts may be one of the following:

- Commercial Portland cement grout or dry-set grout to which a liquid latex is added in the field at the time of application, in lieu of water.
- Commercial Portland cement grout or dry-set grout to which a powdered polymer, such as ethyl vinyl acetate (EVA), is added in the factory, and to which water is added in the field at the time of application.

Latex-Portland cement grout is used in all types of tile, in both interior and exterior applications, and on both vertical and horizontal surfaces. Latex-Portland cement grout on vertical surfaces may be white or colored. Latex-Portland cement grout on floors may be gray or colored. The comments in the "Portland Cement Grout" section earlier about using white or light colored grout on floors also apply to latex-Portland cement grout.

Latex-Portland cement grout may or may not require wetting of wall surfaces before application, as recommended by its producer. Damp curing, however, is usually not required by latex-Portland cement grout manufacturers, except in windy or hot conditions.

Epoxy Grout

Epoxy grouts contain epoxy resin, hardeners, and fillers, such as silica sand.

Epoxy grouts are intended for use where chemical resistance, high temperatures, high bond strength, or impact resistance is needed. They are recommended for use in interior locations on both horizontal and vertical surfaces. They are not generally recommended for use on exteriors, but are often used there anyway.

Furan Grout

Furan grouts contain furan resin and hardeners.

Furan grout is used in industrial and commercial floor areas where exceptional chemical resistance is needed.

Silicone Rubber Grout

Silicon rubber grouts are elastomeric grouts.

Silicon rubber grouts are used in the joints of factory-grouted tile sheets, and in the field for joints in the same tile. They are used often in locations where the tile is subject to hot cooking oils, steam, free oxygen, moisture, staining agents, and extreme temperatures (hot or cold).

Miscellaneous Tile Installation Materials

Membranes

Cleavage Membrane. A cleavage membrane separates a reinforced mortar bed from the substrates and permits differential movement between the two. A cleavage membrane may be one of several materials, including 4-mil polyethylene and 15-pound roofing felt.

Waterproofing Membrane. A variety of membranes, including lead or copper pans and both fluid-applied and preformed sheet elastomeric membranes, are used as waterproofing beneath ceramic tile.

Reinforcement

Horizontal Setting Bed Reinforcement. Setting bed reinforcement is usually a wire fabric. It may be 2 by 2 inch fabric of 16/16 wire, 3 by 3 inch fabric of 13/13 wire, or 1-1/2 by 2 inch fabric of 16/13 wire.

Metal Lath. The metal lath in mortar setting beds should be standard expanded diamond mesh lath. In interior applications, the lath should be painted or galvanized steel. In exterior locations, the lath should be galvanized steel only. Flat lath should be used on studs. Nonrib-type self-furring lath should be used over solid substrates, such as existing tile or masonry.

Board Type Bases

There are two types of boards used as bases for ceramic tile: water-resistant gypsum board and glass mesh mortar units. Both are discussed in more detail in Chapter 4.

Expansion Joint Sealants

Elastomeric sealants complying with ASTM Standard C 920 are recommended. They may be silicone, urethane, or polysulfide. Silicone sealants are used in both interior and exterior vertical locations. They are available with a mildew-resistant additive for use in wet locations, such as at sinks, tubs, and showers. Urethane is used in interior and exterior traffic-bearing locations and exterior vertical locations. Because of their odor, polysulfide sealants are generally restricted to exterior use.

Divider Strips

Sometimes terrazzo divider strips are used to border or divide tile. Such divider strips are brass or zinc alloy.

Tile Installation

Substrates for Field-Applied Tile

Substrate preparation is very important to obtaining a good tile installation. Preparation includes providing the proper degree of surface variation and finish type. The Tile Council of America's *Handbook for Ceramic Tile Installation* includes specific tolerances for smoothness and substrate slab finish type for various substrates. In general, the following guidelines apply.

- Concrete finish and variation for bonded thick beds on floors and decks: Float finish on exterior slabs, screeded finish on interior slabs, accurate to within 1/4 inch in 10 feet. In addition, exterior concrete slabs-on-grade to receive tile should be placed over a subsurface drainage system.
- Concrete finish and variation for thick bed over cleavage or waterproofing membrane: Trowel finish, accurate to 1/4 inch in 10 feet.
- Concrete finish and variation for thin-set beds on horizontal surfaces: Steel trowel and fine broom finish, accurate to within 1/8 inch in 10 feet. In addition, exterior concrete slabs-on-grade to receive tile should be placed over a subsurface drainage system.
- Variation for thin-set beds on horizontal wood surfaces: Accurate to within 1/8 inch in 10 feet.
- Thick beds on vertical surfaces: Bonded mortar beds require substrate accuracy of not more than 1/4 inch in 8 feet from the required plane, but by varying the application methods used, metal lath-supported thick mortar beds can be used over almost every substrate condition,

including irregular, cracked, and smooth surfaces, such as existing ceramic tile.

- Thin-set beds on vertical surfaces: Surfaces for dry-set or latex-Portland-cement mortar, or for epoxy or organic adhesives should be accurately in plane to within 1/8 inch in 8 feet. In addition, surfaces to receive epoxy or organic adhesives should have no variation exceeding 1/16 inch in any foot. Joints in gypsum board and glass mesh mortar units should be taped. Nail and screw heads should be coated.

- Substrates for ceiling or soffit application: Accurate to within 1/8 inch in 8 feet. Accuracy may be obtained with a furring system.

Of course, all substrates should be free of wax, oils, dirt, loose particles, and other foreign substances. Concrete should be free of curing compounds. When concrete surfaces to which tile will be directly applied are contaminated, drastic action may be required. It may be necessary, for example, to remove as much as 1/4 inch of the concrete to obtain a clean surface that is properly roughened to receive tile installed using thin-set materials. Such methods as sand-blasting, grinding with terrazzo machines, scarifying, or power-blast cleaning may be needed. Where the substrates are not contaminated, simply cleaning with brooms, vacuum cleaning equipment, and damp mops will usually produce an adequately clean surface.

Setting Bed Construction for Field-Applied Tile

Setting beds are divided into two categories: Thick beds and thin-set beds.

The applications described in the following paragraphs and shown in Figures 5-2 through 5-8 are generic in nature and intended to show general methods that are most likely to be encountered in existing buildings. Special applications, such as 1-1/4 inch thick heavy chemical-resistant tile in packing houses and sound- and fire-rated floor and wall construction are not included. Refer to the Tile Council of America's *Handbook for Ceramic Tile Installation* for details for specific applications.

Thick Beds.   Thick mortar beds are used for Portland cement, epoxy, and furan mortar applications, and in both interior and exterior locations.

Floor and Deck Applications.   Figures 5-2 and 5-3 show the components of typical thick mortar beds in horizontal applications.

Thick mortar beds on horizontal substrates should be nominally 1-1/2 inches thick.

When the substrate is stable and solidly supported, such as a concrete slab-on-grade, a thick mortar bed should be bonded to the substrate by a Portland cement slurry bond coat.

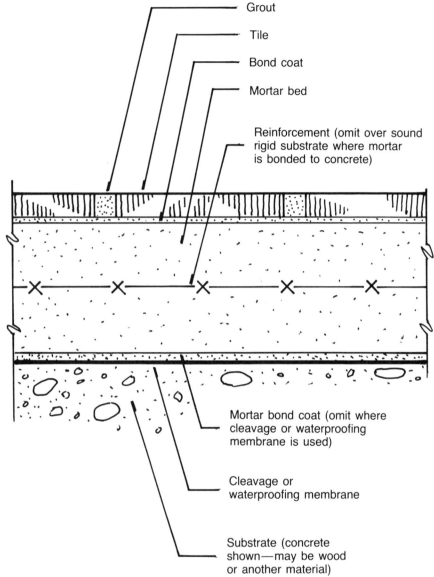

Grout

Tile

Bond coat

Mortar bed

Reinforcement (omit over sound rigid substrate where mortar is bonded to concrete)

Mortar bond coat (omit where cleavage or waterproofing membrane is used)

Cleavage or waterproofing membrane

Substrate (concrete shown—may be wood or another material)

Figure 5-2 Interior thick mortar bed: Floor application.

When the substrate is flexible, such as a supported concrete slab or wood subfloor, a cleavage membrane should be introduced between the substrate and the mortar bed to permit differential movement between the two. Where a waterproofing membrane is required, it can serve as the cleavage membrane.

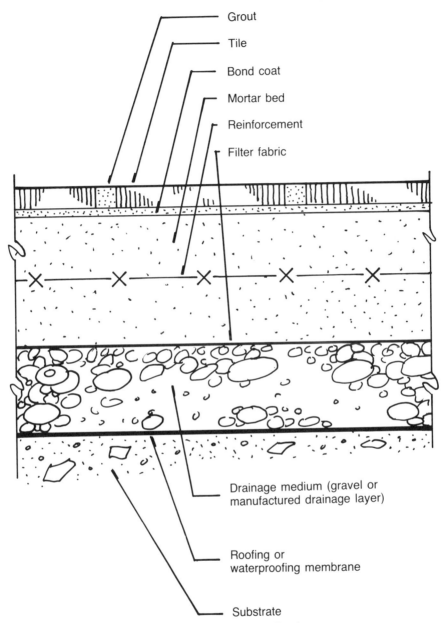

Grout

Tile

Bond coat

Mortar bed

Reinforcement

Filter fabric

Drainage medium (gravel or manufactured drainage layer)

Roofing or waterproofing membrane

Substrate

Figure 5-3 Exterior thick mortar bed: Deck application.

Thick beds over flexible horizontal substrates should be reinforced with wire mesh reinforcement.

Existing tile may have been installed over a wet thick bed in a bond coat of Portland cement paste, or over a cured bed in a layer of regular dry-set mortar, conductive dry-set mortar, latex-Portland cement mortar, or epoxy mortar.

Wall and Other Vertical Applications.   Figures 5-4 and 5-5 show typical thick mortar beds.

Thick mortar beds in vertical applications should be between 3/4 inch and 1 inch thick.

Vertical thick mortar beds in exterior applications should be installed over 15-pound roofing felt or 4-mil polyethylene membrane and supported on metal lath fastened to the substrate (see Fig. 5-4).

Vertical thick mortar beds in interior applications on wood and metal studs should be supported on metal lath fastened to the studs through a

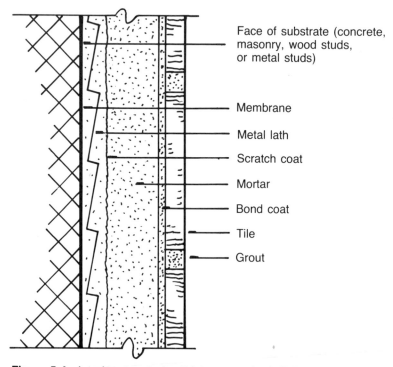

Face of substrate (concrete, masonry, wood studs, or metal studs)

Membrane

Metal lath

Scratch coat

Mortar

Bond coat

Tile

Grout

Figure 5-4   Interior or exterior thick mortar bed: Reinforced vertical application.

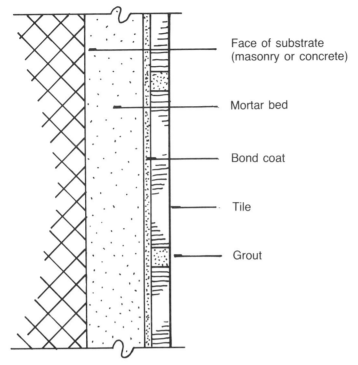

Face of substrate
(masonry or concrete)

Mortar bed

Bond coat

Tile

Grout

Figure 5-5   Interior thick mortar bed: Bonded vertical application.

layer of 15-pound roofing felt or 4-mil polyethylene membrane. On metal studs in dry locations, however, the membrane is sometimes omitted. In some parts of the country, the membrane is routinely omitted even in wet areas, which is in violation of most building codes and the recommendations in ANSI standards and the Tile Council of America's 1988 *Handbook for Ceramic Tile Applications.*

Vertical thick mortar beds in interior applications on solid substrates, such as plaster, masonry, and concrete that are sound and offer a good anchorage for metal lath, but where bonding problems exist, or the surface is cracked or coated, are often installed as a supported system (see Fig. 5-4). Where the substrate is smooth and has minimum variation in plane, a supported system thick setting bed may be installed in one coat. Where the substrate is irregular, a scratch coat may be required to level the surface. This is a good method for applying new tile over an existing smooth surface. The one-coat method is often used in wet areas.

Vertical thick mortar beds in interior applications on smooth masonry or concrete, where the surface is clean, sound, and dimensionally stable, may be applied using a bonded system. In a bonded system (see Fig. 5-5), the mortar bed is applied directly to the substrate. A bonded mortar bed exceeding 3/4 inch thick should be applied in two coats.

Existing tile may have been installed over a wet thick bed in a bond coat of Portland cement paste, or over a cured bed in a layer of dry-set mortar or latex-Portland cement mortar.

Overhead Applications.   Figure 5-6 shows a typical thick mortar bed in an overhead (ceiling or soffit) application.

Thick mortar beds in overhead applications should be between 3/4 inch and 1 inch thick.

A 15-pound roofing felt or 4-mil polyethylene membrane may have been used above the lath, especially in wet areas and where condensation above the ceiling or soffit might have been a problem.

Metal lath may be directly attached to the substrate or may be supported on a wood or metal support system. Where used, support system members should not be more than 16 inches apart.

Existing tile may have been installed over a wet thick bed in a bond coat of Portland cement paste, or over a cured bed in a layer of dry-set mortar or latex-Portland cement mortar.

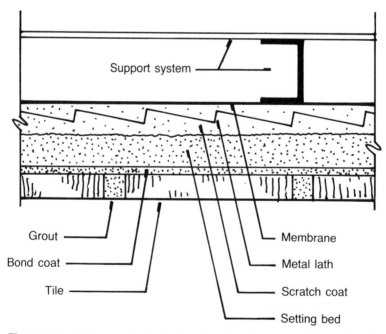

Figure 5-6   Thick mortar bed: Overhead (ceiling or soffit) application.

Thin-Set Beds. Thin-set mortar beds are used for exterior dry-set and latex-Portland cement mortar applications, and for interior organic adhesive and dry-set and latex-Portland cement, epoxy, and furan mortar applications.

Dry-set or latex-Portland cement mortar in a thin-set installation should be a minimum of 3/32 inch thick. Epoxy and furan mortars and epoxy and organic adhesives should be the thickness recommended by their manufacturers.

Floor and Deck Applications.   Figure 5-7 shows the components of typical thin-set mortar beds in horizontal applications.

Dry-set and latex-Portland cement mortar beds are best used on slabs-on-grade. They should not be used on slabs, or other subfloors, that are subject to deflection.

Epoxy and furan grout mortars are used on slabs-on-grade, and sometimes on slabs that are subject to deflection.

Some tile contractors organizations oppose using organic adhesives on floors, but the Tile Council of America's *Handbook for Tile Installation* recommends using them on both wood and concrete floors in residential applications. The TCA *Handbook* also recommends using presanded dry-set and latex-Portland cement mortar over wood construction with a glass mesh mortar unit underlayment; epoxy mortar directly over a wood subfloor; and epoxy adhesives directly on concrete substrates in residential construction.

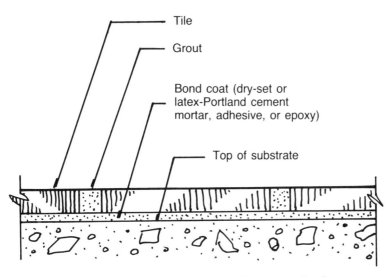

Figure 5-7 Thin-set mortar bed: Floor and deck application.

Most waterproofing membranes require a thick mortar bed, but there are a few that are suitable for direct bonding of latex-Portland cement mortar.

Vertical Applications. Figure 5-8 shows typical thin-set mortar beds in vertical applications.

Dry-set or latex-Portland cement setting beds are installed directly over masonry, Portland cement plaster, gypsum board, or glass mesh mortar units. Gypsum board substrates in wet areas should be the moisture-resistant type. Substrates should have a maximum variation of 1/8 inch in 10 feet and should be smooth and free from cracks. They should be smooth, but not glossy.

Organic adhesive is installed directly over gypsum board, plaster, or glass mesh mortar units. It is best used in dry areas, but sometimes appears in residential tub surrounds and showers.

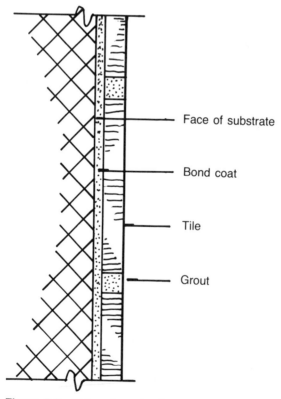

Face of substrate

Bond coat

Tile

Grout

Figure 5-8 Thin-set mortar bed: Vertical application.

Organic adhesives should not be used in very wet areas, such as gang showers, but many such applications exist.

Overhead Applications.   Tile is sometimes installed on ceilings and soffits using thin-set mortar materials and methods. In such installations, substrates should be limited to mortar beds, concrete, masonry, and glass mesh mortar units.

Joints for Field-Applied Tile

Normal tile-to-tile joints vary in width, depending on the tile material, thickness, and laying pattern, and aesthetic results desired. Glazed wall tile and some other tile units have lugs that dictate the minimum joint possible. One criteria for selecting grouting material should be the selected joint width. Sand-Portland cement mix, for example, should be varied from equal parts sand and cement for 1/8-inch wide joints, to one part cement to three parts sand for joints more than 1/2 inch wide.

Expansion, control, and isolation joints are needed for most tile installations. For convenience, the text that follows will refer to them all as "expansion joints." The TCA *Handbook* and ANSI installation standards include specific requirements for expansion joint locations. Generally, the following rules apply:

- Expansion joints should be at least as wide as normal tile-to-tile joints in the same plane.
- Expansion joints in interior glazed wall tile and ceramic mosaic tile surfaces should preferably be 1/4 inch wide, and should never be less than 1/8 inch wide. Expansion joints in interior quarry and paver tile should not be less than 1/4 inch wide. Interior expansion joints not exposed to the sun should be placed between 24 and 36 feet apart in each direction. Where exposed to the sun, interior expansion joints should be placed 12 to 16 feet apart.
- Expansion joints in exterior surfaces should not be less than 3/8 inch wide where up to 12 feet apart, and never less than 1/2 inch wide where up to 16 feet apart, but actual spacings and widths should be increased, depending on the expected temperature of the surface. Decks exposed to the sun often require joints 12 feet apart and 3/4 inch or more wide. In extremely hot locations, even closer spacings and wider joints may be needed. In every case, the joint material selected should be able to accommodate the joint width used. Exterior expansion joints should never be placed more than 16 feet apart.
- Expansion, control, and seismic joints in the substrates, joints between different substrate materials, and even construction (cold) joints in

otherwise homogeneous material forming the substrates, should be carried through the tile. Joints in the tile should not be narrower than the underlying joint in the substrate.

- Expansion joints should also be installed wherever tile abuts a dissimilar material or restraining surface, such as a wall or curb, and around every item that penetrates the tile.
- All expansion joints should be filled with a backer rod (if necessary) and an elastomeric sealant.

Prefabricated Exterior Tile Cladding

Prefabricated exterior tile panels have been used since sometime in the 1950s. While such systems have demonstrated few problems over the years, an existing prefabricated tile installation might develop problems at some time. One type of prefabricated system (Fig. 5-9) usually consists of:

- *Framework:* Metal studs and reinforcing members. Galvanized studs are usually preferred, but painted studs are sometimes used. Welded frames are better, but an existing frame may have been screwed together.
- *Sheathing:* Tongue and groove, water-resistant gypsum sheathing board screwed to the frame. Sheathing is usually 1/2 inch thick, but 5/8-inch thick sheathing may be found.
- Weather-resistant paper.
- *Setting Bed:* A diamond mesh metal lath reinforced, latex-modified Portland cement mortar bed. Beds are usually 1-1/4 inch thick and banded with a casing bead around the perimeter of each panel. Beds may have been constructed as multiple layer plaster beds, conventional mortar setting beds, or one-coat beds.
- *Bond Coat:* A latex-modified dry-set mortar applied over the cured setting bed.
- Tile.
- *Grout:* Latex-modified, dry-set grout.

Prefabricated exterior ceramic tile cladding panels are also manufactured using glass mesh mortar units in lieu of the gypsum sheathing and Portland cement setting bed. Other aspects are the same as described above.

The interior of prefabricated exterior ceramic tile cladding panels is usually finished with a continuous vapor retarder and gypsum board. The stud void is insulated with batt insulation. Joints between panels are filled with elastomeric sealant.

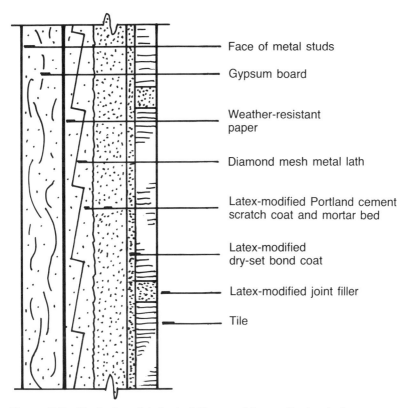

Face of metal studs

Gypsum board

Weather-resistant
paper

Diamond mesh metal lath

Latex-modified Portland cement
scratch coat and mortar bed

Latex-modified
dry-set bond coat

Latex-modified joint filler

Tile

Figure 5-9 Typical prefabricated tile panel for vertical exterior use.

Jess McIlvain's 1984 article, "Prefabricated Exterior Ceramic Tile Cladding," contains a detailed, illustrated description of prefabricated exterior
tile panels. Anyone with a problem related to such systems, or who just
wants to learn more about the method, will find McIlvain's article helpful.

Tile Failures and What to Do about Them

Why Tile Fails

Most tile failures can be traced to one or several of the following sources:
structure failure; structure movement; solid substrate problems; other building element problems; framing or furring problems; plaster substrate failure;
gypsum board substrate failure; glass mesh mortar unit substrate failure;
bad tile; improper design; bad workmanship; poor maintenance procedures;

and miscellaneous sources that are not easily categorized. Occasionally, it will not be possible to ascertain the reason for a tile failure.

It usually takes several improperly selected or installed elements to cause one visible tile failure (Figs. 5-10 and 5-11). Often the individual errors are insignificant alone. For example, a properly constructed reinforced cement mortar setting bed with a cleavage membrane, and with properly located expansion joints, will withstand normal deflection and creep in the supporting concrete slab. The system might not fail if one component, say, part of the cleavage membrane, were omitted. It still might not fail if the reinforcement were laid across an expansion joint in the substrate, or if the substrate were too rough to permit the cleavage membrane portions that were installed to slide freely. But with each omission or improperly constructed part, the chance of failure increases, until one error too many causes the system to fail.

Figure 5-10 Curing compound left on the concrete slab caused a loss of the bond between the slab and the tile setting material shown in this photograph. The problem was exacerbated by the lack of expansion joints in the tile laid over this structural slab. (*Photograph by Jess McIlvain.*)

Figure 5-11 The quarry tile in this photograph sheared from the slab and raised a 1/4 inch above it because contamination was not removed from the slab before the tile was laid and no expansion joints were provided. (*Photograph by Jess McIlvain.*)

Many tile failures result from problems with the tile itself, its setting bed, or joint grout, which are discussed in this chapter. Other tile failures, though, result from problems with the construction underlying the tile and its setting bed. Those problems include structure failure and movement, and problems associated with solid substrates, other building elements, and wood or metal framing or furring, all of which are discussed in Chapter 2.

Many of the problems discussed in Chapter 2, while not the most probable causes of tile failure, are more serious and costly to fix than the types of problems discussed in this chapter. Consequently, the possibility that the types of problems discussed in Chapter 2 are responsible for a tile failure should be investigated. Figure 5-12 shows a case where structure movement caused a tile failure.

Some tile failures are actually a failure in the tile's plaster, gypsum board, or glass mesh mortar unit substrates. In each of these cases, there are too many potential failure causes to repeat them in this chapter. The reader is referred instead to the chapters in which those materials are

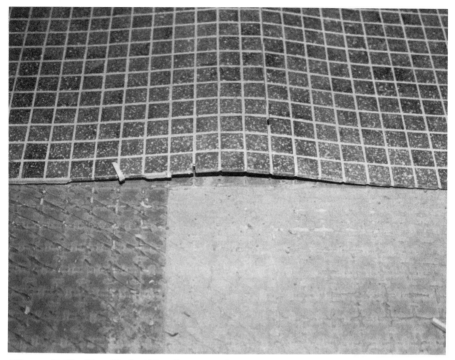

Figure 5-12 The tile in this photograph was installed on a precast concrete plank floor using a thin-set method. Deflection of the precast concrete caused the tile to shear off and pop up. (*Photograph by Jess McIlvain.*)

discussed. Plaster is discussed in Chapter 3; gypsum board and glass mesh mortar units in Chapter 4.

The failure types discussed in Chapters 2, 3, and 4 should be ruled out or, if found to be at fault, rectified before tile repairs are attempted. It will do no good to repair tile, joints, or setting beds, or install new tile, when a failed, uncorrected, or unaccounted-for problem of the types discussed in Chapters 2, 3, and 4 is present. The new tile will also fail.

After the types of problems discussed in Chapters 2, 3, and 4 have been investigated and found to be not present (or repaired if found), the next step is to discover any additional causes for the tile failure, and correct them, before repairing the existing tile or installing new tile. Possible causes include those in the following paragraphs, which contain numbered lists of errors and situations that can cause tile failure. Refer to "Evidence of Failure" later in this chapter for a listing of the types of failure to which the numbered failure causes in this part apply.

Bad Tile. Improperly manufactured tile arriving at a construction site is certainly not unheard of, and that possibility should be considered when tile fails. Many tile imperfections are apparent visually, of course, but many are not. Tiles that appear normal at the time of installation may later become stained or discolored because the tile was manufactured with too high an absorption rate. The number of incidents of bad tile is small, however, when compared with bad design and improper installation.

Many problems blamed on inferior tile actually result from selecting the wrong tile for the installation. For example, tile with a soft glaze may work very well where not subject to abrasion. Using the same tile on a floor, though, is a design error. It is not reasonable to expect any material to do a better job than it was designed to do.

Improper Design. Improper design includes selecting the wrong tile, setting system, or grout material for the location, selecting the wrong installation system, failing to locate or correctly locate expansion joints, or failing to integrate the tile with the adjacent conditions.

Poor Tile Selection. The tile must be suitable for the location and use intended. Errors that will lead to problems include:

1. Selecting a tile that is too thin for the impact loads to be encountered.
2. Selecting tile with a glaze that is too soft for the abrasion it will receive. This problem sometimes occurs because the glaze on some foreign tile is rated using a different system than that used on domestically produced tile. This problem can be prevented if the designer will obtain a sample of the tile contemplated and subject it to a scratch test. If a hand-held 1/4 inch case-hardened drill bit will scratch the tile, it is too soft for use on traffic-bearing surfaces. The surface should have a hardness equal to about 6.5 or more on the 10-point Mohs scale.
3. Selecting tile that is not frost-resistant for use where it will be subjected to freeze-thaw cycles.
4. Selecting a bright glaze, which scratches fairly easily or becomes slippery, for use on floors.
5. Selecting tile that is too slippery for use on floors or decks. This is a particular problem with paver tile, some of which is extremely smooth.
6. Selecting a flat-backed tile for vertical exterior locations.

Incorrect Setting System. The setting system must be suitable for the location and substrate. Examples of errors that will lead to problems include:

1. Selecting a thin-set installation method over a supported horizontal substrate that is subject to deflection. An example is a cast-in-place or precast concrete floor that is not on grade. Slabs that will deflect are unsuitable for most thin-set cementitious materials.

   Thin-set tile on supported slabs fails because the slab changes in shape due to shrinking and deflection. The tile, acting like a diaphragm, maintains its initial shape, or moves differentially from the slab. The result is sheared off, raised, buckled, or cracked tile.

   Adding latex to the setting bed mix does not make thin-set beds adequate for supported slabs. Latex makes mortar less pervious and less brittle, but does not adequately increase its ability to keep tiles bonded to suported slabs.

   Tile does not usually become loose or crack because of initial slab deflection, which takes place as soon as the forms are removed, because such deflection is mostly complete before the tile bed sets. Deflection caused by furniture, people, and other live loads might cause tiles to shear away from the setting bed. But the most common cause of thin-set tile becoming loose and a common cause of tile cracking is permanent slab deformation and size change caused by normal shrinkage of the concrete and continued deflection of the slab over time, which is called "creep." Typically, sheared-off and cracked tile caused by slab creep happens two or three years after the tile is placed.

2. Failing to call for a cleavage membrane over a substrate that is subject to deflection, where a waterproof membrane is not used beneath the setting bed.

3. Failing to call for reinforcement in the setting bed when the substrate is subject to deflection.

4. Failing to call for a waterproofing membrane below tile in wet areas, such as showers and food preparation areas.

5. Using organic adhesives on commercial floors.

6. Using organic adhesives in commercial buildings where the tile so installed is subject to abuse or impact.

7. Using organic adhesives in wet areas.

8. Using organic adhesives on concrete or masonry. Excessive alkalinity in the concrete or masonry joints may burn organic adhesives and make them brittle and non-adhesive.

9. Calling for other than latex-modified mortar for setting porcelain paver tile. Porcelain paver tile is usually flat backed, which provides no mechanical bond with the setting bed. In addition, such tile has a

very low absorption rate, and is large, which reduces the effect of beating it into the setting bed. It is necessary to use latex-modified mortar with such tile if the proper bond strength is to be achieved.

10. Failing to prohibit use of curing compounds beneath ceramic tile installed using thin-set or bonded mortar methods. Alternatively, failing to require subsequent removal of curing compounds that were used. The result can be seen in Figure 5-10.

11. Failing to require removal of oil, grease, dirt, dust, paint, and wax from surfaces to receive ceramic tile (see Fig. 5-11).

Poor Grout Selection.   Most problems that owners have with ceramic tile are related to grout. One recent survey concluded that cleaning tile and its grout is a bigger problem to restaurant owners than cleaning the large grease-collecting hoods that cover their ranges and ovens.

Years ago, most tile grout was just a mixture of sand, cement, and water. Colors, most of which were shades of gray, were achieved by changing the shade of the sand or cement or by using colored sand. Today designers must select from a large array of available grout materials. Much of the cement grout used today contains additives that change its composition and appearance. There are many color pigments, for example, and latex additives. Epoxy, furan, and other high-performance grouts are also available.

Grout selection, then, is more difficult today than it was in the past, but careful attention to the process is essential if failures are to be prevented. The grout selected must be suitable to the location and use of the tiled space. Examples of errors that will lead to problems include:

1. Selecting light-colored grout where it is subject to dirt or stains, such as in heavy traffic or food preparation or service areas. Using white or other light-colored grout on floors is usually a bad idea which leads to maintenance problems later and often becomes unsightly because of dirt and stains. Dirt does not show as much against dark grout joints as it does on light materials. Light-colored grout is a particular problem where the tile has cushion (slightly rounded) edges, as is the case on most paver tile. The cushion edge prevents the grout from finishing flush with the tile surface, which makes cleaning difficult. Commercial cleaning machines simply ride over joints, leaving dirt and stains there. Even when the tile has square edges, unless the installer is particularly careful to leave the grout flush with the tile's wear surface, cleaning equipment may fail to clean off dirt and stains.

2. Selecting grout having a color that contrasts greatly with the tile color. Using light grout with dark tile is more of a problem than using

dark grout with light tile. Unglazed tile, especially unglazed porcelain pavers, some matt glazed tile, and slip-resistant tile have microscopic pores and grain structure into which wet grout will migrate. Unless wax or grout guard is applied to the face of the tile before it is installed, preventing grout entry into the pores and grain structure is not possible, and removal of grout stains is difficult, and often impossible. When the grout color contrasts with the tile, the discoloration may be permanently apparent.

3. Selecting a grout type for use in a location where that grout type is not suitable. Using silicon grout in an exterior location, for example. Using the wrong type may cause it to come out of the joints, or be damaged by chemicals. The TCA *Handbook* includes recommendations for grout type usage.

Improperly Locating or Designing Expansion Joints. Expansion joints must be correctly located and of the appropriate width, if the tile is to function properly. Examples of errors that will cause problems include:

1. Not showing expansion joints on the contract drawings.
2. Showing or specifying joints that are located too far apart or are the wrong width. Concrete will shrink and crack at random. If consideration is not given in the tile design to those random concrete cracks, the tile will eventually also crack. Properly placed expansion joints help alleviate tile cracks due to shrinkage cracks in concrete substrates.
3. Failing to locate joints over all joints, of every kind, in the substrates. Typically, construction (cold) joints are ignored. Ignored substrate joints will eventually show up as cracks in the tile.

Failing to Integrate the Tile with Adjacent Conditions. Tile is a part of the overall construction system that encloses and finishes a building. It must be coordinated and integrated with adjacent construction. The following errors can lead to later problems, including staining, efflorescence, and even shearing of the tile from its setting bed or the bed from the structure.

1. Failing to provide proper flashing in exterior walls finished with tile, permitting water to enter the tile substrate or voids behind the tile.
2. Failing to seal edges and intersections of interior tile with other materials, thus permitting dirt and water from cleaning operations to enter tile substrates or spaces behind the tile.
3. Failing to properly seal the joints between tile and adjacent or penetrating materials and items, or between prefabricated tile panels.

Failing to Require Proper Preparation Methods. Proper preparation is essential if tile failure is to be prevented. The following error will cause problems:

1. Failing to require proper preparation of substrate surfaces and surfaces within the tile system. Specific requirements should be given. Requiring that preparation be in accord with the manufacturer's recommendations is not usually sufficient, especially where existing construction is involved.

Bad Workmanship

Incorrect Installation. Correct installation is essential if tile failures are to be prevented. Examples of installation errors that can lead to problems include:

1. Failing to follow the design and the recommendations of the manufacturer and recognized authorities, such as TCA. Following the manufacturer's instructions is always important, but takes on increased significance when special products, such as large porcelain paver tile, are involved.
2. Improperly cleaning and otherwise preparing the substrates (Figs. 5-13 and 5-14). This is a problem for all tile installations, but is even more acute when a thin-set application is used.
3. Incorrectly proportioning mortar ingredients. Oversanding and using too much water are common problems which can lead to weak or brittle mortar. Mixes varying from equal parts sand and Portland cement up to one part cement and fifteen parts sand on the same project are not uncommon where failures have occurred.
4. Incorrectly adding ingredients and mixing mortar and grout. Improperly mixing latex additives is a common problem, which will weaken mortar or grout. Another common problem is mixing mortar or grout with drills that operate at too many revolutions per minute (150 rpm is the maximum permissible), which traps air in the mixes, making them weak. Improperly mixed grout may be soft, lumpy, or mottled in color.
5. Failing to thoroughly mix colored grout, which will result in a mottled or uneven appearance.
6. Failing to apply sufficient mortar to completely cover the back of the tile, creating voids and insufficient bonding of the tile to the setting bed.
7. Allowing the setting bed bond coat or thin-set mortar to dry (skin) before the tile is applied.

Figure 5-13 This shopping-mall floor tile was installed over terrazzo that had been carpeted. All of the carpet adhesive was not removed and acted as a bondbreaker, which prevented the tile's setting bed from bonding to the terrazzo. (*Photograph by Jess McIlvain.*)

8. Failing to properly wet glazed wall tile before application or to hydrate cement grout by keeping it wet during curing. Unhydrated grout will crumble and disintegrate.

9. Leaving the aluminum oxide bondbreaker on the back of porcelain paver tile. The bondbreaker is added at the factory to prevent the tile from sticking to the rollers used in the roller hearth kiln used to produce the tile. Some manufacturers recommend leaving the bondbreaker in place, saying it will not affect the bond, But recent evidence indicates that a more secure installation is achieved when the bondbreaker is removed before installation.

10. Not properly beating the tile in place, or otherwise assuring the bond (see Fig. 5-14).

11. Improperly installing and finishing grout.

Bad grouting techniques can result in low or uneven grout joints, a rough grout surface, soft grout, or grout that is dirty, streaked, or mottled in appearance. Some techniques will lead to total grout dete-

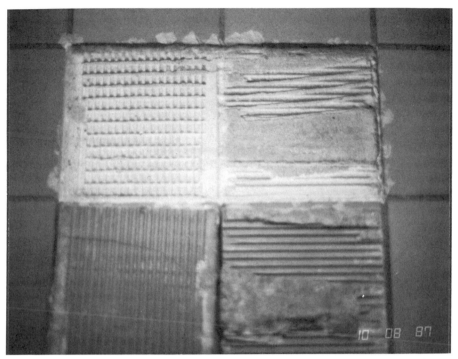

Figure 5-14   The tile in this photograph was not beat in. In addition, the tile on the right was placed over contamination that had not been removed from the slab. (*Photograph by Jess McIlvain.*)

rioration. Filling joints in quarry and paver tile too full with dry spacing mortar mixes, for example, leaves too little room for the surface grout. Under pressure from spike heels and rolling traffic, the too-thin surface grout breaks up and exposes the underlying spacing mortar, which, too weak to be exposed, eventually disintegrates.

The scenario that produced the grout failure shown in Figure 5-15 started when a dry grout was swept into the joint to fill it. A layer of wet grout was then placed over the dry grout and struck with a tool to finish it. Later, water seeped through the thin topping grout into the dry grout where it froze. The resulting dry grout expansion blew the topping grout out of the joint.

Finishing joints too low can make it impossible to clean them with commercial floor cleaning equipment, which passes over the joints without touching the grout.

Dropping of tools, such as the rubber trowels used to remove excess grout from tiles, onto wet grout results in depressions in the

Figure 5-15   Although it may appear that the tile is raised in this photograph, only the grout has moved. (*Photograph by Jess McIlvain.*)

grout which will collect dirt and floor finishing materials which will darken and discolor the tile.

12. Failing to place expansion joints exactly above control or expansion joints in the substrate. The result can be seen in Figure 5-16.

Failing to Protect Tile.   Tile, setting materials, and grout must be protected before, during, and after installation, until the setting beds and grout have been cured. Errors include the following:

1. Permitting the tile, mortar, or grout to freeze.
2. Failing to protect tile from mortar stains. Unglazed tile and other tile with rough surfaces have a tendency to absorb grout. Removal of grout, especially latex-modified grout, from such tile is almost impossible unless the tile is coated with wax or a grout guard before the grout is installed.
3. Permitting abuse after the tile is installed. Abuse includes, but is not limited to, permitting traffic over the tile too soon after installation.

Figure 5-16 The tile joint to the immediate right of the crack in this photograph is an expansion joint. The crack is directly above the control joint in the slab below. (*Photograph by Jess McIlvain.*)

4. Permitting other construction materials to contaminate the grout after it is placed, even after curing is complete (see Fig. 5-11).

Poor Maintenance Procedures. Poor maintenance procedures include:

1. Improper cleaning of tile and grout. Acid cleaners can burn and bleach cementitious grouts, and dull the finish of glazed tile. Abrasive cleaners can scratch tile that has a soft glaze.

2. Using inappropriate commercial sealers to make tile easier to clean. Some sealers, especially those that contain equal parts of linseed oil and mineral spirits, will darken grout. Applying floor polish to tile usually makes the tile slippery.

Miscellaneous. There are also failure causes that do not fall readily into a category, such as the following:

1. Recently, some porcelain tile installations have failed, even when the substrate was apparently properly prepared and the tile was properly installed. There is some reason to believe that the latex in the setting mortar may harden over a period of several years, causing the mortar to lose some of its strength. Another theory, introduced in England, is that such tiles become slightly warped after installation, especially when they are subjected to hot sun and then cooled suddenly by a rain shower. The actual cause has not yet been determined. Often, such tile can be cleaned and reinstalled.
2. Using the wrong size, type, or spacing for the support system framing for prefabricated exterior ceramic tile cladding panels. Using corrodible metal for such supports.
3. Worn tile. Tile, like any other material, will eventually wear out and lose its color or pattern, or become slippery or pitted.

Evidence of Failure

In the following paragraphs, tile failures are listed under the headings "Tile and Setting Bed Failures" and "Joint Failures." These categories are subdivided into failure types, such as "Scratched Tile." Following each failure type are one or more failure sources, such as "Improper Design: Poor Tile Selection." After most failure sources, one or more numbers is listed. The numbers represent possible errors associated with that failure source which might cause that failure type to occur.

A description and discussion of the numbered failure causes for failure types: "Structure Failure," "Structure Movement," "Solid Substrate Problems," "Other Building Element Problems" "Wood Framing and Furring Problems," and "Metal Framing and Furring Problems" appear in Chapter 2 under the same headings, and are listed in the Contents. For example, clarification and explanation of the numbered cause (1) in the example

▪ Metal Framing and Furring Problems: 1 (see Chapter 2).

appears in Chapter 2 under the heading "Metal Framing and Furring Problems," cause 1, which reads

1. Metal framing or furring that is out of alignment.

A description and discussion of the numbered causes that follow failure types: "Improper Design," "Bad Workmanship," "Poor Maintenance Procedures," and "Miscellaneous" appear as subparagraphs and sub-subparagraphs in the part of this chapter titled "Why Tile Fails," which is listed in the Contents. For example, clarification and explanation of the numbered cause (4) listed in the example

▪ Improper Design: Poor Tile Selection: 4.

appears in this chapter under the heading "Why Tile Fails," subparagraph "Improper Design," sub-subparagraph "Poor Tile Selection," cause 4, which reads:

4. Selecting a bright glaze, which scratches fairly easily or becomes slippery, for use on floors.

Some failure sources are not followed by numbers. Those titled "Bad Tile" are discussed under that heading in the part of this chapter titled "Why Tile Fails."

The failure source titled "Standard Thickness Plaster Failures" (which is not followed by numbers) refers to failure types and causes discussed in Chapter 3 under the same heading. That reference is to a cured plaster substrate for tile which will be applied using organic adhesives or other thin-set methods. It does not refer to cementitious tile setting beds, whether or not they are cured before the tile is placed. Failure sources titled "Standard Gypsum Board and Veneer Plaster Gypsum Base Failures" and "Glass Mesh Mortar Unit Failures" refer to failure types and causes discussed in Chapter 4 under these same headings. The data following each of these three failure sources are listed in Chapter 3 or 4 as failure types. Note that only the failure types from Chapters 3 and 4 are listed here. The failure sources and cause numbers are omitted to prevent repetition. Every potential failure source and cause listed in Chapters 3 and 4 for the failure types listed here should be considered as a possible cause for that type of tile failure.

Tile and Setting Bed Failures

Scratched Tile. This failure may be caused by:

▪ Bad Tile.
▪ Improper Design: Poor Tile Selection: 4.
▪ Bad Workmanship: Failing to Protect Tile: 3.
▪ Poor Maintenance Procedures: 1.

Tile Color or Pattern Fading or Excessive Glaze Wear. These problems may be caused by:

- Bad Tile.
- Improper Design: Poor Tile Selection: 2.
- Poor Maintenance Procedures: 1.
- Miscellaneous: 3.

Discolored or Stained Tile.   A failure of this type may be caused by:

- Other Building Element Problems: 1, 2 (see Chapter 2).
- Bad Tile.
- Improper Design: Poor Grout Selection: 1, 2.
- Improper Design: Failing to Integrate the Tile with Adjacent Conditions: 1, 2, 3.
- Improper Design: Failing to Require Proper Preparation Methods: 1.
- Bad Workmanship: Incorrect Installation: 1, 2, 3, 4, 5, 12.
- Bad Workmanship: Failing to Protect Tile: 2.
- Poor Maintenance Procedures: 1, 2.

Slippery Tile.   A problem of this type may be caused by:

- Bad Tile.
- Improper Design: Poor Tile Selection: 4, 5.
- Poor Maintenance Procedures: 2.
- Miscellaneous: 3.

Spalled Tile.   This failure may be caused by:

- Bad Tile.
- Improper Design: Poor Tile Selection: 3.
- Bad Workmanship: Failing to Protect Tile: 1, 2.

Cracked or Broken Tile.   This problem may be caused by:

- Structure Failure: 1 (see Chapter 2).
- Structure Movement: 1, 2, 3, 4, 5, 6, 7, 8 (see Chapter 2).
- Solid Substrate Problems: 2, 3, 4 (see Chapter 2).
- Wood Framing and Furring Problems: 1, 2, 3, 5, 6, 7, 8 (see Chapter 2).
- Metal Framing and Furring Problems: 1, 2, 3, 4, 5 (see Chapter 2).
- Standard Thickness Plaster Failures: Loose Plaster; Soft or Crumbling Plaster; Cracking; Blisters (see Chapter 3).
- Standard Gypsum Board and Veneer Plaster Gypsum Base Failures:

Wavy Board Surface; Loose or Bowing Wall Boards; Board Cracks: Flat Surface and Corner Joint Cracks; Joint Beading or Ridging; Blisters (see Chapter 4).

- Glass Mesh Mortar Unit Failures (see Chapter 4).
- Bad Tile.
- Improper Design: Poor Tile Selection: 1, 3.
- Improper Design: Incorrect Setting System: 1, 2, 3.
- Improper Design: Improperly Locating or Designing Expansion Joints: 2, 3.
- Bad Workmanship: Incorrect Installation: 1, 6, 12.
- Bad Workmanship: Failing to Protect Tile: 1, 3.
- Miscellaneous: 2.

Loose Tile.   This may appear as hollow-sounding tile, raised tile, tile sliding beneath adjacent tile, tile bowing away from the substrate anywhere from 1/16 inch to 6 inches. Sometimes tile along a grout joint will raise up as much as forty-five degrees, forming a tent-shaped ridge. Tile may loosen due to:

- Structure Failure: 1 (see Chapter 2).
- Structure Movement: 1, 2, 3, 4, 5, 6, 7, 8 (see Chapter 2).
- Solid Substrate Problems: 1, 2, 3, 4 (see Chapter 2).
- Other Building Element Problems: 1, 2 (see Chapter 2).
- Wood Framing and Furring Problems: 1, 2, 3, 4, 5, 6, 7, 8 (see Chapter 2).
- Metal Framing and Furring Problems: 1, 2, 3, 4 (see Chapter 2).
- Standard Thickness Plaster Failures: Loose Plaster; Soft or Crumbling Plaster: Cracking; Blisters; Efflorescence (see Chapter 3).
- Standard Gypsum Board and Veneer Plaster Gypsum Base Failures: Wavy Board Surface; Loose or Bowing Wall Boards; Soft or Disintegrating Boards (see Chapter 4).
- Glass Mesh Mortar Unit Failures (see Chapter 4).
- Bad Tile.
- Improper Design: Poor Tile Selection: 6.
- Improper Design: Incorrect Setting System: 1, 2, 3, 4, 5, 6, 7, 8, 9, 10, 11.
- Improper Design: Improperly Locating or Designing Expansion Joints: 2, 3.
- Improper Design: Failing to Integrate Tile with Adjacent Conditions: 1, 2, 3.

- Improper Design: Failing to Require Proper Preparation Methods: 1.
- Bad Workmanship: Incorrect Installation: 1, 2, 3, 4, 7, 8, 9, 10, 11.
- Bad Workmanship: Failing to Protect Tile: 1, 3.
- Miscellaneous: 1, 2.

Joint Failures

Crumbled or Disintegrated Regular Tile Joints. Failure causes include:

- Structure Failure: 1 (see Chapter 2).
- Structure Movement: 1, 2, 3, 4, 5, 6, 7, 8 (see Chapter 2).
- Solid Substrate Problems: 1, 2, 3, 4 (see Chapter 2).
- Wood Framing and Furring Problems: 1, 2, 3, 5, 6, 7, 8 (see Chapter 2).
- Metal Framing and Furring Problems: 1, 2, 3, 4, 5 (see Chapter 2).
- Standard Thickness Plaster Failures: Loose Plaster; Soft or Crumbling Plaster; Cracking (see Chapter 3).
- Standard Gypsum Board and Veneer Plaster Gypsum Base Failures: Wavy Board Surface; Loose or Bowing Wall Boards; Board Cracks: Flat Surface and Corner Joint Cracks (see Chapter 4).
- Glass Mesh Mortar Unit Failures (see Chapter 4).
- Improper Design: Incorrect Setting System: 1, 2, 3, 4, 5, 6, 7, 8, 9.
- Improper Design: Poor Grout Selection: 3.
- Improper Design: Improperly Locating or Designing Expansion Joints: 2, 3.
- Bad Workmanship: Incorrect Installation: 1, 3, 4, 9, 12.
- Bad Workmanship: Failing to Protect Tile: 1, 3.
- Miscellaneous: 2.

Stained or Discolored Regular Tile Joints: These problems may be caused by:

- Other Building Element Problems: 1, 2.
- Improper Design: Poor Grout Selection: 1.
- Improper Design: Failing to Require Proper Preparation Methods: 1.
- Bad Workmanship: Incorrect Installation: 1, 2, 5, 12.
- Bad Workmanship: Failing to Protect Tile: 3, 4.
- Poor Maintenance Procedures: 1, 2.

Repair, Replacement, and Cleaning of Existing Tile and Joints

Tiles are seldom repaired. Only when tile has historic significance or is irreplaceable is it repaired. Such repair requires expert knowledge and experience and is beyond the scope of this book. When repair of historic tile is necessary, contact one of the historical societies mentioned in the Appendix for guidance in finding a person or organization to make the repairs. Start with the National Trust for Historic Preservation. When the tile needing repair is contemporary, contact the tile's producer.

Tile repair, then, usually means removing the existing tile and installing new tile in its place. The new tile, should, of course, be installed using properly selected tile, setting beds, and grout, and proper, recognized installation methods. Since many tile failures are due to improper installation methods for the conditions, reinstalling tile using the same methods may well lead to a recurrence of the tile failure. If the problem, for example, resulted from using a thin-set tile over a supported slab, such as in Figure 5-12, installing new tile using the same method will probably result in the same failure. It may be possible to reinstall the new tile in a different type of thin-set bed, such as an organic or urethane adhesive. Some epoxy materials are now being used for this purpose. But any such applications will remain a gamble until time has proven their effectiveness, and they are accepted by recognized authorities, such as TCA and ANSI.

Most dirt, oil, and other applied stains and soiling that are not a part of the tile or grout can usually be removed. Different methods work for different stains, different grout materials, and for different tile materials and glazes. A glazed tile may not be cleaned in the same way as an unglazed tile of the same type, for example. A meaningful discussion of the many cleaning products and methods necessary to clean everyday stains and dirt from every type of tile and grout would be longer than this book, which makes it impractical to try to include such information here. Most of the cleaning methods included in the following paragraphs are for conditions that are not always discussed in manufacturer's maintenance manuals.

Similarly, many of the conditions requiring repair, and the repair methods discussed in the following paragraphs, are not addressed in TCA or manufacturer's standard literature.

Loose Tile.   Cleaning grout and setting materials from, and reinstalling, tile that has fallen off or is loose but still in place is usually more expensive than removing the tile and installing new tile. There is, however, at least one exception. Porcelain tile that has fallen off because the latex-modified setting bed has lost its bond can sometimes be cleaned and reinstalled economically.

Under some circumstances, it might be appropriate to try to re-adhere loose floor tile without removing it, even though this is not the most economical solution to the problem, when:

- The loose tile represents a small portion of the total tiled area, usually 10 percent or less.
- No substrate problem exists.
- A major tile removal and replacement operation would disrupt the building owner's or occupants' activities more than is tolerable.
- The in-place tile is not replaceable and would probably be damaged beyond repair by a removal and cleaning operation.

There are two available methods for re-adhering loose tile without removing it: the pressure injection method, and the vacuum injection method.

In the pressure injection method, a liquid epoxy adhesive is forced beneath the tile under pressure. Sometimes the pressure necessary will lift the tile or even blow it from the surface, making major replacement necessary.

The vacuum injection method is usually more successful. In this method, the floor is sealed with a plastic film, the space beneath the tile is evacuated by a vacuum pump, and a thin, highly viscous liquid adhesive is drawn into the vacuum.

Both methods require expert knowledge, and both are expensive. There are only a few firms in the nation capable of properly performing the vacuum injection procedure.

Slippery Tile.   Paver tile that is slippery when wet or dusty can be successfully roughened using a hydrofluoric acid solution.

Tile Stained with Grout and Dirt.   Where dirt or contrasting colored grout has entered the pores and grain structure of unglazed porcelain, matt glazed, or slip-resistant tile, attempt removal as follows:

- It is sometimes possible to remove grout that does not contain a latex additive by scrubbing with a stripping pad on a floor cleaning machine, using scouring powder and water.
- Mortar that contains latex can sometimes be removed using methylene chloride, but it is usually impossible to completely remove latex-modified mortar that is trapped in tile pores. Methylene chloride, which is found in most paint strippers and many floor finish strippers, is highly corrosive to plastics and paints. Its use requires special precautions and ventilation.

- It is sometimes possible to use silica sand and scouring powder with a black stripping pad on a floor cleaning machine to polish off some raised grain to permit removal of dirt and discolorations.
- Staining mortar and dirt can sometimes be removed from matt glazed tile using a scouring pad on a floor cleaning machine and methylene chloride.

No amount of cleaning will remove black or other dark-colored grout that has entered the pores and grain structure and has thereby stained white tile.

After unglazed porcelain, matt glazed, or slip-resistant tile has been cleaned, it is sometimes possible to reduce additional staining by applying a commercial floor finish (sealer and wax) to the tile. Such a finish may, unfortunately, make the tile more slippery.

Expansion Joint Problems.   Where tile or joints have failed because expansion joints were omitted or improperly located, the condition can be corrected by removing the damaged tile and installing new tile. Often, however, especially if the problem has existed for a while and is not getting worse, or if the only sign of expansion joint failure is hollow-sounding, but not raised, tile, it may be best to ignore expansion joint problems. The cure can be expensive, and, sometimes, creates problems worse than those it is supposed to solve. Saw-cutting installed tile, for example, when the tile is on a bonded mortar bed or thin-set directly over concrete, will often cause the entire tile field to shear away from the substrates. Once the decision is made to remove damaged or raised tile and install new tile, it makes some sense to, at the same time, correct the underlying cause, as follows:

- Where joints in the substrates fall beneath a tile joint, install an expansion joint in lieu of the tile joint. Such joints may be constructed by removing the tile joint grout and underlying setting material to expose the substrate joint below. The joint is then filled with a backer rod and finished with elastomeric sealant. Where the tile joint is not as wide as the substrate joint, the tile along the joint must be cut to the width of the joint or removed, and new tile cut to fit and installed on each side of the joint, so that the final tile joint is at least as wide as the substrate joint.
- Where the substrate joint falls within tile (not beneath joints) and the design permits, an expansion joint at least as wide as the substrate joint can be saw-cut in the tile, and filled with backer rod and elastomeric sealant.
- Where the substrate joint falls in a location which is undesirable in the

tile, an isolation membrane may be installed and the new tile expansion joint placed slightly offset from the substrate joint. To construct an offset joint, remove a 24-inch wide strip of tile and setting bed, install a 12-inch wide isolation membrane of about 40- to 50-mil elastomeric sheet material over the joint and feather the edges using latex-Portland cement mortar. Then install new tile using the same latex-Portland cement mortar. Leave an expansion joint at least as wide as the substrate joint and fill it with backer rod and elastomeric sealant.

Crumbled or Disintegrated Grout. Crumbled or disintegrated grout may be symptoms of other problems, such as unbonded tiles, improper substrate, or improper substrate preparation. If tiles are bonded, crumbled or disintegrated grout should be blown out by air under pressure, or ground out of the joint to expose sound material. The joint should be dampened down and new grout applied and properly cured. Latex-modified grout will adhere to existing grout better than will regular cement grout.

Discolored Grout. Colored grout that is stained by dirt, construction debris, or other materials can sometimes be cleaned. Colored grout in which the pigments have been improperly mixed, or that has been burned by acid cleaners, or darkened by sealers, can sometimes be dyed using special stains. Some stains, however, are actually paint that will coat the grout's surface but not penetrate deeply. Stains that do not penetrate may wear away, leaving the original discoloration visible.

The gypsum dust in the grout shown in Figure 5-17 was partly removed by cleaning and the appearance was improved still further by sealing the grout with linseed oil and mineral spirits.

Paver tile is particularly difficult to install so that the joints are filled close enough to the tile surface to make cleaning easy, because this tile type has cushioned edges. More force and more cleaning machine passes are necessary to clean grout joints in paver tile than in tile types that have square edges. Some owners find it best to apply a floor finish on paver tile to seal the joints and make them easier to clean.

When cleaning does not remove dirt and discolorations from grout, one way to solve the problem is to remove the discolored grout and install new grout. It is also possible to grind down stained grout and apply a grout topping. The ground-down joint is coated with an acrylic bonding agent. Then the topping, which also contains an acrylic resin, is applied. Both methods are expensive. There are only a few organizations in the nation who have demonstrated success with the grout topping procedure.

Efflorescence. Efflorescence occurs when water leaches out impurities, usually salts, causing white powdery stains on tile and joint surfaces. Ef-

Figure 5-17   The grout in the tile joints shown in this photograph is dark. The light coloring was caused by the grout being impregnated, after curing, with gypsum dust. (*Photograph by Jess McIlvain.*)

florescence can sometimes be reduced by washing with a mild detergent using stiff bristle brushes. Hardened efflorescence can be improved by washing with an acid solution, but may not be eliminated altogether. The problem is that the products used to remove the white stains will wet the cleaned joints, which causes further efflorescence. In addition, acids strong enough to remove efflorescence will damage glazed tiles and grout. Acids must be neutralized, of course, which may cause other problems.

The tile and cleaner manufacturers' recommendations should be followed closely when using any acid cleaner on tile, because of the potential for harm to glazed tile and joints.

Installing Tile over Existing Surfaces

Ceramic tile may be installed over almost any existing surface by varying the installation methods. The TCA *Handbook* includes extensive recommendations for such installations. The first recommendation is that, where possible, the existing finish be removed and the tile installed as recommended for new surfaces.

Where removal is not practicable, wall surfaces can be covered with new gypsum board or glass mesh mortar units, or surfaces can be properly prepared and new tile installed directly over them. Recognizing that removal of existing finishes may not be reasonable, the TCA *Handbook* details installation methods for most existing materials. The installation method recommended is dictated by the surface to be covered. Tile may be installed over smooth surfaces using thin-set methods. Where the existing surfaces are rough or cracked, mortar bed methods are recommended.

Since no one should attempt to specify or install ceramic tile without access to the current TCA *Handbook*, no useful purpose would be served by repeating its recommendations here.

Where to Get More Information

The Tile Council of America's (TCA) *Handbook for Ceramic Tile Installation* is the most widely accepted reference for tile installation available today. Its conclusions depend on adherence to ANSI and ASTM standards, but it also includes additional recommendations and drawings illustrating its recommendations. No one should attempt to design or install ceramic tile without ready access to the TCA *Handbook. Sweet's Catalog Files* contains a copy. Copies can also be obtained from the Tile Council of America. The ANSI standards listed in this book's Bibliography that relate to tile application are all referenced in the TCA *Handbook*.

The ANSI standards referenced in the TCA *Handbook* are available from ANSI, but may also be available from TCA. Every designer and installer of tile should obtain a copy of them. Most are listed in the Bibliography and followed by a [5].

Every designer should have a full complement of applicable ASTM Standards available for reference, of course, but anyone who needs to understand ceramic tile should definitely own a copy of each ASTM standard listed in the Bibliography and followed by a [5].

The Ceramic Tile Institute's (CTI) *Ceramic Tile Manual* contains copies of ANSI standards and also test procedures for glazed and unglazed special-purpose and faience tile. These types will probably not comply with ANSI Standard A137.1-1980, as should the other tiles discussed in this chapter, but existing tile of these types might comply with the "CTI Standard for Glazed and Unglazed Special Purpose and Faience Tile" and CTI "Test Procedure CTI-69-5."

The National Association of Tile Contractors was revising its excellent publication, *Reference Manual and Specifications*, at the time of this writing (late 1988). The new edition may have a somewhat different title, but the content of the new edition is an improvement over the earlier version. This manual is designed to help solve ceramic, marble, and granite tile problems, including those associated with cementitious and noncementitious grouts, thin-set tile applications, and substrate problems, such as curing compounds and release agents on concrete that is to receive tile. It discusses the causes, prevention, and correction of tile problems. The manual is primarily intended for use by tile contractors, but architects, general contractors, and building owners will also find it a useful reference for preventing and dealing with tile problems.

Joan F. Blatterman's 1988 article, "Details Underfoot," discusses damaged grout replacement, expansion joints, and the installation of ceramic tile, with particular emphasis on industry standards, such as ANSI and Tile Council of America publications.

Jess McIlvain's articles listed in the Bibliography are excellent sources of information about tile.

The Materials and Methods Standards Association's *Bulletins 1 through 14* include quality standards for ceramic tile materials and installations, as well as information about efflorescence. Bulletin No. 9, for example, includes descriptions and information to help in selecting and installing grout. Bulletin No. 12 discusses grout release agents and temporary protective coatings. Bulletin No. 14 addresses latex and emulsion additives for mortar and grout.

The American Olean Tile *Maintenance Guide Manual* is an excellent source of data about cleaning glazed and unglazed tile and grout. It covers many types of soil and stain removal. Anyone responsible for maintaining tile or specifying the maintenance of tile should purchase a copy from American Olean.

AIA Service Corporation's *Masterspec* Basic: Section 09300, Tile, contains descriptions of the materials and installations that are the subject of this chapter. Unfortunately, this section contains little that will help with troubleshooting failed ceramic tile.

Ramsey/Sleeper's *"Architectural Graphic Standards"* contains data about ceramic tile.

The Association of Tile, Terrazzo, Marble Contractors and Affiliates' 1983 *Guide for Grouting and Cleaning Ceramic Floors with Latex Grout* is an excellent guide. Techniques suggested in it are also suitable for standard grout types consisting of sand, cement, and water.

Also refer to items listed in the Bibliography and followed by [5].

APPENDIX

Data Sources

NOTE: The following list includes sources of data referenced in the text, included in the Bibliography, or both. **HP** following a source indicates that the source also contains data of interest to those concerned with historic preservation.

Adhesive and Sealant Council (ASC)
1500 Wilson Boulevard, Suite 515
Arlington, VA 22209
(703) 841-1112

Advisory Council on Historic
   Preservation
1100 Pennsylvania Avenue, Suite 809
Washington, DC 20004
(202) 786-0503 **HP**

AIA Service Corporation
The American Institute of Architects
1735 New York Avenue, N.W.
Washington, DC 20006
(202) 626-7300

American Association of State and
   Local History
172 Second Avenue, North, Suite 102
Nashville, TN 37201
(615) 255-2971 **HP**

American Council of Independent
   Laboratories (ACIL)
1725 K Street, N.W.
Washington, DC 20006
(202) 887-5872

The American Institute of Architects
1735 New York Avenue, N.W.
Washington, DC 20006
(202) 626-7300

American Institute of Architects
   Committee on Historic
   Resources
1735 New York Avenue, N.W.
Washington, DC 20006
(202) 626-7300 **HP**

American Institute of Timber
   Construction
333 West Hampden Avenue
Englewood, CO 80110
(303) 761-3212

American Insurance Association
85 John Street
New York, NY 10038
(212) 669-0400

American Iron and Steel Institute
1133 15th Street, Suite 300
Washington, DC 20005
(202) 452-7100

American National Standards
Institute (ANSI)
1430 Broadway
New York, NY 10018
(212) 354-3300

American Olean Tile Company, Inc.
1000 Cannon Avenue
Landsdale, PA 19446
(215) 855-1111

American Plywood Association
(APA)
P.O. Box 11700
Tacoma, WA 98411
(206) 565-6600

American Society of Heating, Refrigerating and Air-Conditioning
Engineers, Inc.
1791 Tullie Circle, N.E.
Atlanta, GA 20329
(404) 636-8400

American Wood Preservers
Association
P.O. Box 5283
Springfield, VA 21666
(703) 339-6660

American Wood Preservers Bureau
P.O. Box 6058
2772 South Randolf St.
Arlington, VA 22206
(703) 931-8180

Architectural Technology
The American Institute of Architects
1735 New York Avenue, N.W.
Washington, DC 20006
(202) 626-7300

Architecture
The American Institute of Architects
1735 New York Avenue, N.W.
Washington, DC 20006
(202) 626-7300

Association for Preservation
Technology
Box 2487 Station D

Ottawa, ONT K1P 5W6, Canada
(613) 238-1972 **HP**

Association of Tile, Terrazzo, Marble
Contractors and Affiliates, Inc.
P.O. Box 12140
Jackson, MS 39211
(601) 939-2071

Association of the Wall and Ceiling
Industries—International
1600 Cameron Street
Alexandria, VA 20002
(703) 684-2924

ASTM
1916 Race Street
Philadelphia, PA 19103-1187
(215) 299-5585

Building Design and Construction
Cahners Plaza
1350 East Touhy Avenue
P.O. Box 5080
Des Plaines, IL 60018
(312) 635-8800

Campbell Center for Historic
Preservation Studies
P.O. Box 66
Mount Carroll, IL 61053
(815) 244-1173

Ceramic Tile Institute
700 North Virgil Avenue
Los Angeles, CA 90029
(213) 660-1911

Chicago Plastering Institute
6547 North Avondale
Chicago, IL 60631
(312) 774-4500

Commercial Standard (U.S.
Department of Commerce)
Government Printing Office
Washington, DC 20402
(202) 377-2000

Construction Research Council
1800 M Street, N.W., Suite 1040

Washington, DC 20036
(202) 785-3378

The Construction Specifier
The Construction Specifications
   Institute
601 Madison Street
Alexandria, VA 22314-1791
(703) 684-0300

Council of Forest Industries of
   British Columbia
1055 West Hastings Street
Vancouver, B.C. V6E 2H1

Craftsman Book Company
6058 Corte del Cedro
Carlsbad, CA 92009
(619) 438-7828

Department of Commerce
14th Street and Constitution Avenue,
   N.W.
Washington, DC 20230
(202) 377-2000

Environmental Protection Agency
401 M Street, S.W.
Washington, DC 20460
(202) 829-3535

ETL Testing Laboratories, Inc.
P.O. Box 2040
Route 11, Industrial Park
Cortland, NY 13045
(607) 753-6711

Exteriors
1 East 1st Street
Duluth, MN 55802
(218) 723-9200

Exterior Insulation Manufacturers
   Association
P.O. Box 75037
Washington, DC 20013
(202) 783-6582

Factory Mutual System
1151 Boston–Providence Turnpike
Norwood, MA 02062
(617) 762-4300

Federal Housing Administration
(U.S. Department of Housing and
   Urban Development)
451 7th Street, S.W.
Washington, DC 20201
(202) 755-5995

Federal Specification (General
   Services Administration)
Specifications Unit (WFSIS)
7th and D Streets, S.W.
Washington, DC 20406
(202) 472-2205

Forest Products Laboratory
U.S. Department of Agriculture
Gifford Pinchot Drive
P.O. Box 5130
Madison, WI 53705
(698) 264-5600

General Services Administration
General Services Building
18th and F Streets, N.W.
Washington, DC 20405
(202) 655-4000

Greater Portland Landmarks
165 State Street
Portland, ME 04101
(207) 774-5561

Gypsum Association
1603 Orrington Avenue
Evanston, IL 60201
(312) 491-1744

Hartford Architecture Conservancy
130 Washington Street
Hartford, CT 06106
(203) 525-0279 **HP**

Heritage Canada Foundation
Box 1358 Station B
Ottawa, ONT K1P 5R4, Canada
(613) 237-1867 **HP**

Historic Preservation (Magazine)
(See National Trust for Historic
   Preservation) **HP**

Illinois Historic Preservation Agency
Division of Preservation Services
Old State Capitol
Springfield, IL 62701
(217) 782-4836 **HP**

Industrial Risk Insurers
85 Woodland Street
Hartford, CT 06102
(203) 520-7300

Institute for Applied Technology/
  Center for Building Technology
National Bureau of Standards
U.S. Department of Commerce
Washington, DC 20540
(202) 342-2241

International Institute for Lath and
  Plaster
c/o W. F. Pruter Associates
3127 Los Feliz Boulevard
Los Angeles, CA 90039
(213) 660-4644

Italian Tile Center
499 Park Avenue
New York, NY 10022
(212) 980-8866

Library of Congress
1st Street, N.E.
Washington, DC 20540
(202) 287-5000 **HP**

Materials and Methods Standards
  Association
614 Monroe Street
Grand Haven, MI 49417
(616) 842-7844

McGraw-Hill Book Company
1221 Avenue of the Americas
New York, NY 10020
(212) 997-2271

Metal Lath/Steel Framing
  Association
600 South Federal Street, Suite 400
Chicago, IL 60605
(312) 922-6222

National Alliance of Preservation
  Commissions
Hall of the States
444 North Capitol Street, N.W.,
  Suite 332
Washington, DC 20001
(202) 624-5490 **HP**

National Association of Tile
  Contractors
626 Lakeland East Drive
Jackson, MS 39208
(601) 939-2701

National Bureau of Standards (NBS)
(See National Institute of Standards
  and Technology)

National Concrete Masonry
  Association
P.O. Box 781
Herndon, VA 22070
(703) 435-4900

National Fire Protection Association
Batterymarch Park
Quincy, MA 02269
(617) 770-3000

National Forest Products Association
1619 Massachusetts Avenue, N.W.
Washington, DC 20036
(202) 797-5800

National Institute of Standards and
  Technology
(Formerly National Bureau of
  Standards)
Gaithersburg, MD 20234
(301) 975-2000

National Institute of Standards and
  Technology
(Formerly National Bureau of
  Standards)
Center for Building Technology
Gaithersburg, MD 20234
(301) 975-5900

National Preservation Institute
P.O. Box 1702

Alexandria, VA 22313
(703) 393-0038 **HP**

National Trust for Historic
  Preservation
1785 Massachusetts Avenue, N.W.
Washington, DC 20036
(202) 673-4000 **HP**

Occupational Safety and Health
  Administration (U.S. Department
  of Labor)
Government Printing Office
Washington, DC 20402
(202) 783-3238

The Old-House Journal
69A Seventh Avenue
Brooklyn, NY 11217
(718) 636-4514

Portland Cement Association
5420 Old Orchard Road
Skokie, IL 60077
(312) 966-6200

The Preservation Institute for the
  Building Crafts
Main Street, P.O. Box 1777
Windsor, VT 05089
(802) 674-6752

The Preservation Press
National Trust for Historic
  Preservation
1785 Massachusetts Avenue, N.W.
Washington, DC 20036
(202) 673-4000 **HP**

Preservation Resource Group
5619 Southampton Drive
Springfield, VA 22151
(703) 323-1407 **HP**

Product Standards of NBS (U.S.
  Department of Commerce)
Government Printing Office
Washington, DC 20402
(202) 783-3238

Sealant Engineering and Associated
  Lines Assoc. (SEAL)

P.O. Box 24302
San Diego, CA 92124
(619) 569-7906

Sealant and Waterproofing Institute
3101 Broadway, Number 300
Kansas City, MO 64111-2416
(816) 561-8230

Sheet Metal and Air Conditioning
  Contractors National Associa-
  tion, Inc.
8224 Old Courthouse Road
Vienna, VA 22180
(703) 790-9890
    For publications contact:
SMACNA Publications Department
P.O. Box 70
Merrifield, VA 22116
(703) 790-9890

Society for the Preservation of New
  England Antiquities
141 Cambridge Street
Boston, MA 02114
(617) 227-3956 **HP**

Southern Pine Inspection Bureau
4709 Scenic Highway
Pensacola, FL 32504
(904) 434-2611

Thermal Insulation Manufacturers
  Association (TIMA)
7 Kirby Plaza
Mt. Kisco, NY 10549
(914) 241-2284

Tile Contractors Association of
  America
112 North Alfred Street
Alexandria, VA 22314
(703) 836-5995

Tile Council of America, Inc.
P.O. Box 326
Princeton, NJ 08542
(609) 921-7050

Tile and Decorative Surfaces
20335 Ventura Boulevard, Suite 400

Woodland Hills, CA 91364
(818) 704-5555

Tile Letter
P.O. Box 13629
Jackson, MS 39236
(601) 939-2071

Truss Plate Institute
583 D'Onofrio Drive, Suite 200
Madison, WI 53719
(608) 833-5900

U.S. Department of Agriculture
14th Street and Independence
    Avenue, S.W.
Washington, DC 20250
(202) 447-4929

U.S. Department of Commerce
    for PS (Product Standard of NBS)
Government Printing Office
Washington, DC 20402
(202) 783-3238

U.S. Department of the Interior
National Park Service
P.O. Box 37127
Washington, DC 20013-7127
(202) 343-7394 **HP**

U.S. General Services Administration
Historic Preservation Office
Washington, DC 20405
(202) 655-4000 **HP**

Technical Preservation Services
U.S. Department of the Interior,
Preservation Assistance Division
National Park Service
Washington, DC 20013-7127 **HP**

Underwriters Laboratories
333 Pfingsten Road
Northbrook, IL 60062
(312) 272-8800

United States Gypsum Company
101 South Wacker Drive
Chicago, IL 60606
(312) 606-4000

Van Nostrand Reinhold
115 Fifth Avenue
New York, NY 10003
(212) 254-3232

West Coast Lumber Inspection
    Bureau
P.O. Box 23145
Portland, OR 97223
(503) 639-0651

Western Wood Products Association
1500 Yeon Building
Portland, OR 97204
(503) 224-3930

John Wiley & Sons
605 Third Avenue
New York, NY 10158
(212) 850-6000

BIBLIOGRAPHY

NOTE: Each item in the Bibliography is followed by one or more numbers in brackets. The numbers list the chapters in this book to which the bibliographical entry applies.

The **HP** following some entries in the Bibliography indicates that the entry has particular significance for historic preservation projects.

Sources for many of the entries, including addresses and telephone numbers, are listed in the Appendix.

AIA Service Corporation. *Masterspec,* Basic: Section 06100, Rough Carpentry, 8/86 Edition. The American Institute of Architects. [2]

———. *Masterspec,* Basic: Section 07241, Exterior Insulation and Finish System—Class PB, 5/87 Edition. The American Institute of Architects. [3]

———. *Masterspec,* Basic: Section 07242, Exterior Insulation and Finish System—Class PM, 5/87 Edition. The American Institute of Architects. [3]

———. *Masterspec,* Basic: Section 09200, Lath and Plaster, 2/85 Edition. The American Institute of Architects. [2, 3, 4]

———. *Masterspec,* Basic: Section 09215, Veneer Plaster, 2/88 Edition. The American Institute of Architects. [2, 3, 4]

———. *Masterspec,* Basic: Section 09250, Gypsum Drywall, 8/87 Edition. The American Institute of Architects. [2, 4]

———. *Masterspec,* Basic: Section 09270, Gypsum Board Shaft Wall Systems, 2/88 Edition. The American Institute of Architects. [2, 4]

———. *Masterspec,* Basic: Section 09300, Tile, 2/86 Edition. The American Institute of Architects. [5]

Allen, Edward. 1985. *Fundamentals of Building Construction: Materials and Methods.* New York: Wiley. [2, 3, 4, 5]

American Institute of Timber Construction. *Timber Construction Standards*. Englewood, CO: American Institute of Timber Construction. [2]

————. *Timber Construction Manual*. Englewood, CO: American Institute of Timber Construction. [2]

American National Standards Institute. Standard A10.20-1977, Safety Requirements for Ceramic Tile, Terrazzo, and Marble Work. ANSI. [5]

————. Standard A108.1-1985, Glazed Wall Tile, Ceramic Mosaic Tile, Quarry Tile and Paver Tile Installed with Portland Cement. ANSI. [5]

————. Standard A108.4-1985, Ceramic Tile Installed with Organic Adhesive or Water-Cleanable Tile Setting Epoxy Adhesive. ANSI. [5]

————. Standard A108.5-1985, Ceramic Tile Installed with Dry-Set Portland Cement Mortar or Latex-Portland Cement Mortar. ANSI. [5]

————. Standard A108.6-1985, Ceramic Tile Installed with Chemical-Resistant, Water-Cleanable Tile-Setting and Grouting Epoxy. ANSI. [5]

————. Standard A108.7-1985, Electrically Conductive Ceramic Tile Installed with Conductive Dry-Set Portland Cement Mortar. ANSI. [5]

————. Standard A108.8-1985, Ceramic Tile Installed with Chemical-Resistant Furan Mortar and Grout. ANSI. [5]

————. Standard A108.9-1985, Ceramic Tile Installed with Modified Epoxy Emulsion Mortar/Grout. ANSI. [5]

————. Standard A108.10-1985, Installation of Grout in Tilework. ANSI. [5]

————. Standard A118.1-1985, Dry-Set Portland Cement Mortar. ANSI. [5]

————. Standard A118.2-1985, Conductive Dry-Set Portland Cement Mortar. ANSI. [5]

————. Standard A118.3-1985, Chemical-Resistant, Water-Cleanable Tile-Setting and Grouting Epoxy and Water-Cleanable Tile-Setting Epoxy Adhesive. ANSI. [5]

————. Standard A118.4-1985, Latex-Portland Cement Mortar. ANSI. [5]

————. Standard A118.5-1985, Chemical-Resistant Furan Mortar and Grout. ANSI. [5]

————. Standard A118.6-1985, Ceramic Tile Grouts. ANSI. [5]

————. Standard A118.7-1985, Modified Epoxy Emulsion Mortar/Grout. ANSI. [5]

————. Standard A136.1-1985, Organic Adhesives for Installation of Ceramic Tile. ANSI. [5]

————. Standard A137.1-1980, Ceramic tile. ANSI. [5]

American Olean Tile Company, Inc. *Maintenance Guide Manual*. Landsdale, PA: American Olean Tile Company, Inc. [5]

American Wood Preservers Association. *Book of Standards*. Springfield, VA: American Wood Preservers Association. [2]

Architectural Technology. 1986. Technical Tips: Metal Lathing—Then and Now. *Architectural Technology*, March/April: 64–65. [2, 3]

————. 1982. Guide Specification for Military Construction, CE-240.01, Furring (Metal), Lathing, and Plastering. Corps of Engineers, Office of the Chief of Engineers, Department of the Army. [2, 3]

Ashurst, John. 1988. *Practical Building Conservation, Volume 2*. England: Gower. [3]

Association for Preservation Technology. 1969. *Bulletins of APT, Volume 1*. Ottawa, Ontario: APT. **HP**

Association of Tile, Terrazzo, Marble Contractors and Affiliates, Inc. 1983. *Guide for Grouting and Cleaning Ceramic Floors with Latex Grout*. Jackson, MS: Association of Tile, Terrazzo, Marble Contractors and Affiliates. [5]

Association of the Wall and Ceiling Industries—International. *Veneer Plaster Manual*. Washington, DC: Association of the Wall and Ceiling Industries—International. [2, 3, 4]

ASTM. 1986. *Annual Book of ASTM Standards, Section 4 (Cement, Lime, Gypsum)*. ASTM. [3, 4, 5]

————. Standard A 123, Specifications for Zinc (Hot-Galvanized) Coatings on Products Fabricated from Rolled, Pressed, and Forged Steel Shapes, Plates, Bars, and Strip. ASTM. [2]

————. Standard A 446, Specifications for Sheet Steel, Zinc-Coated (Galvanized) by the Hot-Dip Process, Structural (Physical) Quality. ASTM. [2]

————. Standard A 525, Specifications for General Requirements for Steel Sheet Zinc-Coated (Galvanized) by the Hot-Dip Process. ASTM. [2]

————. Standard A 570, Specifications for Hot-Rolled Carbon Steel Sheet and Strip, Structural Quality. ASTM. [2]

————. Standard A 611, Specifications for Steel, Cold-Rolled Sheet, Carbon, Structural. ASTM. [2]

————. Standard A 641, Specifications for Zinc-Coated (Galvanized) Carbon Steel Wire. ASTM. [2]

————. Standard C 11, Definition of Terms Relating to Gypsum and Related Building Materials. ASTM. [2, 3, 4]

————. Standard C 35, Specifications for Inorganic Aggregates for Use in Gypsum Plaster. ASTM. [3]

————. Standard C 36, Specifications for Gypsum Wallboard. ASTM. [4]

————. Standard C 37, Specifications for Gypsum Lath. ASTM. [3, 4]

————. Standard C 59, Specifications for Gypsum Casting and Molding Plaster. ASTM. [3]

————. Standard C 61, Specifications for Gypsum Keene's Cement. ASTM. [3]

————. Standard C 79, Test Method for Gypsum Sheathing Board. ASTM. [4]

————. Standard C 91, Specifications for Masonry Cement. ASTM. [3]

————. Standard C 150, Portland Cement. ASTM. [3, 5]

———. Standard C 206, Specifications for Finishing Hydrated Lime. ASTM. [3]

———. Standard C 207, Specifications for Hydrated Lime for Masonry Purposes. ASTM. [3]

———. Standard C 242, Standard Definitions of Terms Related to Ceramic Whitewares and Related Products. ASTM. [5]

———. Standard C 287, Specifications for Gypsum Plasters. ASTM. [3]

———. Standard C 442, Specifications for Gypsum Backing Board and Coreboard. ASTM. [4]

———. Standard C 475, Specifications for Joint Treatment Materials for Gypsum Wallboard Construction. ASTM. [4]

———. Standard C 514, Specifications for Nails for the Application of Gypsum Wallboard. ASTM. [4]

———. Standard C 557, Specifications for Adhesive for Fastening Gypsum Wallboard to Wood Framing. ASTM. [4]

———. Standard C 578, Specifications for Adhesive for Preformed Cellular Polystyrene Thermal Insulation. ASTM. [3]

———. Standard C 587, Specifications for Gypsum Veneer Plaster. ASTM. [3, 4]

———. Standard C 588, Specifications for Gypsum Base for Veneer Plasters. ASTM. [3, 4]

———. Standard C 627, Evaluating Ceramic Floor Tile Installation Systems. ASTM. [5]

———. Standard C 630, Water-Resistant Gypsum Backing Board. ASTM. [4, 5]

———. Standard C 631, Specifications for Bonding Compounds for Interior Plastering. ASTM. [3]

———. Standard C 645, Specifications for Non-Load (Axial) Bearing Steel Studs, Runners (Track), and Rigid Furring Channels for Screw Application of Gypsum Board. ASTM. [2]

———. Standard C 646, Specifications for Steel Drill Screws for Application of Gypsum Board to Light-Gage Steel Studs. ASTM. [2]

———. Standard C 754, Specifications for Installation of Steel Framing Members to Receive Screw-Attached Gypsum Wallboard, Backing Board, or Water-Resistant Backing Board. ASTM. [2]

———. Standard C 840, Specifications for Application and Finishing of Gypsum Board. ASTM. [4]

———. Standard C 841, Specifications for Installation of Interior Lathing and Furring. ASTM. [2, 3]

———. Standard C 842, Specifications for Application of Interior Gypsum Plaster. ASTM. [3]

———. Standard C 843, Specifications for Application of Gypsum Veneer Plaster. ASTM. [3, 4]

————. Standard 847, Specifications for Metal Lath. ASTM. [3]

————. Standard C 897, Specifications for Aggregate for Job-Mixed Portland Cement-Based Plasters. ASTM. [3]

————. Standard C 919, Practices for Use of Sealants in Acoustical Applications. ASTM. [2, 4, 5]

————. Standard C 920, Specifications for Elastomeric Joint Sealants. ASTM. [4, 5]

————. Standard C 926, Specifications for Application of Portland Cement-Based Plaster. ASTM. [3]

————. Standard C 931, Specifications for Exterior Gypsum Soffit Board. ASTM. [4]

————. Standard C 932, Specifications for Surface-Applied Bonding Agents for Exterior Plastering. ASTM. [3]

————. Standard C 955, Specifications for Load-Bearing (Transverse and Axial) Steel Studs, Runners (Track), and Bracing or Bridging, for Screw Application of Gypsum Board and Metal Plaster Bases. ASTM. [2]

————. Standard C 960, Specifications for Predecorated Gypsum Board. ASTM. [4]

————. Standard C 1002, Specifications for Steel Drill Screws for Application of Gypsum Board. ASTM. [4]

————. Standard C 1007, Installation of Load-Bearing (Transverse and Axial) Steel Studs and Accessories. ASTM. [2]

————. Standard C 1047, Specifications for Accessories for Gypsum Wallboard and Gypsum Veneer Base. ASTM. [3, 4]

————. Standard C 1063, Specifications for Installation of Lathing and Furring for Portland Cement-Based Plaster. ASTM. [2, 3]

————. Standard D 226, Specification for Asphalt-Saturated Organic Felt Used in Roofing and Waterproofing. ASTM. [2]

————. Standard D 578, Specification for Glass Fiber Yarns. ASTM. [3]

————. Standard E 84, Test Method for Surface Burning Characteristics of Building Materials. ASTM. [2]

Blatterman, Joan F. 1988. Details Underfoot. *Architectural Record,* July: 118–121. [5]

Blumer, H. Maynard and Stephanie Stubbs. 1987. Technical Tips: Choosing Stucco Systems. *Architecture,* January: 110–111. [3]

Bodner, James. 1985. Ceramic Tile Makes a Comeback. *The Construction Specifier,* October, 38(10): 58–63. [5]

Brunnell, Gene. 1977. *Built to Last: A Handbook on Recycling Old Buildings.* Washington, D.C.: The Preservation Press. **HP**

California Lathing and Plastering Contractor's Association. 1981. *Plaster/Metal Framing System/Lath Manual.* Los Angeles, CA: California Lathing and Plastering Contractor's Association. [2, 3, 4]

Cattell, D. 1988. *Specialist Floor Finishes: Design and Installation.* London: Blackie and Sons Ltd. [5]

Ceramic Tile Institute. *Ceramic Tile Manual.* Los Angeles, CA: Ceramic Tile Institute. [5]

Chalmers, Ray. 1985. Selecting the Proper Tile Application Method. *Building Design and Construction,* September, 26(9): 118–120. [5]

———. 1985. A Review of Related Products for Ceramic Tile. *Building Design and Construction,* September, 26(9): 124–125. [5]

Chalmers, Ray and Margaret Doyle. 1985. Ceramic Tile Case Studies. *Building Design and Construction,* September, 26(9): 128–132. [5]

Chicago Plastering Institute. *Restoring Plaster in Older Structures.* Chicago, IL: Chicago Plastering Institute. [1, 3]

Commerce Publishing Corporation. 1988. *The Woodbook.* Seattle, WA: Commerce. [2]

Commerce, United States Department of. *PS 1—U.S. Product Standard for Construction and Industrial Plywood.* Washington, DC: United States Department of Commerce. [2]

———. *PS 20—American Softwood Lumber Standard.* Washington, DC: United States Department of Commerce. [2]

Commercial Renovation. 1986. Technique: Fiberglass Wall System Saves New England Church Interiors. *Commercial Renovation,* December, 8(6): 18.

———. 1987. The 1987 Premier Renovation Architects. *Commercial Renovation,* December: 24–44. **HP**

Construction Specifications Institute, Construction Specifications Canada. 1983. *Masterformat.* Alexandria, VA: The Construction Specifications Institute.

Construction Specifier, The. 1987. A Resource Guide to the 3Rs: Restoration, Renovation and Rehabilitation. *The Construction Specifier,* July, 40 (7): 102–114. [1, 2, 3, 4, 5]

Diehl, John R. 1965. *Manual of Lathing and Plastering, Gypsum Association Edition.* New York: M. A. C. [2, 3, 4]

Doyle, Margaret. 1985. Ceramic Tile Suits a Variety of Uses. *Building Design and Construction,* September, 26(9): 114–117. [5]

———. 1988. Trends in Specifying EIFS. *Building Design and Construction,* August, 29(8): 58–62. [3]

Erwin, Gene. 1986. Exterior Insulation: Specs with Style. *Exterior,* Spring, 4(1): 34–40. [3]

———. 1987. Trouble-Shooting Guide for Exterior Insulations. *Exterior,* Spring, 5(1): 83–86. [3]

Exterior Insulation Manufacturers Association. *EIMA Guide Specifications for Exterior Wall Insulation and Finish Systems Class PB, Type A.* Washington, DC: Exterior Insulation Manufacturers Association. [3, 4]

———. *EIMA Guide Specifications for Exterior Wall Insulation and Finish Systems*

Class PM, Type A. Washington, DC: Exterior Insulation Manufacturers Association. [3, 4]

———. EIMA Classification of Exterior Insulation Systems. Washington, DC: Exterior Insulation Manufacturers Association. [3, 4]

Factory Mutual Systems. *Approval Guide*. Factory Mutual Systems. [3, 4, 5]

———. *Loss Prevention Data Sheets*. Factory Mutual Systems. [3, 4, 5]

Forest Products Laboratory. *Handbook No. 72—Wood Handbook*. Washington, DC: United States Department of Agriculture. [2]

Frane, James T. 1987. *Drywall Contracting*. Carlsbad, CA: Craftsman. [4]

Freund, Eric C. and Gary L. Olsen. 1985. Renovating Commercial Structures: A Primer. *The Construction Specifier*, July, 38(7): 36–47. [2]

Garrison, John Mark. 1985. Casting Decorative Plaster. *The Old-House Journal*, November, 13(9): 186–189. [3]

General Services Administration. 1970 (April). Public Building Services Guide Specifications, Section 0910, Plaster Repairs. United States General Services Administration. [3]

Gorman, J. R. 1982. Smooth Specifying for Architectural Textures in Plaster. *The Construction Specifier*, July, 35(5): 76–82. [3]

Gypsum Association. 1984. *Fire Resistance Design Manual: Eleventh Edition (GA 600-84)*. Evanston, IL: Gypsum Association. [2, 4]

———. 1985. *Recommended Specifications for Application and Finishing of Gypsum Board (GA-216-85)*. Evanston, IL: Gypsum Association. [4]

———. 1985. *Gypsum Board Products Glossary of Terminology (GA-505-85)*. Evanston, IL: Gypsum Association. [2, 4]

———. 1985. *Using Gypsum Board for Walls and Ceilings (GA-201-85)*. Evanston, IL: Gypsum Association. [2, 4]

———. 1986. *Recommended Specifications: Gypsum Board Types, Uses, Sizes and Standards (GA-223-86)*. Evanston, IL: Gypsum Association. [2, 4]

———. 1986. *Recommendations for Covering Existing Interior Walls and Ceilings with Gypsum Board (GA-650-86)*. Evanston, IL: Gypsum Association. [2, 4]

———. 1986. *Fire Resistant Gypsum Sheathing (GA-252-86)*. Evanston, IL: Gypsum Association. [4]

———. 1988. *Recommended Specifications: Recommendations for Installation of Steel Fire Door Frames in Steel Stud-Gypsum Board Fire-Rated Partitions (GA-219-86)*. Evanston, IL: Gypsum Association. [2, 4]

Harvey, John. 1972. *Conservation of Buildings*. London, England: Baker. **HP**

Illinois Heritage Association. Technical Insert No. 17—Plaster: A Primer on Techniques and Terms. September/October. [3]

Insall, Donald W. 1972. *The Care of Old Buildings Today: A Practical Guide*. London: The Architectural Press. **HP**

Italian Tile Center. *The Designer's Guide to Italian Tiles and Their Installation*. New York: Italian Tile Center. [5]

Johnston, Clay M. 1987. Lath and Plaster: A Capsule Look. *The Construction Specifier*, February, 40(2): 54–58. [2, 3, 4]

Jowers, Walter. 1986. Textured Plaster Finishes. *The Old-House Journal*, March, 14(2): 75–77. [3]

Kincaid, Mary. 1983. Color in the Squares. *The Construction Specifier*, June, 36(5): 70–76. [5]

Ladygo, Andrew. 1988. New Techniques for Restoring Decorative Plasterwork. *The Construction Specifier*, July, 41(7): 105–112. [2, 3]

Leeke, John. 1987. Saving Irreplaceable Plaster. *The Old-House Journal*, November/December: 51–55. [2, 3]

Loza, Don. 1985. Using Exterior Insulating Systems for Renovation. *The Construction Specifier*, July, 38(7): 54–56. [3]

Maruca, Mary. 1984. 10 Most Common Restoration Blunders. *Historic Preservation*, October: 13–17. **HP**

Materials and Methods Standards Association. *Bulletins 1 through 14*, Grand Haven, MI: Materials and Methods Standards Association. [5]

McIlvain, Jess. 1982. The Problem With Dry-Set Mortars. *Tile and Decorative Surfaces*, September: 17–20. [5]

———. 1982. Ceramic Tile Maintenance. *Tile and Decorative Surfaces*, October/November: 48–57. [5]

———. 1982. The Preconstruction Conference. *Tile and Decorative Surfaces*, December: 102–103. [5]

———. 1983. Caution: Latex-Portland Cement Mortar Over Plywood. *Tile and Decorative Surfaces*, January/February. [5]

———. 1983. Plaster vs. Mortar Beds. *Tile and Decorative Surfaces*, April: 41–56. [5]

———. 1983. Never Again. *Tile and Decorative Surfaces*, July: 138–140. [5]

———. 1983. Dodging the Dry-Set Mortar Gremlins. *The Construction Specifier*, June, 36(5): 77–82. [5]

———. 1984. Prefabricated Exterior Ceramic Tile Cladding, Part 1. *Tile and Decorative Surfaces*, January/February: 80–85. [5]

———. 1984. Prefabricated Exterior Ceramic Tile Cladding, Part 2. *Tile and Decorative Surfaces*, March: 41–53. [5]

———. 1984. Prefabricated Exterior Ceramic Tile Cladding, Part 3. *Tile and Decorative Surfaces*, April: 50–58. [5]

———. 1984. Prefabricated Exterior Ceramic Tile Cladding, Part 4. *The Construction Specifier*, June, 37(6): 76–91. [5]

———. 1984. Let's Talk Tile. *Tile and Decorative Surfaces*, June: 69–74. [5]

———. 1984. Mortar Beds. *Tile and Decorative Surfaces*, September: 118–120. [5]

———. 1984. The Preconstruction Conference. *Tile Letter*, October: 32–33. [5]

———. 1985. Floor Renovation. *Tile and Decorative Surfaces*, April: 48–49. [5]

———. 1985. Moisture Expansion. *Tile and Decorative Surfaces*, June: 72–86. [5]

———. 1985. The Goose That Laid the Rotten Egg. *Tile Letter*, August: 42–46. [5]

———. 1986. Writing Ceramic Tile Specifications. *Tile and Decorative Surfaces*, March: 78–80. [5]

———. 1986. The Effects of Light on Tile. *Tile and Decorative Surfaces*, October/November: 81–82. [5]

———. 1986. Lights, Action. *Tile Letter*, July: 36–40. [5]

———. 1987. Selecting Ceramic Tile Floor Installation Methods. *Tile and Decorative Surfaces*, August: 38–42. [5]

———. 1988. Grout: It Doesn't Have to Be a Problem. *Tile and Decorative Surfaces*, June: 42–45. [5]

McKee, H. J. 1983. *Introduction to Early American Masonry, Stone, Brick, Mortar, and Plaster, No. 1 Technology of Early American Building Series*. Washington, DC: Columbia University/National Trust for Historic Preservation. [3]

Metal Lath/Steel Framing Association. 1985. *Lightweight Steel Framing Systems Manual (2nd Edition)*. Chicago, IL: Metal Lath//Steel Framing Association. [2]

———. 1986. *Technical Information File*. Chicago, IL: Metal Lath/Steel Framing Association. [2]

———. Technical Bulletin No. 18: Fire Rated Metal Lath/Steel Stud Exterior. Chicago, IL: Metal Lath/Steel Framing Association. [2, 3]

———. *Technical Bulletin No. 101: Types of Metal Lath and Their Uses*. Chicago, IL: Metal Lath/Steel Framing Association. [3]

———. *Technical Bulletin No. 120: Ceramic Tile Applied to Metal Lath and Plaster*. Chicago, IL: Metal Lath/Steel Framing Association. [3]

———. 1986. *Specifications for Metal Lathing and Furring*. Chicago, IL: Metal Lath/Steel Framing Association. [2, 3]

Minnery, Catherine, and Donald Minnery. 1979. Repairing Stucco. *The Old-House Journal*, July, 7(7): 73, 77–79. [3]

Moreno, Elena Marcheso, 1987. Failures Short of Collapse. *Architecture*, July: 91–94.

National Association of Tile Contractors. *Reference Manual and Specifications*. Jackson, MS: National Association of Tile Contractors. [5]

National Concrete Masonry Association. 1983. *Exterior Insulation of Block Walls*. National Concrete Masonry Association. [3]

———. 1985. *Portland Cement Plaster (Stucco) for Concrete Masonry*. National Concrete Masonry Association. [3]

National Forest Products Association. *National Design Specifications for Wood Construction*. Washington, DC: National Forest Products Association. [2]

———. *Manual for House Framing*. Washington, DC: National Forest Products Association. [2]

————. *Span Tables for Joists and Rafters.* Washington, DC: National Forest Products Association. [2]

National Trust for Historic Preservation. 1985. *All About Old Buildings—The Whole Preservation Catalog.* Washington, DC: The Preservation Press. (This is an extensive reference work containing the names and addresses of many organizations active in the historic preservation field and lists of publications sources. Anyone facing a preservation problem should obtain this catalog as soon as possible. It will save much time in finding the right organization or data source.) **HP**

Naval Facilities Engineering Command. 1983 (March). Guide Specifications Section 06100, Rough Carpentry. Department of the Navy. [2]

————. 1984 (February). Guide Specifications Section 09100, Metal Support Systems. Department of the Navy. [2]

————. 1982 (August). Guide Specifications Section 09110, Lathing. Department of the Navy. [3]

————. 1985 (July). Guide Specifications Section 09150, Plastering and Stuccoing. Department of the Navy. [3]

————. 1985 (March). Guide Specifications Section 09250, Gypsum Board. Department of the Navy. [4]

————. 1984 (March). Guide Specifications Section 09310, Ceramic Tile, Quarry Tile, and Paver Tile. Department of the Navy. [5]

The Old-House Journal. 1984. Restoration Products: Self-Stick Drywall Mesh Tape. *The Old-House Journal,* January/February, 12(1): 30. [4]

Olson, Christopher. 1987. Improved Products Broaden Tile Applications. *Building Design and Constructions,* April, 28(4): 98–101. [5]

Phillips, Morgan W. Adhesives for the Reattachment of Loose Plaster. Association for Preservation Technology, *APT Bulletin V,* XII(2): 37–63. [3]

Piper, Richard. 1988. Special Report: Troubles with Synthetic Stucco. *New England Builder,* June: 34–38. [3]

Poore, Jonathan. 1983. Making the Perfect Drywall Patch. *The Old-House Journal,* December, 11(10): 220–221. [4]

Poore, Patricia. 1983. "What's Behind Sagging Plaster." *The Old-House Journal,* January/February: 24–25. [2, 3]

————. 1983. Old-House Basics: What's Possible in Plaster Restoration. *The Old-House Journal,* November, 11(9): 200. [3]

Portland Cement Association. *Portland Cement Plaster (Stucco) Manual.* Chicago, IL: Portland Cement Association. [3]

————. *Bonding Concrete or Plaster to Concrete.* Chicago, IL: Portland Cement Association. [3]

————. 1988. *Design and Control of Concrete Mixtures, Thirteenth Edition.* Skokie, IL: Portland Cement Association. [3]

Ramsey/Sleeper, The AIA Committee on Architectural Graphic Standards. 1981. *Architectural Graphic Standards, Seventh Edition*. New York, NY: Wiley. [2, 3, 4, 5]

Rehab Age. 1981. Interior Solutions—Some Wall Problems You Can Repair Yourself. *Rehab Age,* November: 44–57. [3]

Smith, Baird, M. 1984. Moisture Problems in Historic Masonry Walls: Diagnosis and Treatment. Technical Preservation Services, U.S. Department of the Interior, Technical Report. **HP**

Southern Pine Inspection Bureau. *Standard Grading Rules for Southern Pine Lumber*. Pensacola, FL: Southern Pine Inspection Bureau. [2]

Staehli, Alfred M. 1985. Historic Preservation: Where to Find the Facts. *The Construction Specifier,* July, 38(7): 50–53. **HP**

Stahl, Frederick A. 1984. *A Guide to the Maintenance, Repair, and Alteration of Historic Buildings*. New York: Van Nostrand. **HP**

Stover, Alan B. 1987. The Specifier's Guide to Construction Warranties. *The Construction Specifier,* November, 40(11): 110–120.

Tile Council of America, Inc. 1988. *Handbook for Ceramic Tile Installation*. Princeton, NJ: Tile Council of America, Inc. [5]

Tile Contractors Association of America. *Products and Materials Guide*. Alexandria, VA: Tile Contractors Association of America. [5]

Truss Plate Institute. *Design Specifications for Light Metal Plate Connected Wood Trusses*. Madison, WI: Truss Plate Institute. [2]

Underwriters Laboratories. *Building Materials Directory—Class A, B, C: Fire and Wind Related Deck Assemblies*. Underwriters Laboratories. [2, 3, 4]

———. *Fire Resistance Directory—Time/Temperature Constructions*. Underwriters Laboratories. [2, 3, 4]

United States Department of the Army. *Technical Manual TM 5-801-2,* Historic Preservation Maintenance Procedures. Washington, DC: Department of the Army. [3]

United States Gypsum Company. 1972. *Red Book: Lathing and Plastering Handbook, 28th Edition*. Chicago, IL: United States Gypsum Company. [2, 3, 4]

———. 1987. *Gypsum Construction Handbook, Third Edition*. Chicago, IL: United States Gypsum Company. [2, 3, 4]

Van Den Branden/Hartsell. 1971. *Plastering Skill and Practice*. Chicago, IL: American Technical Society. [2, 3, 4]

West Coast Lumber Inspection Bureau. *Standard Grading Rules for West Coast Lumber*. Portland, OR: West Coast Lumber Inspection Bureau. [2]

Western Lath, Plaster, and Drywall Contractor's Association. 1988. *Plaster/Metal Framing System/Lath Manual*. New York: McGraw-Hill. [2, 3, 4]

Western Wood Products Association. *Grading Rules for Western Lumber*. Portland, OR: Western Wood Products Association. [2]

————. *Grade Stamp Manual.* Portland, OR: Western Wood Products Association,
[2]

————. *A-2, Lumber Specifications Information.* Portland, OR: Western Wood
Products Association. [2]

————. *Western Woods Use Book.* Portland, OR: Western Wood Products Association. [2]

————. *Wood Frame Design.* Portland, OR: Western Wood Products Association.
[2]

Wilson, Forrest. 1984. *Building Materials Evaluation Handbook.* New York: Van
Nostrand. [2, 3]

————. 1985. Building Diagnostics. *Architectural Technology,* Winter: 22–41. [2, 3]

Wright, Gordon. 1988. EIFS Offer Variety of Aesthetic Options. *Building Design
and Construction,* August, 29(8): 64–66. [3]

Zulandt, David F. 1985. Consider an Alternative: Veneer Plaster. *The Construction
Specifier,* July, 38(7): 84–85. [2, 3, 4]

Index

Acoustical plaster, 70, 111. *See also* Plaster, standard thickness
AIA Service Corporation, 65, 124, 230, 277. *See also Masterspec*
American Institute of Architects, 5, 6
American Institute of Timber Construction (AITC), 20
Timber Construction Manual, 20
Timber Construction Standards, 20
American Lumber Standards Committee, 21
American National Standards Institute (ANSI), 233, 234, 235, 237, 238, 251, 271, 276. *See also* text Bibliography
Standard A136.1, 238
Standard A137.1-1980, 233, 234, 235
American Olean Tile, 277
American Plywood Association, 22, 25
American Wood-Preservers Association (AWPA), 20, 23, 24
American Wood-Preservers Bureau (AWPB), 23
Maintenance Guide Manual, 277
Architects, 5–6, 9–12

as help for building owners, 5–6
as help for other architects and engineers, 9–10
prework on-site examinations by, 11–12
professional help for, 9–10
Architectural Graphic Standards, 30, 51, 123, 230, 277
Associated General Contractors of America, 5
Association for Preservation Technology, 123, 124
"Bulletin Vol. XII, No. 2," 123
Association of Tile, Terrazzo, Marble, Contractors and Affiliates, Inc., 7, 277
Guide for Grouting and Cleaning Ceramic Floors with Latex Grout, 277
ASTM. *See also* text Bibliography
guides applicable to ceramic tile, 242, 276
guides applicable to framing and furring, 22, 23, 41, 42, 44, 46, 47, 65–66

ASTM *(cont.)*
    guides applicable to gypsum board,
        129, 130, 131, 132, 137, 160,
        207, 230–31
    guides applicable to lath and
        plaster, 70, 71, 73, 75, 76, 101,
        124–25

Blatterman, Joan F., 277
"Details Underfoot," 277
Blue board. *See* Veneer plaster
    gypsum base
Building contractors. *See* General
    building contractors
Building materials manufacturer. *See*
    Product manufacturer
Building owners. *See* Owners,
    building

California Lathing and Plastering
    Contractors Association. *See*
    Western Lath, Plaster, and
    Drywall Contractors
    Association
Cement plaster, 70–76, 82–84,
        85–100, 101–13, 122–25
    accessories for, 74–75, 103, 106
    bases for, 71–73, 75–76, 103, 106
    bonding agents for, 75
    definitions, 70
    failure in, evidence of, 93–100
    failure in, reasons for, 85–93
    finishes for, 83–84, 107, 112
    installing new bases for, 75–76
    installing new plaster, 82–84
    installing plaster over existing
        materials, 112–13
    lath for, 71–73, 76, 83, 103–6, 113
    placing unsupported loads on lath
        for, 19
    plaster materials, 70–71, 103–4
    repairing and extending of, 101–12
    solid substrates for, 71, 75, 82–83,
        113
    thickness of, 84
    where to get more information,
        122–25
Ceramic tile, 233–77
    adhesives for, types and uses, 238–
        39
    board type base for, 241 (*see also*
        Glass mesh mortar units *and*
        Gypsum board, standard types)
    definitions
        of ceramic tile, 233
        of general terms, 236–37
        of grout types, 230–41
        of mortar and adhesives, 237–39
        of tile types, 233–36
    divider strips for, 242
    expansion joint sealants for, 242
    failure in, evidence of, 266–70
    failure in, reasons for, 253–66
    grout types and uses, 239–41
    installing new materials, 242–53
    installing over existing materials,
        275–76
    joints for field-applied tile, 251–52
    membranes, cleavage and
        waterproofing, 241
    metal lath for, 241
    mortar types and uses, 237–38
    prefabricated tile panels, 252–53
    reinforcement, setting bed, 241
    repair, replacement, and cleaning
        of, 271–75
    standards for, 233–34 (*see also*
        American National Standards
        Institute, ASTM, *and* Tile
        Council of America)
    substrates for, 242–43
    thick-setting beds for field-applied
        tile, 243–48
    thin-setting beds for field-applied
        tile, 248–51
    tile types, accessories, and uses
        ceramic mosaic tile, 234–35
        glazed wall tile, 234
        paver tile, 236
        quarry tile, 236
        special purpose tile, 236
    where to get more information,
        276–77
Ceramic Tile Institute (CTI), 160, 276
    Ceramic Tile Manual, 276
    "CTI Standard for Glazed and

Unglazed Special Purpose and
Faience Tile,'' 276
''Test Procedure CTI-69-5,'' 276
Cold-formed metal framing. *See*
Metal framing and furring
Concrete substrates, 17–18. *See also*
Solid substrates
Condensation, as a cause of damage,
19
Construction Specifications Canada,
127
Constructions Specifications Institute,
127
Consultant. *See* Specialty consultant
Creep, failures due to, 17, 18, 184

Damage consultant. *See* Forensic
consultant *and* Specialty
consultant
Deflection
allowing for, 25, 33, 47, 51, 54, 56
failures due to, 16, 17, 18, 36, 60
Design Specifications for Light Metal
Plate Connected Wood
Trusses, 22
Diehl, John R., 122
Drywall Contracting, 232

Efflorescence
on ceramic tile, 274–75, 277
on plaster, 111
on substrates, 18, 118, 141, 183
EIFS. *See* Synthetic stucco
Emergencies, 4
Engineers
as help for architects and other
engineers, 9–10
as help for building owners, 5–6
prework on-site examinations by,
11–12
professional help for, 9–10
Expansion and contraction
allowing for, 25, 47, 51, 88
failures due to, 16, 18, 88, 89
of wood, 17
Exterior insulation and finish systems
(EIFS). *See* Synthetic stucco

Exterior Insulation Manufacturers
Association, 67, 115, 124, 232

Finish, definition, 2
Finish failure, definition, 2
Forensic consultant. *See also*
Specialty consultant
definition and responsibilities, 7
Forest Products Laboratory, 65
*Handbook No. 72—Wood
Handbook,* 65
Framing, metal, 15–17. *See also*
Metal framing and furring
Framing, wood, 31–34. *See also*
Wood framing and furring
Frane, James T., 232
Furring, metal. *See* Metal framing
and furring
Furring, wood, 30–31. *See also*
Wood framing and furring

General building contractors
as help for building owners, 6
prework on-site examinations by,
12–13
professional help for, 10–11
Georgia Pacific Corporation, 224
Glass mesh mortar units, 224–32, 241
available products, 224–25
definition, 224
failure in, evidence of, 228–30
failure in, reasons for, 227–28
finishing, 227
installing new units, 226–27
installing units over existing
materials, 230
materials, 224–25
Glazed tile. *See* Ceramic tile
Gorman, J. R., 66, 122
Greater Portland Landmarks, 124
Grout for ceramic tile. *See* Ceramic
tile
Gypsum Association, 66, 88, 125,
132, 140, 141, 142, 160, 172,
183, 207, 222, 223, 230–32
*Fire Resistance Design Manual:
Eleventh Edition (GA-600-84),*
66, 125, 140, 231

Gypsum Association (cont.)
  Fire Resistance Gypsum Sheathing
    (GA-252-86), 232
  Gypsum Board Products Glossary
    of Terminology (GA-505-85),
    66, 231
  Recommendations for Covering
    Existing Interior Walls and
    Ceilings with Gypsum Board
    (GA-650-86), 66, 232
  Recommended Specifications for
    Application and Finishing of
    Gypsum Board (GA-216-85), 231
  Recommended Specifications:
    Gypsum Board Types, Uses,
    Sizes and Standards (GA-223-
    86), 232
  Recommended Specifications:
    Recommendations for
    Installation of Steel Fire Door
    Frames in Steel Stud-Gypsum
    Board Fire-Rated Partitions
    (GA-219-86), 66, 232
  Using Gypsum Board for Walls
    and Ceilings (GA-201-85), 231–
    32
Gypsum board, backing boards. See
    Gypsum board, standard types
Gypsum board, coreboards. See
    Gypsum board, standard types
Gypsum board, exterior soffit boards.
    See Gypsum board, standard
    types
Gypsum board, foil-backed. See
    Gypsum board, standard types
Gypsum board, liner boards. See
    Gypsum board, standard types
Gypsum board, miscellaneous
    special-purpose boards, 132.
    See also Gypsum board,
    special-purpose types
Gypsum board, predecorated, 132,
    134–35, 137–38, 140–41, 175–
    91, 206, 208–9, 219, 220–24,
    230–32. See also Gypsum
    board, special-purpose types
  accessories for, 134, 208

  adhesives for, 137–38
  board material, 127–29, 132, 208
  failure in, evidence of, 191–92, 206
  failure in, reasons for, 179–91
  fasteners for, 134–35, 137
  installing new materials, 140–41,
    175–79
  installing over existing materials,
    220–24
  preparation for installation, 140–41,
    208–9
  repairing and extending of, 219
  where to get more information,
    230–32
Gypsum board, regular. See Gypsum
    board, standard types
Gypsum board, special-purpose
    types, 19, 127–28, 131–32. See
    also each individual type
  definitions, 127–28
  glass mesh mortar units (see Glass
    mesh mortar units)
  types, listing of, 131–32 (see also
    each specific type)
  unsupported insulation over, 19
Gypsum board, standard types, 19,
    126–63, 179–201, 207–19, 219–
    24, 230–32, 241
  accessories for, 132–34, 208
  adhesives for, 137–38
  board materials, 127–31, 208
  definitions, 127–28
  failure in, evidence of, 191–201
  failure in, reasons for, 179–91
  fasteners for, 134–36, 208
  installing new materials, 140–63
  installing over existing materials,
    220–24
  joint treatment materials, 138–39
  preparation for installation, 140–41,
    208–9
  repairing and extending of, 207–19
  textured finishes, 139, 219–20
  types, listing of, 129–31
  unsupported insulation over, 19
  where to get more information,
    230–32

Gypsum board, type X (fire rated).
      See Gypsum board, standard
      types
Gypsum board, water-resistant. *See*
      Gypsum board, standard types
Gypsum Construction Handbook, 66,
      122, 232
Gypsum lath. *See* Gypsum plaster
      lath
Gypsum plaster, 69–70, 71–82, 85–
      100, 101–13, 122–25. *See also*
      Plaster, standard thickness *and*
      Plaster, veneer
   accessories for, 73–74, 103, 106
   bases, 71–73, 75–76, 103, 106
   bonding agents for, 75
   definitions, 69
   failure in, evidence of, 93–100
   failure in, reasons for, 85–93
   finishes for, 81–82, 107, 111–12
   installing new bases for, 75–77
   installing new plaster, 77–82
   installing plaster over existing
      materials, 112–13
   Keene's cement plaster, 69, 70, 82,
      87, 107
   lath for, gypsum, 73, 76, 80–81,
      103–6, 113
   lath for, metal, 72–73, 76, 78–80,
      103–6, 113
   lath for, wood, 72, 76, 104, 106,
      108–10
   placing unsupported loads on lath
      for, 19
   plaster material, 69–70, 103–4
   repairing and extending of, 101–12
   solid substrates for, 71, 75, 77, 113
   thickness of, 82
   where to get more information,
      122–25
Gypsum plaster lath, 73–74, 76, 80,
      87, 105, 106, 108–9, 131–32,
      134–37, 140–41, 173–75, 179–
      92, 203–6, 207–18, 220–24,
      230–32. *See also* Gypsum
      board, special-purpose types
   accessories for, 73–74, 208

   applying plaster over, 80
   board material, 127–29, 131–32,
      208
   failure in, evidence of, 191–92,
      203–6
   failure in, reasons for, 179–91
   fasteners for, 134–37
   installing new materials, 140–41,
      173–75
   installing over existing materials,
      220–24
   preparation for installation, 140–41,
      208–9
   repairing and extending of, 207–19
   where to get more information,
      230–32
Gypsum sheathing, 115, 116, 118,
      126, 127–29, 131, 134–35, 136,
      140–41, 171–73, 179–92, 201–
      3, 207–19, 220–24, 230–32.
      See also Gypsum board,
      special-purpose types
   board material, 127–29, 131, 208
   failure in, evidence of, 191–92,
      201–3
   failure in, reasons for, 179–91
   fasteners for, 134–35, 136, 208
   installing new materials, 140–41,
      171–73
   installing over existing materials,
      220–24
   as part of an EIFS system, 115,
      116, 118, 201–2
   preparation for installation, 140–41,
      208–9
   repairing and extending of, 207–19
   where to get more information,
      230–32

International Institute for Lath and
      Plaster, 67, 122

Joints in ceramic tile. *See* Ceramic
      tile

Keene's cement plaster. *See* Gypsum
      plaster

Ladygo, Andrew, 109, 111, 123
Lath, gypsum. *See* Gypsum plaster
lath
Lath, metal. *See* Plaster lath
Lath, wood. *See* Plaster lath
Lath, Plaster, and Drywall
Information Bureau, 66
Leaks, as a cause of damage, 18
Leeke, John, 123
"Saving Irreplaceable Plaster," 123
*Lightweight Steel Framing Systems
Manual,* 66, 125
Lime plaster. *See* Sand-lime plaster

Manual for House Framing, 20, 25,
31
Manual of Lathing and Plastering,
122
McIlvain, Jess, 253, 277
"Prefabricated Exterior Ceramic
Tile Cladding," 253
Masonry substrates, 17–18. *See also*
Solid substrates
Masterformat, 127
Masterspec, 65, 124, 230
Section 07241, Exterior Insulation
and Finish System—Class PB,
124
Section 07241, Exterior Insulation
and Finish System—Class PM,
124
Section 09200, Lath and Plaster,
65, 124, 230
Section 09250, Gypsum Drywall,
65, 230
Section 09270, Gypsum Board
Shaft Wall Systems, 65, 230
Section 09300, Tile, 277
Section 09215, Veneer Plaster, 65,
124, 230
Materials manufacturer. *See* Product
manufacturer
Materials and Methods Standards
Association, 8, 277
Bulletins 1 through 14, 277
Metal framing and furring, 15–17, 41–
64

anchors, fasteners, and accessories,
45–46
cold-formed metal framing, 41, 45,
58–59
failures and what to do about
them, 60–63
finishes, 41
furring installation, 51–53, 63–64
furring member types, 41–43
installing metal framing and furring
over existing materials, 63–64
installing new metal framing and
furring, 46–60
materials, 41–46, 61
proprietary ceiling suspension
systems, 43
repairing and extending metal
framing and furring, 61–63
sealants in, 59
shaftwalls, 41, 45, 59–60
sound insulation in, 59
spacing of members, 47–51
wall and partition framing,
nonbearing types (studs), 43–
45, 54–57
Metal lath. *See* Plaster lath
Metal Lath/Steel Framing
Association, 47, 66, 125
*Lightweight Steel Framing Systems
Manual,* 66, 125
*Specifications for Metal Lathing
and Furring,* 47, 66, 125
Modulars, Incorporated, 224
Mosaic tile. *See* Ceramic tile

National Association of Tile
Contractors, 276–77
*Reference Manual and
Specifications,* 276–77
National Concrete Masonry
Association, 123
National Forest Products Association
(NFPA), 20, 21, 25, 31
Manual for House Framing, 20,
25, 31
*National Design Specifications for
Wood Construction,* 20, 21

Span Tables for Joists and Rafters, 20

National Trust for Historic Preservation, 271

"New Techniques for Restoring Decorative Plasterwork," 111, 123

Owners, building, 4–8, 11
  prework on-site examinations by, 11
  professional help for, 4–8
  what to do in an emergency, 4–5

Paver tile. *See* Ceramic tile
Phillips, Morgan W., 109, 123
Plaster, cement. *See* Cement plaster
Plaster, gypsum. *See* Gypsum plaster
Plaster, standard thickness, 68–114, 122–125. *See also* individual plaster types
  accessories for, 73–75, 106
  bases for, 71–73, 106
  bonding agents for, 75
  failure in, evidence of, 93–100
  failure in, reasons for, 85–93
  installing new bases for, 75–77
  installing new plaster, 77–84
  installing plaster over existing materials, 112–13
  lightweight aggregates, 70
  placing unsupported loads on lath, 19
  plaster materials, 69–71, 103–4
  repairing and extending of, 101–12
  where to get more information, 122–25
Plaster, veneer, 68, 71–72, 73, 75–76, 84–94, 100–1, 112, 113–14, 122–25
  accessories for, 75
  base for, 71–73
  failure in, evidence of, 93–94, 100–1
  failure in, reasons for, 85–93
  installing new bases for, 75–77
  installing new plaster, 84

  installing plaster over existing materials, 112–14
  plaster materials, 69–71, 112
  placing unsupported loads on lath, 19
  repairing and extending of, 112
  where to get more information, 122–25
Plaster base. *See* Plaster lath
Plastering Skill and Practice, 123
Plaster lath, 68, 71, 72–73, 76, 78–79, 83, 86, 89, 103–6, 108–10, 113. *See also specific lath types*
  gypsum lath (*see* Gypsum plaster lath)
  metal lath, 72–73, 76, 78–80, 83, 89, 105, 106, 108, 113
  veneer plaster base (*see* Veneer plaster gypsum base)
  wood lath, 72, 76, 106, 108, 109
  where to get more information, 122–25
Plaster/Metal Framing System/Lath Manual, 66, 122
Plaster of Paris, 69
Poore, Patricia, 67, 123
  "What's Behind Sagging Plaster," 67, 123
Portland Cement Association, 88, 106, 123
  "Bonding Concrete or Plaster to Concrete," 106, 123
Portland Cement Plaster (Stucco) Manual, 123
Portland Cement Plaster (Stucco) for Concrete Masonry, 123
Portland cement plaster. *See* Cement plaster
Prefabricated tile cladding panels. *See* Ceramic tile
Product manufacturer
  as help for architects and engineers, 10
  as source of contractor names for owner, 6
Professional help
  architects and engineers, 9–10

Professional help *(cont.)*
  building owners, 4–8
  general building contractors, 10–11
Pruter, Walter F., 67, 122
*PS 1—Construction and Industrial
    Plywood,* 20, 22
*PS 20—American Softwood Lumber
    Standard,* 20, 21

Quarry tile. *See* Ceramic tile

*Red Book: Lathing and Plastering
    Handbook,* 66, 122–23, 232

Sand-lime plaster, 69, 103. *See also*
    Standard thickness plaster
Setting beds for tile. *See* Ceramic tile
Settlement, as a damage cause, 15,
    16, 18
Shaftwalls, 162. *See also* Metal
    framing and furring
Society for the Preservation of New
    England Antiquities (SPNEA),
    109, 123
Solid substrates, 17–18
  as a base for synthetic stucco, 114,
    115, 116, 117
  as a plaster base, 71–72, 75–76,
    82–83, 113
  problems that can cause failures in,
    18
Southern Pine Inspection Bureau
    (SPIB), 20
*Standard Grading Rules for
    Southern Pine Lumber,* 20
Span Tables for Joists and Rafters,
    20
Specialty consultant. *See also*
    Forensic consultant
  as help for an architect or
    engineer, 10
  as help for a building owner, 7–8
  as help for a general contractor,
    10–11
  prework on-site examinations by,
    11–13
  qualifications, 7–8

Specialty contractor
  as help for a building owner, 6–7
  as subcontractor for general
    contractor, 10–11, 12
Specialty subcontractor. *See*
    Specialty contractor
*Specifications for Metal Lathing and
    Furring,* 47, 66, 125
Standard thickness plaster. *See*
    Plaster, standard thickness *or
    individual plaster types*
  definition, 68
Structural framing systems, 15–17.
    See also Wood framing and
    furring *and* Metal framing and
    furring
  failure of, 15–16
  movement of, 16–17
Studs, metal. *See* Metal framing and
    furring
Studs, wood, 32–33. *See also* Wood
    framing and furring
Substrates. *See* Solid substrates
Synthetic stucco, 68, 114–24
  accessories for, 115
  base for, 115
  definition, 68, 114–15
  failures in evidence of, 119–21
  failures in reasons for, 117–19
  finish materials, 114–15
  installing new base for, 116
  installing new finish, 116–17
  installing over existing materials,
    121–22
  repairing of, 121
  where to get more information,
    115, 124

Tile cladding, prefabricated. *See*
    Ceramic tile
Tile Council of America (TCA), 8,
    239, 242, 243, 247, 249, 251,
    260, 261, 271, 275, 276, 277
*Handbook for Ceramic Tile
    Installation (Handbook),* 239,
    242, 243, 247, 249, 251, 260,
    275, 276
Truss Plate Institute, 22

Underwriter's Laboratories
	Incorporated (UL), 24, 46, 60
United States Department of
	Commerce (DOC), 20, 21, 22.
	See also PS 1 and PS 20
United States Gypsum Company, 66,
	122, 224, 232
	Gypsum Construction Handbook,
	66, 122, 232
	*Red Book: Lathing and Plastering
	Handbook,* 66, 122–23, 232

Van den Branden/Hartsell, 123
Veneer plaster. *See* Plaster, veneer
Veneer plaster gypsum base, 73, 76,
	84, 85, 92, 112, 113, 126–29,
	131, 134–41, 163–201, 207–19,
	220–24, 230–32
	accessories for, 134, 208
	adhesives for, 137–38
	applying plaster over, 84
	board material, 127–29, 131, 208
	failure in, evidence of, 191–201
	failure in, reasons for, 179–91
	fasteners for, 134–36
	installing new materials, 140–41,
		163–71
	installing over existing materials,
		220–24
	joint treatment materials, 138–39
	preparation for installation, 140–41,
		208–9
	repairing and extending of, 207–19
	where to get more information,
		230–32
Vibration, failures due to, 17, 18

Warranties, construction, 4–5
West Coast Lumber Inspection
	Bureau (WCLIB), 20
	*Standard Grading Rules for West
	Coast Lumber,* 20
Western Lath, Plaster, and Drywall
	Contractors' Association, 66,
	122
Western Wood Products Association
	(WWPA), 20
	*A-2, Lumber Specifications
	Information,* 20
	Grade Stamp Manual, 20
	*Grading Rules for Western
	Lumber,* 20
	Western Woods Use Book, 20
	Wood Frame Design, 20
Wood framing and furring, 17, 19–40
	anchors and fasteners, 22–23, 25–
		26
	failures and what to do about
		them, 34–39
	fire-retardant treatment, 24
	installing new wood framing and
		furring, 24–34
	installing wood framing and furring
		over existing materials, 39–40
	materials, 20–23, 37
	preservative treatment, 23–24
	repairing and extending wood
		framing and furring, 36–39
	roof trusses, 22
	shrinkage of wood, 17, 20, 38
	spacing of members, 26–30
	truss-type floor joists, 22
Wood lath. *See* Plaster lath